KONSULT

Electracy and Transmedia Studies

Series Editors: Jan Rune Holmevik and Cynthia Haynes

The Electracy and Transmedia Studies Series publishes research that examines the mixed realities that emerge through electracy, play, rhetorical knowledge, game design, community, code, and transmedia artifacts. This book series aims to augment traditional artistic and literate forms with examinations of electrate and literate play in the age of transmedia. Writing about play should, in other words, be grounded in playing with writing. The distinction between play and reflection, as Stuart Moulthrop argues, is a false dichotomy. Cultural transmedia artifacts that are interactive, that move, that are situated in real time, call for inventive/electrate means of creating new scholarly traction in transdisciplinary fields. The series publishes research that produces such traction through innovative processes that move research forward across its own limiting surfaces (surfaces that create static friction). The series exemplifies extreme points of contact where increased electrate traction might occur. The series also aims to broaden how scholarly treatments of electracy and transmedia can include both academic and general audiences in an effort to create points of contact between a wide range of readers. The Electracy and Transmedia Series follows what Gregory Ulmer calls an image logic based upon a wide scope—"an aesthetic embodiment of one's attunement with the world."

Books in the Series

KONSULT: Theopraxesis by Gregory L. Ulmer (2019)

Exquisite Corpse: Art-Based Writing Practices in the Academy, edited by Kate Hanzalik and Nathalie Virgintino (2019)

Tracing Invisible Lines: An Experiment in Mystoriography by David Prescott-Steed (2019)

The Internet as a Game by Jill Anne Morris (2018)

Identity and Collaboration in World of Warcraft by Phillip Michael Alexander (2018)

Future Texts: Subversive Performance and Feminist Bodies, edited by Vicki Callahan and Virginia Kuhn (2016)

Play/Write: Digital Rhetoric, Writing, Games, edited by Douglas Eyman and Andréa D. Davis (2016)

Sites

Gregory Ulmer's *Konsult Experiment*: http://konsultexperiment.com/

KONSULT

Theopraxesis

Gregory L. Ulmer

Parlor Press
Anderson, South Carolina
www.parlorpress.com

Parlor Press LLC, Anderson, South Carolina, USA
© 2019 by Parlor Press
All rights reserved.
Printed in the United States of America on acid-free paper.

S A N: 2 5 4 - 8 8 7 9

Library of Congress Cataloging-in-Publication Data on File

978-1-64317-067-1 (paperback)
978-1-64317-068-8 (hardcover)
978-1-64317-069-5 (PDF)
978-1-64317-070-1 (ePub)

1 2 3 4 5

Electracy and Transmedia Studies
Series Editors: Jan Rune Holmevik and Cynthia Haynes

Cover image: Gregory L. Ulmer
Cover design: David Blakeslehy

Parlor Press, LLC is an independent publisher of scholarly and trade titles in print and multimedia formats. This book is available in paper, cloth and eBook formats from Parlor Press on the World Wide Web at http://www.parlorpress.com or through online and brick-and-mortar bookstores. For submission information or to find out about Parlor Press publications, write to Parlor Press, 3015 Brackenberry Drive, Anderson, South Carolina, 29621, or email editor@parlorpress.com.

Contents

Preface   ix

1 Justice   3

Interlude: Murphy's Well-Being (1)   37

2 Allegory   46

Interlude: *Murphy's Well-Being* (2)   81

3 Enjoyment   87

Interlude: *Murphy's Well-Being* (3)   117

4 Trace   126

Interlude: *Murphy's Well-Being* (4)   163

5 Choragraphy   170

Interlude: *Murphy's Well-Being* (5)   207

6 Rhythm   216

Interlude: *Murphy's Well-Being* (6)   247

Works Cited   257

Index   265

About the Author   279

for Hayden, Claire, Raya, and Anjali

We can thus hope to reach a plane where logical properties, as attributes of things, will be manifested as directly as flavors or perfumes.

—Claude Lévi-Strauss

Figure 1. "Installation." *Murphy's Well-Being*, Florida Research Ensemble, in "Region4: Transformation through Imagination," Gainesville, Florida, February 2012. Photo by Jack Stenner.

Preface

ELECTRACY

In recent years collaborations with my colleagues have taken the form of an effort to revisit heuretics as pedagogy, to clarify and reconfigure it to serve as the basis for learning in the emerging conditions of global online education, including MOOCs, ubiquitous computing, mixed reality, and related initiatives. These chapters originally were addressed less formally to my colleagues and students (the "we" of this text), as theorizing how to teach the invention of electracy online. The proposal is that learning includes the construction of a genre called *konsult* (pronounced KON-sult) that in turn mediates all learning, relative to the complete interactive environment of systems and institutions, not only for degrees but also for life-long education and citizenship.

What is the role and future of literate school (a redundancy) in electracy? Perhaps it is not surprising that not everyone thinks education needs to change, or not in the way that we envision. We know in advance and in principle how the world works—that change happens in a certain way (the propensity of things). There seems to be an isotopy of being across all levels of existence, from atoms to galaxies, including the human dimension both biological and cultural, intuited in the design of mandalas. Any one level in this cosmology may function as a *mise en abyme* (miniaturization) figuring the organization of the whole (if one has the craft of allegory in mind). Here for example is an account of change in this holistic perspective, with reference to the atomic level, that resonates with cultural history.

> Change begins slowly, uncertainly, and in places that are highly dependent upon local circumstances because the nuclei necessarily are misfits in the existing structure or orthodoxy. The nuclei are unpredictable (except perhaps by the Witch of Endor of whom Banquo demanded "If you can look into the seeds of time, and say which grains will grow and which will not, Speak then to me") because no system can by itself know ahead of time what, if any, new structure can supplant it. Nuclei do form, however, in those regions of the old structure that are least contented. A phase change is analogous to a political revolution; not the destruction of all individuals but the rearrangement of most of them into a new pattern of interaction. A revolution, driven by the injustices of the old regime, needs its formative nucleus, and its growth (which occurs in an interface of high disorder) is slowed by the need to accommodate or eliminate dissenters. Eventually, however, the structure that began as the highly creative work of a successful innovator becomes an ideology and as it spreads it becomes indoctrination, not creation. (Smith 42)

What remains for us to decide is not whether to participate in change, but the locus of our position in the array: with the normative lock, the gaps, or the misfits (the resistance, the opportunity, or the trouble).

Our collaboration begins with a review of the rationale for undertaking a more radical reform of education, to be practiced as a transition from literate to electrate learning. The first reason to change education ("Apparatus") is the historical analogy, associated with the reality of the migration of the archive accumulated during the 2500-year epoch of literacy due to information overload. Historically, each apparatus first put its archive into a new medium of storage, and in the process invented a fundamentally different metaphysics (orientation to reality). School itself is a product of this invention within orality of the institution that created literacy. School is relative to the apparatus of literacy, and as such will continue within electracy, even adapting to digital technology, while having to accommodate the new dimension of civilization emerging within electracy. Part of the purpose of *Konsult* is to articulate the nature of this new metaphysics, to determine the most appropriate and effective operation of school in this transforming reality. We speak from within the institution of school, looking back on the historical relationship of school with church and religion, and forward to the emerging relationship of school with corporation and entertainment

HEURETICS

Although Digital Humanities is a disciplinary location most immediately relevant to this proposal, it also concerns the leading institution of STEM education, which is on record as intending to reform its curriculum for a digital apparatus. The task force on the future of MIT education produced "Recommendations" that are a useful point of departure for innovation. The list of intentions is insightful, relative to projections of apparatus theory. For now, the point to emphasize is that however appropriate the recommendations are, they do not attempt to describe, let alone prescribe, the nature of the innovations in pedagogy and curriculum they call for, beyond reminders of the traditions and commitments that historically made MIT successful. This hesitation at the threshold of invention is not a shortcoming but an invitation to the institution at large to begin the process of invention. This invitation is intriguing and challenging in referring to "the magic of MIT" (an emergent and unpredictable effect of a complex system), and in implying that MIT as an institution or collective entity is as intelligent and creative as are the individuals who staff it. The basic assumption is that MIT twenty years from now will function differently, perhaps radically so, from the way it works now. In other words, the imagined future of education is not just "media literacy."

Between recommendations and implementation comes invention. Electracy as a mode of study includes "heuretics" (the logic of invention), assuming that the transformation that it proposes must be and can be invented. Critical analysis of the discourse on method in the Western tradition revealed that every text introducing what proved to be a fundamental innovation in thought, reason, and procedure, beginning with Plato's *Phaedrus* and continuing through avant-garde manifestos in modernism, was organized around a rhetorical matrix, a device consisting of five operators: Contrast, Analogy, Theory, Target, tale. The challenge of creative thinking is that the outcome is unknown (by definition). Or rather, we have a goal that guides the process—the design of an electrate mode of learning that is global, syncretic, holistic, online (blended), including service, engaging with real-world problems, and the other principles itemized in the recommendations. How exactly are these principles to be enacted?

The first step of invention is to outline the function of each operator of the heuretic matrix known as the CATTt. The generator retains the primary literate procedure: problem/solution. The Problem is articulated in terms of the pair Contrast-Target: *Contrast* is being rejected (obsoleted in McLuhan's matrix). Plato in outlining his ideal city and its literate education rejected Homeric models of learning. *Target* describes the affordances of the new condition for which the method is being created (in Plato's case, the Academy with its devices of reading and writing, and mathematics). The Solution is (experimentally) articulated in the pair Analogy-Theory. *Analogy* identifies an existing discourse in a different domain that manifests some of the desired features. For Plato, medical diagnosis demonstrated the powers of analysis in the physical realm that he desired for metaphysics. *Theory* is an existing account of reality adopted (provisionally) to guide the choices and direction of the design. Plato worked in the tradition of Pythagoras, with Socrates as his immediate inspiration. *Tale* refers to the mode or genre, the form, in which to assemble and integrate the four sets of resources (each resource being inventoried for its relevant features), to bring them into conversation. The tale partially explains the emergent instructions, and partly demonstrates them (it does what it says). Plato invented the dialogue form as the means to support the bootstrapping of the Academy into literacy (Maranhao). The dramatized conversations of Socrates (usually) with one or more interlocutors constituted an interface metaphor—the scene of conversation brought students natively oral into the experience of dialectic, the mode of reasoning native to literacy.

CATTt

A meta-CATTt has guided my experiments with electracy. A useful feature of the CATTt is that it accomodates any group of resources, and produces or generates a poetics or set of instructions specific to those resources. Each of my graduate seminars over the past decades tested a different CATTt, but the category of resource for each slot in the template repeated. Here is an overview of the genre formulated for the seminars. The CATTt slots function like a spread in Tarot reading (or in any template, such as Lacan's four discourses): the slot itself is active and inflects any resource it receives. The syntax of CATTt begins with the articulation of a problem: Contrast repels; Target attracts. Contrast: the extant metaphysics of literacy are fine as far as they go, but are relative to their alphabetic apparatus. Target: The Internet requires a digitally native metaphysics. The Contrast and Target are kenotic, emptying out, opening a site for invention. The procedure is to inventory the respective resources to understand the terms of the problem, both what is being rejected, that for which an alternative is sought, and the affordances of the new condition. Solution is generated from an inventory of Analogy and Theory. Analogy is an extant related practice suggesting possibilities of the new discourse; Theory identifies the principles structuring the invention as a whole (the What of the enterprise). The CATTt produces four inventories, four lists, each list inflected by its slot. A pattern of correspondences emerges in the intertext created by the juxtaposition of lists. This pattern is configured into a poetics, a formula or recipe of instructions for composing (in our case) an electrate metaphysics. This book supports and organizes the process of collection, inventory, and correlation, dictating therefore that for now the poetics remains literate, and only describes a practice that is implemented elsewhere. The poetics described here may serve as relay for your own invention, and will guide the online extension of this book, *Konsult Experiment*.

Target

A point of departure is Target, establishing the contemporary circumstances calling for fresh thinking. The MIT Recommendations outline a plan of desired innovations that correlate with apparatus projections. The most relevant proposals documented in the Recommendations include the following:

- Initiative for educational innovation (#1)
- Engaging in bold experiments (#2)
- Strengthening teaching of communications (#4)
- Creating service opportunities (#5)
- Extending new pedagogical approaches to the world (#7): modularity, game-based learning, partnering to encourage blended learning, seeding global discussions, increasing diversity.
- Harnessing the knowledge of a lasting global community (#8)

- Engaging with the world (#10)

The implied scenario imagines students combining residential, blended, and online modalities of pedagogy and curriculum, undertaking a holistic learning integrating pure and applied study, engaging with real-world, global problems directly in their actual setting, ones that challenge and resist business-as-usual public-policy solutions, performed through service learning, internships, flexible residencies, and partnering with relevant institutions, in collaboration with peers and cohorts from the broader community of schooling as well as other institutions of society. The electrate character of this vision is its commitment to relational, holistic, collective dimensions of education, needed to overcome the isolating, rigid divisions separating the various institutional dimensions of the life-world, resulting in significant obstacles for an ecology of learning that is at the same level of complexity as the problems inhibiting global thriving. The remainder of the CATTt resources supplies the materials for a poetics generating instructions for how to conduct schooling that accomplishes the purposes of Target.

Specifically, the heading "Extending MIT's Educational Impact" included five recommendations, most already adopted within the EmerAgency project to invent electrate consulting. Item 7d, for example, especially resonates with programs already explored in a number of konsultancies by the Florida Research Ensemble for the EmerAgency (Ulmer et al., *Miami Virtue*).

> Using open problems to seed global discussions. Problem-based learning is at the heart of an MIT education. While understanding the foundation and principles of a particular discipline is essential, the Task Force feels that the investment of students in learning is most successful when they apply their learning to real-world problems. Many such problems do not have clearly defined solutions and they enable a continuing conversation that also often spans departmental silos. The Task Force recommends encouraging departments to develop classes or series defined by the challenges they seek to address. For instance, one might imagine an MITx series on air pollution. Within that series, a student would find a number of classes—including air purification, urban planning, politics, and poverty—that are intended to aid the understanding and examination of air pollution from a variety of

perspectives. This might require a student to work on projects with students from different corners of the world who may already be addressing the nuances of air pollution in their individual communities. This connection will help create a global community of thought and practice around global challenges, and a cadre of sophisticated problem solvers. ("Institute-Wide Task Force").

Konsult

Konsult is to the invention of electrate learning what dialogue was to Plato's Academy. Plato invented a new genre to support written learning, and we may use his dramatized conversation as a relay and analogy for developing a similar unifying genre for learning in the digital apparatus. A related relay is the memory palace technique used in manuscript pedagogy to facilitate memorization of large quantities of information. Memory palaces consisted of three layers: a familiar street, often from one's hometown; strong memorable images from general culture; specialized information. Konsult functions by means of mobile ubiquitous computing, enabling the *egent* (electrate consultant) freedom of movement in space and time (GPS and EPS [Existential Positioning System]). The genre supports holistic learning, mediating collective attunement among collaborating consultants and institutions. The holistic orientation requires receiving resources not only from one's specialized discipline but from the divisions of knowledge as a whole.

The other primary institutions of society must be integrated into the interface as well, such as governments and corporations. Finally, and most importantly, the egent's home and family context play a central role. Digital learners are distributed globally. The konsultation is grounded in a site of disaster (a public policy aporia) selected by the egent, and this problem resistant to all solutions provides the boundary object guiding the learning. The genre functions as avatar in the proper sense (Ulmer, *Avatar Emergency*), meaning that the egent is in the receptive position of Arjuna to whom Krishna revealed himself as god in order to explain Hindu ethos, in the original account of epic crisis (*Bhagavad Gita*). Arjuna acted based on his reception of total knowledge relative to his episteme and epoch. Konsult manages this advisory function relative to contemporary global civilization.

"Theopraxesis" is a portmanteau word formulated to express the syncretic integration of the three virtues, capacities or faculties organizing intellectual endeavor in the Western tradition: Theory, Praxis, Poiesis (versions include: Thinking, Doing, Making; Knowledge, Purpose, Affect; Pure Reason, Practical Reason, Judgment of Taste). In practice, three genres or modes of representation were associated with the respective faculties: Philosophy, History, Literature. The relationship among these three modalities throughout literacy has been that of hostility, hierarchy, rivalry or competition, each one claiming to have a greater access to reality (Ought, Is, What If). Literacy required analysis, separation and even isolation of parts for its economy of information: "clear and distinct ideas," relative to the fundamental practice of producing concepts through "definition." Electracy inversely is integral, requiring in principle a syncretism of the three virtues. Theopraxesis is an integrated practice of the three virtues (capacities).

STIGMERGY

Egents collaborate through the interface of konsult, treating aporetic disasters as boundary objects. From the first time I read about stigmergy, perhaps in something by Lewis Thomas, it seemed like a good analogy for collaboration. The Internet created conditions that made the figure literal, as generalized in the first definition one finds, a mechanism of indirect coordination between agents or actions. The principle is that the trace left in the environment by an action stimulates the performance of a next action, by the same or a different agent. The original coinage by Pierre-Paul Grasse to describe the behavior of termites has been extended to cover open source distributed group collaboration, especially in networked environments. The passage is from social insects to social media, further extensible to algorithms.

The figure triggers some further contexts, such as that of dung beetles and their more exotic label, scarab. There is a general possibility of finding relays in the natural world for literal and figurative guidance with systems relations. Dung beetles, for example, are the only known creatures to navigate and orient themselves according to the Milky Way. Aesop's fables offer a prompt, with the Ant and the Grasshopper coming to mind especially. Michel Serres, *Parasite*, has shown the philosophical potential of this material. Parasitism operates through the logic of taking without giving or "abuse value." But the parasite nevertheless makes exchange possible by creating connections between otherwise incommensurable forms of ordering.

Stigmergy is a figure suggesting how an electrate polis might function. Electracy includes new identity formations (individual and collective), beyond selfhood and the democratic state. I proposed elsewhere that a fifth estate (adding a new dimension to the three estates of governing and the fourth estate of journalism) is forming, assisted by social media and mobile ubiquitous computing, observed in such movements as Occupy or groups such as Anonymous. The film about Wikileaks founder Julian Assange (*The Fifth Estate*) adds to the usefulness of this analogy. Ants communicate, for example, by leaving trails of pheromones as chemical signals. Ant stigmergy is a suggestive figure for how Internet technology and Derrida's trace may support an emergent dispersed global theopraxesis.

New Ratios

The stigmergy figure alludes to a primary question of invention. The construction of metaphysics includes establishing a Measure (Limit). The humanistic tradition of literacy proposed "man" as the measure, and there is a certain irreducible anthropomorphism in epistemology, and perhaps even ontology (if these modalities are even distinguishable today). The modernist revolution that is part of electracy supports an alternative ratio (proportion as a relation of ratios). Various species behaviors such as rhizomatic swarming evoke possibilities as relays guiding design thinking relative to digital computing. Peter Eisenman comes to mind as exemplary of this movement, his discussion of slime mold as a measure orienting parametric design.

> What I am saying is that in other disciplines there exists the possibility of modeling voids. In other words, to model such structures as slime molds, which are self-generating internalized mechanisms that have their own laws and behavior and which do not start from a fixed profile, they do not start from a recognizable profile. Slime mold does not look like anything. In fact, it mutates and takes its shape from the container that it is in. It will take on various formal structural organizations depending on its own internal movement and growth.
>
> If architecture had the capacity to begin from such modeling, we would begin to have a kind of new architecture, an

architecture that was no longer phallocentric. Now that does not mean that we would not be sheltering and containing, rather the containing would be seen as the residue of the process, and not metaphoric of the process. In other words, the process image and its analogous meanings would come from the self-generating activity as opposed to the enclosing activity. In this sense nobody is saying that architecture would not shelter, enclose, contain, etc. but it will not necessarily make metaphors of these organizations. (Peter Eisenman, in Selim Koder, "Interview").

The theorist Charles Jencks, discussing "thinking with objects," noted slime molds as examples of self-organizing systems studied in complexity theory. "In 1992 I gave Eisenman a sealed bottle labeled by the producer New Orleans Cajun Slime, and I added the word Mould. He accepted the gift, as a fitting symbol of the new paradigm in architecture." (1). The larger point suggested by this polysemy is not any one organic system (not "slime mold is the measure of all things"), but the pattern, this heuristic analogy bringing together certain instances of natural systems, contemporary mathematics, computation, design. This vector may be extended into apparatus invention, creating an electrate alternative to form (Idea).

POPCYCLE

The biological models of complex adaptive systems are central to the relational metaphysics of electracy. Learning is itself an instance of a complex adaptive system, and an aspect of what we are exploring is the extent to which there is a certain isomorphism transversing all such systems. Heuretic pedagogy is describable within a systems perspective, beginning with the popcyle of institutions within which identity is constructed. Mystory (electrate equivalent of historiography) maps the position of a subject within the popcycle of institutions. The premise of heuretics is that there is an equivalent in learning of the four-color theorem in mapping (chorography maps learning). In mathematics (according to one definition), the four-color map theorem states that, given any separation of a plane into contiguous regions, producing a figure called a map, no more than four colors are required to color the regions of the map so that no two adjacent regions have the same color. The analogy is that the four institutions of the popcycle suffice as interface relating a learner with every possible dimension of reality.

The name "popcycle" alludes to the process of invention/discovery, to call attention to the fact that inventions draw upon the full range of cultural institutions and experience. Acting on the EmerAgency slogan, "follow the invention," I have shown how innovation traverses multiple disciplines. A symptom of the popcycle at work may be found in the metaphors and images innovators use in describing their process of insight: The rebus puzzles Freud found in a humor magazine; the parlor game that inspired the Turing test; the duck/rabbit optical illusion central to Wittgenstein's "aspect"; the children's encyclopedia analogy that Einstein took as the basis for his thought experiment (riding a beam of light); the Japanese ukiyo-e prints Claude Lévi-Strauss received as rewards beginning at age six from his portrait-painter father. Heuretics as pedagogy assumes that learning correlates strongly with creativity. Mystory maps (choragraphy) one's position in the institutions of the popcycle, to track interpellation (construction of identity). Konsult appropriates and adapts these practices, developed for electrate learning, to an education conducted online. Konsult conducts interface bringing into relation aporetic problems, expert schemas, mystory wide images, and electrate annotation in the context of what Benjamin Bratton calls the Stack (Earth, Cloud, City, Address, Interface, User).

The mise-en-abyme layout (interpenetration of strata) of the interface is not formally motivated, nor is there any one structure required to register the dimensions. The affordances of the technology are being updated constantly, but there is less attention given to the other dimensions of the interface. Derrida's reference to heraldry was one inspiration for our approach, having in mind his ambivalent explorations of abyssal figures, extending not only to modernist tropes, but to the structure of Plato's *Timaeus* and the operations of Chora. I referred to it in terms of the Fibonacci geometry of the whirling square (in *Internet Invention*), to call attention to its dynamics as vortex (Pound). The figure may be unpacked further, since I have used it to think together every four (+1) series and set that presents itself, in the spirit of the four-color theorem: four causes (ancient and modern), suits of cards, divination systems, four (or five) tastes, the cardinal tropes, cardinal and ordinal directions, and more.

When it comes to the image of wide scope (four or five fundamental images structuring imagination, and central to the history of invention) tested in the pedagogy of *Internet Invention*, the prototype is Einstein's compass (received from his father as a gift at age four or five): any wide image functions as compass for the existential positioning system of learning, to orient egents tracking the vector of invention. Literacy established education as an institution of knowledge, constituting an archive of information, history, and craft skills and schemas, but it neglected the creative invention of the disciplines. Electrate learning shifts emphasis from reproduction of verification to an institution of invention, designed as an existential positioning system that individual learners use to innovate within received systems (hence syncretism of literate and electrate education). Learners (inventors) intuit a certain path or direction, that is also experienced in everyday life as conatus, a striving to persist in one's own being (to live). Heidegger supplemented literate instrumental calculation with the poetics of following a path (Cristin, *Heidegger and Leibniz*). It turns out that Heidegger's Dasein, his existentialia as electrate categories, opens the dimension of "disposition" that is exactly the one identified by Gerald Holton as the site of an inventor's image of wide scope. In *Contributions to Philosophy*, Heidegger goes further, framing thought as such as creative.

> One of the *Contributions'* most striking words for the new thinking is *Er-denken*, which we can render as "bethinking." *Erdenken* ordinarily means to think something up, to invent it (*erfinden*). Heidegger seems to be daring us to raise some typical objecitons to his thought: it is fantastic, arbitrary, nonobjective. The conception of truth as correct representation looks on inventiveness with suspicion: creativity must be subordinated to the way things are. The very word *Er-denken* is part of Heidegger's assault on representational thought. Bethinking tries to step beyond being as presencing, and thus beyond the present-indicative tonality of traditional thought." (Polt, *The Emergency of Being* 109).

The name for someone practicing heuretics is "heuretes" (one who finds), corresponding with "bethinking" in Heidegger's turn from concepts to incepts (inceptive thinking). Einstein's compass, embodying the concrete logic of his personal disposition (pre-disposition Holton would say) has as much to do with his revolutionary science as do the disciplines of physics and mathematics.

Aporia Disaster

We may introduce here another organizing feature of konsult after apparatus and heuretics: *disaster*. The egent (electrate learner, heuretes), konsults on disaster (the "k" marks the practice as "inventional" rather than conventional). This disaster is such because aporetic—an actual condition of public policy debate that is fundamentally resistant to the best solutions of conventional practice (scientific, political, social). For the EmerAgency prototype this site is the Cabot/Koppers Superfund Site in Gainesville, Florida, addressed in the konsult entitled "Murphy's Well-Being." The design of MWB is developed through a series of units interpolated as interludes between the chapters. Conventional consulting is in the Contrast slot in our CATTt. Contrast does not mean that conventional consulting ("consulting" with a "c") is wrong or bad, but that it is inadequate to the entangled ecology of disaster. Let the empirical utilitarian (literate) practices do their best. The disasters persist. Konsult is thus motivated to seek experimental alternatives.

Konsult is to electracy what dialogue is to literacy: the genre created to support learning in the new apparatus. Dialogue is structured by an interface metaphor of "conversation," albeit in written form. Conversation is a practice familiar in the oral apparatus, and the conceptual persona of "Socrates" alludes to the practice of an historical person. Within the dramatized conversations, students encountered dialectic (the logic native to literacy). Konsult similarly appropriates "consulting" as a practice familiar to literacy and central to applied knowledge in specialized disciplines. Egents konsulting on a disaster are like interlocutors conversing with Socrates. *Disaster is the Socrates of electracy*. The challenge of heuretics is to design konsulting (electrate consulting) in a way that brings egents into relation with practices native to the affordances of the digital apparatus. Socrates was skilled in conceptual reasoning (many of the dialogues are exercises in defining of terms, as well as in inferential reasoning applying the definitions to circumstances). What is the writing of the disaster (to allude to Blanchot)? Disasters are expressions, communications, replies, feedback loops, revelations of Avatar. What may be counter-intuitive is that, given its status as pedagogy, konsult introduces between pure and applied disciplinary knowledge the wide image (autobiography of interpellation, predisposition) of the egent. Wide-image is simulacrum (a claim to be developed further). Part of heuretics as pedagogy is to learn how to translate a unique wide image into an original hypothesis addressing a collective aporia. Analogies for the relation of egents with disasters might be analysands with analysts, or auteurs with Hollywood B movies.

POETICS

Here is an overview of the poetics of konsult, to be tested and adapted for your own case. Experiments select specific operators within the resources for probes and projects.

1. Konsult: Egents create konsult to organize all learning. The genre as interface brings into relation the popcycle system (field, network) of institutions. Egents may be: a) enrolled in a college program; b) MOOC participant; c) fifth estate movement; d) activist, artist, citizen; e) lifelong learner; f) professional consultant; g) other. The practice itself correlates collaboration across institutions and among disparate egents. The purpose is choragraphy: to map a process interfacing literacy with electracy: the isolated divisions of the university and of culture put into connection with the entangled holistic events of disaster. One becomes educated, even if the aporia remains.

2. Interface: The genre appropriates existing practice of consulting as the interface metaphor conjoining literate schooling (specialized knowledge, applied science), with electrate metaphysics. The guiding stand is that egents konsult on aporetic problems of personal concern: disasters natural and cultural, matters resistant to public policy initiatives. The disaster is a boundary object, gathering heterogeneous specializations into collaborative groups.

3. Pedagogy: the function of the genre is not to replicate or mime consulting but to propose an electrate supplement for it. Konsult supports learning, from the side of creativity and invention. The CATTt poetics is needed to design and test a system of annotation that reconfigures the disaster accord-

ing to electrate metaphysics. The genre reconfigures not only consulting (disciplinary practices) but pedagogy itself (learning practices). Pedagogy is understood to be a representation of disciplinary knowledge (not the knowledge itself) and as such is open to the revolution in representation that is a feature of the passage from literacy to electracy.

4. Theory (CATTt): The theory informing konsult poetics is poststructuralism: French reading Germans reading Greek philosophy. Apparatus (*dispositif*) is the fundamental organizing concept of this reading relevant to us—the insight that civilization evolves through an adaptive system interrelating technology, institution invention, identity formation. The three most recent epochs are orality, literacy, electracy, each epoch opening a new dimension of capability relevant to human thriving. A shorthand version of the relationship among the epochs is found in Kant's three critiques, which in turn may be condensed in the truism that the three relevant virtues (powers, capabilities) are the Good (Right/Wrong, orality, religion), the True (True/False, literacy, science), the Beautiful (Attraction/Repulsion, electracy, entertainment). The crucial point is that electracy addresses the power of desire (attraction/repulsion). Electracy does not replace science and religion but supplements them (reconfiguration among the apparati). Religion and science continue and transform to accommodate the third power of desire within the project of well-being. The keywords (synonyms) directing this orientation are: Enjoyment (Heidegger); Jouissance (Lacan); Trace (Derrida). This latter term shows the stakes, since Derrida's "trace" is folded into "electracy." The list could be extended (Bataille's General Economy; Klossowski's simulcrum). Deleuze's reading of Spinoza's conatus (joy/sadness) is important, not to mention desiring machines (Deleuze and Guattari)

5. Analogy (CATTt): The resource for articulating electrate logic is the vanguard revolution in the arts, originating in Montmartre cabarets and culminating in its first phase in Zurich Dada. The avant-garde opened a space of pure creativity, pure invention, in Bohemian Paris in the nineteenth century. A general description of this logic is that it does for desire (drive, affect,

emotion, feeling) what Aristotle's propositional logic did for reason. All the resources of *signifiance* are legitimated, beyond the propositional and mathematical configuration of literacy, across all media. The break and redirection again is sited in Kant, Third Critique, bringing aesthetics into equal standing with scientific understanding and moral reason. Everything follows from Kant's proposal of reflective judgment, which is thought ordered through aesthetic relations without concepts or topical logics. Much of what has happened in culture during the past two centuries may be characterized as working out the consequences of reflective judgment, which accesses the dimension of life-death, a primoridal or primal scene (*obscenario*), Unconscious, primary process (to use phrases from psychoanalysis, which is the fullest rational account of these operations). In more conventional terms, articulated most fully in the work of Hannah Arendt, Kant's third Critique (of Judgment) concerns not thinking or will but imagination. Electracy is to the virtue of imagination what literacy is to the virtue of thinking. Arts innovations (bachelor machine construction) provide the rhetoric with which to organize multimodal annotations of disaster as scene of instruction.

6. Experiment: The hypothesis of our framing is that electrate learning requires students to design and test konsult. Konsult extends the form of conventional consultant scenarios and other annotations into a mental model (cognitive map, memory palace, wide image, existential positioning system — EPS) locating learner orientation within the forces shaping the situation of the disaster. Countering the realist poetics of consultant scenarios, the experiment uses resources selected from the CATTt archives to produce New Wave modernist obscenarios. The larger goal of the collective process is to design and test a metaphysics for electracy (the operating rhetorics equivalent of ontology, logic, ethics and the like for literacy). The experiment uses reflective judgment with Dada forms to experience the powers of desire (appetite) expressed in the disaster. Keeping in mind a definition of learning as undergoing change, the primary effect of konsult is a revelation of egent participation in collective events in the ecosystem of reality. The cumulative effects of these experiments have implications for all parts of

the apparatus, including transformations of values and behaviors. EmerAgency motto: *Problems B Us*.

Murphy's Well-Being

Between each chapter there is a section describing a konsult performed by the Florida Research Ensemble, as a point of reference, but not as a model or prescription. These interludes sample an archive of notes, documents, posts, conversations, and images produced during the design process (2011–2012), the collaboration creating an interactive installation experimenting with the genre of konsult. Participants in the production group include FRE members Gregory Ulmer, Barbara Jo Revelle, Jack Stenner, along with graduate students Lu Cao, Samuel Lopez de Victoria, and Zach Castedo. The konsult addresses the ongoing disaster of ground and air pollution associated with a Superfund site—the wood-treatment operation at the Cabot-Koppers facility in Gainesville, Florida, in continuous operation from 1911 until its closing in 2010. Entitled "Murphy's Well-Being," the konsult uses arts and letters knowledge and methods to support community theopraxesis.

The installation consisted of two, synchronized video projections and an interactive, multi-touch table that allowed participants the ability to investigate and navigate a database archive, a representation of the Cabot-Koppers Superfund site and adjacent neighborhood. The interactive surface used the Diffused Surface Illumination method to respond to presses on the screen. For example, homes in the adjacent Stephen Foster neighborhood function as buttons. The viewer touches a house, thus triggering playback of contextually related video projected on the nearby walls. The projection on the left is an interview with an occupant from the home, and the adjacent video is a clip programmatically selected from one of the popcycle categories (History, Entertainment, Philosophy). "Murphy's Well-Being" was created for the Superfund Art Project exhibition titled, "Region 4: Transformation Through Imagination," Thomas Center Gallery, Gainesville, FL, March 2—April 28, 2012. Support for the project was provided by the University of Florida Fine Arts Scholarship Enhancement Fund, the Superfund Art Project via the City of Gainesville, and The Florida Department of Environmental Protection.

This project continues online in a blog—Konsult Experiment—affiliated with the Electracy and Transmedia series, edited by

Cynthia Haynes and Jan Rune Holmevik for Parlor Press (www.konsultexperiment.com).

Acknowledgments

The design and testing of konsult have been undertaken in the context of collaboration with colleagues and students. Thanks especially to members of the Florida Research Ensemble—Jack Stenner, Barbara Jo Revelle, Jan Rune Holmevik, John Craig Freeman. Mark Goulthorpe, Professor of Architecture at MIT, provided motivation, support, and insight in the context of his Design Stream colloquium. Victor Vitanza and Craig Saper are continuing sources of inspiration. The inventive projects of the students in my graduate seminars at the University of Florida demonstrated the practical value of heuretics. It should not go without saying that research is not sustainable without the support of family. I am especially grateful to Kathy Ulmer, with whom this year (2018) I am celebrating fifty years of marriage, and to our grandchildren for their affirmation of the joys of learning.

KONSULT

Figure 2. "The Well." *Murphy's Well-Being*, Florida Research Ensemble. Installation. Photo by Jack Stenner.

1 Justice

ELECTRATE LEARNING

Learning is the greatest pleasure, and an inherent *capability*, perhaps the definitive one, for human beings. There are many ways to learn, and perhaps *pleasure* is the more important entry in the equation. At the same time, there are complaints about how hard it is to learn, or at least how difficult learning becomes in the institution of education. Where are we when we learn? With whom am I speaking? What if learning were conducted not as communication between clearly positioned sender and receiver, but in another way, according to the protocols of poetic making? We are proposing for electracy an autodidactic pedagogy. *Here is the first lesson*, but how is it to be taken, composed by an American academic, in English, for a globally dispersed education across all institutions? I am addressing myself, composing in the *middle voice*, neither active nor passive, but reflexive. You, overhearing me, address yourself in turn. Konsult is invented by the learner.

I benefitted from at least four educations, pedagogy of four institutions (and then some), and so did you. We live within these institutions that collectively are called the popcycle: Family, Entertainment (popular culture), School, Career (profession, craft). For some of us Church may displace one of the others, or function as a fifth register. It often is in conflict with Street, the emergent institution of leisure, clubs, parties, gangs. In the epoch of literacy, Western alphabetic civilization, the popcycle institutions remained apart, analytically compartmentalized. In the emerging apparatus of electracy (digital civilization, beginning in the industrial revolution), the popcycle registers begin to converge, hybridize, syncretize, blend into one complex arrangement. An apparatus is a set-up, dispositif, a framing configuration that guides all thought and action of its subjects (Agamben, *What Is an Apparatus?*). How to learn in this new apparatus of electracy? How to think and act within the holistic popcycle? That is what we will explore together, each in our own situation.

REOCCUPYING AVATAR

We are proposing a scene, a process of electrate instruction from a particular point of view, addressing ourselves (each one of us participating). The program is not asserted but described, and its relevance may be tested by one who feels addressed. We: the egents of EmerAgency. EmerAgency is an online virtual consultancy (with Konsult Experiment as one instantiation), self-appointed advisers committed to adapting social media to the formation of a "fifth estate." "Egent" names the electrate "agent," and evokes macaronically the Latin verb "they lack." "They," the anonymous mass, is (are) becoming individuated. Why is lack important to digital egency? We may recognize "lack" as a fundamental condition of Subject in contemporary theory of identity. Apparatus formation includes the invention of identity behaviors (individual and collective), and we will argue that all the theory devoted to "Subject" articulates in fact a new modality of experience beyond soul and self, and native to a digital milieu. Given this attitude, let me review the argument of my recent book, *Avatar Emergency*, in order to clarify the state of the question for me, the point of departure for further instruction (for myself, first of all).

The Sanskrit term "avatar" (meaning "descent") has been appropriated within popular culture, first by the creators of cyberpunk science fiction, to name the manifestation of a player's persona in cyberspace. The usage extended to virtual reality sites such as Second Life, referring to the characters one played online, and on into one's online identity in general. This usage offered an opportunity for expropriation, to open popular culture to electracy—the recognition that identity behaviors individual and collective are invented within an apparatus along with technologies of equipment and rhetorics of practice. The cyberpunk usage, however, is more descriptive of *brand behavior*, certainly relevant but expressing the extension and continuation of literate selfhood into electracy. Brands are self-conscious, willed, deliberately designed, projections of ego (and self). Electrate individuals are brands but not avatars.

The theological, mythological, and cultural experience to which the term avatar refers has little to do with brand: it is not projected by self, but received from Outside. The prototype of avatar is the scene in the Hindu classic, *Bhagavad Gita*, itself a part of the epic *Mahabharata*. Prince Arjuna arrives at the site where two great armies are preparing for battle, awaiting only his order to begin what will have been a terrible civil war. Arjuna expresses doubts to his charioteer and best friend, Krishna. Krishna reveals himself at that moment as Avatar, representative on earth of the god Vishnu. Avatar descends in conditions of crisis. The Song (Gita) consists of an interlude in the epic, a scene of instruction in which Krishna explains to Arjuna the ethos, the metaphysics, of his apparatus: the notions of hero, duty (Dharma), and how one achieves liberation (Moksha).

This narrative is a prototype for a certain *functionality* that we seek also for electracy: not theology, but the scene through which an individual person receives instruction from Absolute (relative to an epoch). William Gibson's cyberpunk science fiction used the analogy of possession by a god (Haitian Vodun) to dramatize the experience of an individual "jacked in" to databases circulating total information. It is important to adjust our usage of avatar, as relay for understanding collective identity creation today. There is an actant position "god" in civilization. How does it function? I am not god, nor am I passively determined by some external force. In what way do I participate in the collective construction of reality? The historical relationship between the macrocosm and microcosm collapsed during modernity, as literacy achieved closure, and needs to be reinvented for electracy. One definition of konsult as education is just this interface correpondence between microcosm and macrocosm. Avatar is the name for an emergent collective Subject position (capitalized, to reflect this theoretical status), or rather, for this relation between person and world (inside and outside). "Egency" is to Avatar what "agency" is for self. The heuretic method for this invention borrows from Hans Blumenberg the insight into how each epoch learns to *reoccupy* the metaphysics of its predecessors, to accumulate an historical palimpsest in which most of the questions remain the same, and most of the answers are "obsoleted" (McLuhan), archived and replaced. Blumenberg's context was a history of secularization, the passage of Europe out of the Middle Ages into modernity (Blumenberg, *The Legitimacy of the Modern Age*). Our curriculum includes in its program the development of this function of collective subject (egent), experienced as a scene of instruction respecting a contemporary Absolute or *measure of limit*.

The Conflict of Institutions

Shall we speak of education proper, the one organized in the institution of School, by means of books, reading and writing, literacy, the attitude that evolved into science? Citizens of some societies take this institution for granted, although it is of recent date. What if attending school put your life at risk? News of a certain confrontation reached me through global media, in the comfort of my study, concerning a young woman named Malala Yousafzai. Here is Malala's own account of the event.

> When our bus was called that afternoon, the other girls all covered their heads before emerging from the door and climbing into the white Toyota van with benches in the back. I sat with my friend Moniba and a girl called Shazia Ramzan, holding our exam folders to our chests and with our school bags under our feet. The bus turned right off the main road at the army checkpoint as always and rounded the corner past the deserted cricket ground. I don't remember any more. But I now know that a young bearded man stepped into the road and waved the van down. As he spoke to the driver another young man approached the back. "Who is Malala?" he demanded. No one said anything but several of the girls looked at me. I was the only girl with my face not covered. He lifted up a black pistol, a Colt .45. Some of the girls screamed and Moniba tells me I squeezed her hand. The man fired three shots. The first went through my left eye socket and out under my left shoulder. I slumped forward on to Moniba, blood coming from my left ear, so the other bullets hit those near to me. One went into Shazia's left hand. The third went through her left shoulder and into the upper right arm of another girl, Kainat Riaz. My friends later told me the gunman's hand was shaking as he fired. By the time we got to the hospital my long hair and Moniba's lap were full of blood. I was rushed to the intensive care unit of the Combined Military Hospital, Peshawar. (Myall)

A Taliban commander, Adnan Rasheed, in an open letter addressed to Malala, defended the attack by explaining that the problem was not education as such, but which kind, which institution (which apparatus). It was true that Pakistani Taliban had blown up hundreds of schools in the SWAT region, but those were schools teaching "a satanic or secular curriculum." Rasheed's advice and appeal to Malala was to return to Pakistan and enroll in an Islamic school for women. "Use your pen for Islam," he wrote, "and plight of Muslim ummah (community) and reveal the conspiracy of tiny elite who want to enslave the whole humanity for their evil agendas in the name of a new world order." (Associated Press, July 18, 2013).

Rasheed's appeal registers a fundamental (fundamentalist) division, cutting across any individual popcycle: that between two apparatuses (apparati)—orality and literacy, Religion and Science, Church and School. It is possible to understand the drama of Rasheed and Yousafzai in this historical context, as representatives of these two orders, each fully institutionalized, with historical traditions and deep cultural heritage, each with its own ethos. The differences are metaphysical, referring to the set-up of reality itself. *Reality*. Literate theologians will tell you: belief in the full sense represented by Rasheed requires not just a suspension of reason (science), but its abandonment as a value. At the same time, it would be possible to develop a syncretic relationship with Islamic mysticism as a relay for collective electrate identity, along the same lines as the reoccupation of Avatar from Hindu tradition. I have in mind Henry Corbin, whose work on the Sufi mystics influenced Harold Bloom's extension of the modern crisis poem into the dimension of gnosis (Bloom, *Omens of the Millennium*). The mystic's personal relationship with the Angel, creating "Person" in the *imaginal order*, may be recognized as itself reflecting a syncretism with the Greco-Roman Daimon (Cheetham, *The World Turned Inside Out*). The digital apparatus, in fact, (re)opens a place and opportunity for a mystic actant in the narrative register of general culture, as relay for electrate collective identity.

Meanwhile, a glimpse of optimism may be available in the fact that the two parties in Malala's narrative are from the same culture and society, language and region, with the difference being rather gender, a man and woman. Hollywood knows how to tell that story: Rasheed and Yousafzai meet at an international United Nations conference and fall in love. But that story happens in a third apparatus—electracy—concerned not with religion or science, but entertainment.

Terror

Why does learning provoke violence? Before Malala and the Taliban there was the *fatwa* issued by Ayatollah Khomeini of Iran in February, 1989, calling for the death of Salman Rushdie, the Indian British author of *The Satanic Verses*, a novel that was accused of blaspheming Islam. The metaphysics of electracy is invented out of aesthetic judgment, the capability of imagination, as distinct from the virtues of scientific and ethical judgment. Salman Rushdie's encomium for Gabriel Garcia Marquez, on the occasion of the latter's passing, shows the promise of the arts as a scene of global community. "When I first read García Márquez I had never been to any Central or South American country. Yet in his pages I found a reality I knew well from my own experience in India and Pakistan. In both places there was and is a conflict between the city and the village, and there are similarly profound gulfs between rich and poor, powerful and powerless, the great and the small. Both are places with a strong colonial history, and in both places religion is of great importance and God is alive, and so, unfortunately, are the godly" (*New York Times Book Review*, May 18, 2014: 26). It is this kind of analogy, finding the equivalent in one's own place, that is fundamental for electrate community.

Rushdie's cosmopolitan attitude is not universally embraced. A jihadist murdered the filmmaker Theo Van Gogh, a relative of the artist Vincent Van Gogh, for making a film depicting the abuse of women in Muslim communities. The pattern continues in the violence provoked by the publication in newspapers of cartoon caricatures of the Prophet Mohammed. Freedom of the press or of expression, a primary value of secular society, conflicts with principles condemning blasphemy in religious culture. We are still within this historical process of secularization, the separation of science from religion (the dissociation of apparati), a progression whose prototype was the execution of Socrates by the City State of Athens (by democratic vote). The equally famous case is that of Galileo, forbidden by the Catholic authorities from publishing his work supporting heliocentric cosmology, on pain of torture and death—a history given definitive form in the play by Bertolt Brecht.

And lest we think that the violence cuts only one way, we should remember that the age of revolution born of the Enlightenment, unleashed destruction and murder targeting the Church as institution of oppression. Both the French and Soviet revolutions, in the name of enlightenment against superstition and corruption, attempted to eliminate religion cast as enemy of the people. Both also resulted in their respective versions of a reign of political terror. There is a name for a byproduct of apparatus adjustment: *terror*. Must this movement from one epoch and one apparatus to the next always require and promulgate violence? Is it happening again? The terror produced in the emergence of literacy out of orality alerts us to the possibility of violence associated with the emergence of electracy out of literacy.

Metaphysical Twerks

How does this history of terror appear from the framing (the set-up, the apparatus) of electracy? History shows the pattern, providing the analogy to understand what is happening today. The nation state eventually separated from the church (the Holy Roman Empire, for we are speaking of the Western tradition), and science separated from religion, by forming its own societies and institutions. Similarly, in electracy, the capitalist corporation is separating from the nation state, and entertainment is becoming an autonomous global popular culture. This most recent version of the shifting of historical "tectonic plates" is documented in Benjamin R. Barber, *Jihad Vs. McWorld: How Globalism and Tribalism Are Reshaping the World*. His title reminds us of the three orders of apparatus creation: communications technology, institutional practices, identity behaviors (individual and collective). Tribe and Spirit (soul) are to orality what State and Self are to literacy. The apparatus analogy tells us that these givens are undergoing transformation again.

Barber's point is that what instigated the contemporary conditions of terrorism is not church vs. state, tribe vs. nation, but (as the title says), Jihad vs. McWorld. The trigger is the emerging force of the capitalist corporation and its promotion of global entertainment, fronting an enormous jingle of consumerism. An electrate set-up does not replace that of the established apparati (right vs. wrong in orality; true vs. false in literacy), but takes up its own metaphysics, addressing the capacity of the human body to be affected: pleasure-pain, attraction-repulsion—*jouissance* (to use the French term). Well-being, individual thriving against suffering, such is the purpose and commitment of electrate metaphysics.

We will discuss in more detail elsewhere the specifics of electracy, but for now we can identify the analogy: the Athens of electracy is nineteenth-century Paris, Montmartre specifically; its Academy is the cabaret scene of Bohemian Paris (*Le Chat Noir*, for example, beginning in the 1880s), culminating in Zurich, the Cabaret Voltaire, during World War I. What topical logics are to literacy (codified by Aristotle, Plato's student and founder of his own academy, the Lyceum), Dadaism and the bachelor machine are to electracy. The cabaret venues from Montmartre to Zurich and beyond continue in the casinos of Las Vegas today, and their true heirs circulate globally in American popular culture and theme parks. Entertainment is metaphysics, an institutional grounding for the electrate apparatus, dubbed McWorld, to alert us to its own manner of violence. Still in the early stages of emergence, the institutionalization of electracy remains open to invention. Aristophanes' comedy, *The Clouds*, dramatized the disturbance created within Greek society by emerging institutions of literacy such as sophism. Chinua Achebe's novel, *Things Fall Apart*, is a serious treatment of the consequences for an oral society of advanced literacy in the form of colonialism. A moment of confrontation between the different literacies of the West and China is recounted in Jonathan D. Spence's *The Memory Palace of Matteo Ricci*. The film *The Matrix*, inspired in part by Jean Baudrillard's theory of "simulacra," dramatizes a possible electrate future from the point of view of literacy. In a conventional course on apparatus history such works would be on the syllabus.

The nation state (Barber argues) contends with both Jihad and McWorld. The Taliban fear not so much Malala becoming a medical doctor (which is her ambition), for women with MDs are not uncommon in Pakistan. How did the medical profession gain such prestige? Many of the girls who escaped their Boko Haram ("Western Education is a sin") kidnappers also expressed a desire to use their education to become physicians. Jihad fears Malala and her peers will go to Vegas and learn to twerk (like Miley Cyrus). Meanwhile, McWorld also opposes science (literacy) in the interests of profits, as in the denials of climate science, as part of a cynical alliance with Christian fundamentalism. Science and democracy are caught between prophets and profits.

The Right to Learn

Electrate learning is configured in a specific way. We said it is self-addressed (auto-portrait, autodidactic), and its motivation is an experience of justice, or of injustice. There is a disturbance in the world (in the force, as our pop mythology has it). You experience it, recognize it. Justice apart from duty, utility, advantage. It calls, as Heidegger says. Such is the experience of Dasein, of being in the world: care (*Sorge*) is a condition of personal *disposition* (Daimon gives it voice). No one has to explain it at this immediate level. It addresses you, which is what the Ancients said about beauty. It is radiant, it appears, is manifest, not hidden. It impinges upon attention. We mark it as the Absolute effect, point of departure for collective identity formation. The prototype for us, as egents, konsultants for the EmerAgency, from which I was called (like many others), is the attempted assassination of Malala Yousafzai. This act was unjust, wrong, a symptom of chaos, disorder, oppression, in the world as I know it. Some want to relativize this event, within a pluralist order of incommensuable civilizations. Lyotard proposed the term *differend* to cover confrontations of interests with no mediating conventions or codes. Time out of joint. There is much more to understand and invent with respect to justice. If not that particular act then some other one touches you. Here is an instruction: select that event and appropriate it for your archive of learning, as the target for konsult.

We may take as a point of departure, as a declaration of purpose, the address Malala gave before the United Nations, July 12, 2013:

> So here I stand . . . one girl among many. I speak—not for myself, but for all girls and boys.
>
> I raise up my voice—not so that I can shout, but so that those without a voice can be heard.
>
> Those who have fought for their rights:
>
> Their right to live in peace.
>
> Their right to be treated with dignity.
>
> Their right to equality of opportunity.
>
> Their right to be educated. (Yousafzai).

Her appeal raises a framing question for the global society emerging within electracy. The limitation of "right" is that there must be some institution that recognizes one's standing. One deserves justice, but who or what is charged with the responsibility to provide it? Malala's appeal for rights resonates with that of Michael Hardt and Antonio Negri in *Empire*: "Rather than global security, then, what is proposed here is a global constitutionalism, or really this amounts to a project of overcoming state imperatives by constituting a global civil society. These slogans are meant to evoke the values of globalism that would infuse the new international order, or really the new transnational democracy" (7). The imperative is not new. Hardt and Negri's proposal of a global civil society resonates with the propensity of electracy as an apparatus to produce new institution formations, in which the Internet is envisioned as the seat of this global public sphere. For better or worse, global society includes McWorld and its experience economy. Let this challenge constitute a context and motivation for electrate education. It is a call to form a fifth estate that is to the coming community of electracy what journalism is to the nation state in literacy.

Justice as Apparatus

You are recruited, solicited to become egent, as a framework for electrate learning, to testify and give testimony with respect to Justice (the virtue, beyond but including justice "before the law"), whatever your personal experience of it will have been. *Avatar Emergency* approached electrate learning through the virtue of Prudence (*phronesis*). We (becoming Subject, EmerAgency egents) undertake the invention of electracy as an update of Justice for our epoch and apparatus. Electracy is not invented "in general." The prototype for our project is provided by Plato, founder of the first school (the Academy in Athens), one of the inventors of literacy. He is credited by the grammatologist Eric Havelock with inventing the first concept (the fundamental cognitive unit and communicational device of literacy), specifically, the concept of Justice (Havelock, *The Greek Concept of Justice*). Plato did not invent "Justice" as experience, event, virtue, history, but rather the literate means of addressing, understanding, and acting, for individuals and states, to create Justice for the apparatus of literacy.

There was already in place an oral modality of Justice. We find it recorded in Homer's epics, for example, as in the story of the anger of

Achilles, his withdrawal from the battle at Troy in response to the injustice suffered at the hands of his commander, Agamemnon, over the distribution of booty. Two hundred and fifty years before Plato, Hesiod collected an archive of examples of actions just and unjust, displaying a pattern. Plato asked the question that founds Philosophy: what is Justice, itself? The universal principle, the definition of the written term, identifies the properties necessary to the function or purpose of Justice as such. The terms of this definition provide a measure with which to assess the claims of any particular condition to be just or not. This new literate metaphysics transformed the individual and collective behaviors associated with Justice. The proposal for an electrate Justice takes up where oral and literate versions leave off. There is continuity, persistence across apparati concerning the goal of well-being, secured by Justice, but a profound discontinuity on the nature and manner of realization.

What is our prototype, to guide invention? Heuretics (the logic of invention) proposes the tactic of rhetorical invention: adopt a model (Ulmer, *Heuretics*). An inventory of Plato's *Republic* as relay produces the following set of integrated, nested creations:

- Technology: the availability of alphabetic writing, accumulating over several centuries a documentation of the cultural archive (epics of Homer for example), the transitional form of tragedy, recording for storage and retrieval the spoken Greek language.
- Institution: the Academy, the first "school" in the Western tradition, devoted to the design and testing of the practices of writing, opening a place for exercising the faculty and capacity of pure disinterested reason.
- Form: Dialogue, a discourse genre for creating, testing, and disseminating literate learning, using dramatizations of conversations as an interface metaphor to introduce newly literate (oral) learners to dialectical thinking.
- Persona: Socrates, Plato's mentor and predecessor, whose history was appropriated by Plato to function as an "image of thought," to perform and model the life of a lover of wisdom, applying critical reason to questions of how to live the best life.

The heuretic procedure is to accept or reoccupy this inventory as a template, and to propose equivalents for electracy. Meanwhile, there is a further specification. The dialogue in question is the *Republic*, in which the new concept of Justice is develops within a general account of the kind of education necessary for literacy, the one capable of producing a just society. At the heart of this dialogue is one of the most famous, most familiar, fables in the Western tradition — the allegory of the cave. The theme is that people in everyday oral society are likened to prisoners chained in a cave, absorbed in shadow plays performed with firelight by puppeteers. A prisoner is unchained, turned around, and led out of the dark into the sunlight, figure of enlighenment. Our method is to propose an equivalent, an allegory that expresses the core of a new educational model, a figure of electrate metaphysics.

What is an analogy for experiencing the reality of electracy from within a literate civilization? Here is the assignment undertaken in this book and continued online (Konsult Experiment). The question motivates an exercise for which there is no predetermined outcome. It is worth remembering that the cave holding the prisoners alludes in the original context to the rituals of the Orphic cults, the Eleusinian Mysteries, constituting the religion dominant in tribal, oral, Ancient Greece. The prisoner is released from chains, turned around (conversion), led out of the cave into the light of day, to experience full sunlight for the first time. This Sun represents the Good: the eye is to the sun what the soul is to the Good (there is an eye in the soul). This ratio itself is part of our relay: A : B: C : D. The fundamental experience (what the learner undergoes) is conversion (turning about). Are we prepared to receive this clue? The literate student must leave the oral metaphysics. Must the electrate student similarly "turn around"? The imaginal realm is invoked and reoccupied in every apparatus. Our visualization technologies support not just sensory perception, but the "mind's eye" (as we tend to call it) — Emerson's "transparent eyeball," or the "two eyes of the heart" referenced by the Sufi Ibn' Arabi.

Ascent

Let the transformation (remake, adaptation) of the *Republic* serve as an exercise or assignment in our course on the invention of electrate learning. Our project is to design a passage from literacy to electracy, or better: from the contemporary disjunction of orality and literacy to electracy as syncretic integration (theopraxesis). The generation of our contemporary reoccupation of the allegory is framed with a series of prompts or advisories, suggesting analogies for the cave allegory of literacy in Plato's *Republic*, with a similar context for an allegory in electracy. These prompts may be summarized in a representative work, as an emblem and mise-en-abyme of the larger issue. To confirm the continuing relevance of Plato's allegory as a prompt for imagining our own condition, there is the example of William Kentridge, who focused his first of six lectures in Harvard's Charles Eliot Norton series on Plato's cave (Kentridge, *Six Drawing Lessons*).

> The lights dim, and an excerpt of one of William Kentridge's animated films begins. A parade of silhouette puppets marches from the left side of the screen to the right, seen in profile. Bowed over, most carry something on their backs: baskets, guns, bodies, shovels, children. A wordless voice half-sings, half-moans the melody of "What a Friend We Have in Jesus" to the accompaniment of an accordion in the background. Kentridge is a South African filmmaker whose work has been celebrated for its direct engagement with political and social issues. This film, *Shadow Procession* (1999), immediately calls to mind various historical displacements, exiles, and genocides, even as it avoids pinning the work to any specific time or place.
>
> Once the video finished, Kentridge cleared his throat and announced, "Let us begin in 360 B.C." He then quoted, at length, the allegory of the cave from Plato's *Republic*. As he worked to write a film capturing this story, he said, he struggled to find a setting in which to place the prisoners who can see nothing but the play of shadows and sunlight on the cave's wall, and who when released can see the world outside the cave as a liberation into a higher reality, out of a half-aware deception. "While making the film, I could not find a destination that felt possible," he said. "The procession could not end with a fête galante on the island of Cythera, like Watteau; it could not arrive at a civic state, as in David; nor could it arrive at a collective farm" — hence his choice to tell the story using shadows in an indeterminate setting. (Lenfield)

A preliminary lesson is formal: konsult design begins within a precursor text (of any sort), appropriated for reoccupation (in the manner of what Harold Bloom calls a crisis poem). The first prompt concerns theme: *Republic* is about the new kind of education required to support a literate civilization. A variation on the allegory is found in the *Symposium*, in Socrates's account of his conversation with Diotima on the nature of love. His point is that the ascent to contemplation of the Good (Absolute Form) begins in physical desire: Eros as sexual attraction. Renaissance Neoplatonism, the Humanism of the Florentine Academy, represents the full syncretism of Greco-Roman, Judeo-Christian civilization in the midst of a turn to modernity. One of most famous versions of this allegory of Reason is *The Birth of Venus*, by Sandro Botticelli, commissioned by the Medici family.

The Neoplatonic interpretation of this painting assumed Plato's understanding of the soul originating with the gods, descent (avatar) into a body, striving thereafter to return "home," ascent, to pure spirit. The pedagogy of the painting was that the path of ascent begins in (male) physical desire (first response to nude beauty), which triggers a natural movement towards what is most real, beyond merely material perishable beauty to the Idea (Form) of beauty itself, as such. This intelligible beauty leads in turn to love of the divine creator (the Absolute). The insight of (all) metaphysics (that which persists from one apparatus to the next) concerns this fundamental orientation of the body within nature, the undergoing of these forces, the vectors of descent and ascent. Such is the "diegesis" of metaphysics. The commonplace reference is to the Great Chain of Being: that all things and creatures are hardwired so to speak with this orientation or nature, except for human beings, who are not determined in advance, and who in fact choose, construct, and invent their direction. Or rather, what differs in the metaphysics of each apparatus is just the account of this human direction and movement in and through and out of material reality. Konsult takes up this question in turn, in our project to design and test an existential positioning system (EPS). Education is futural, oriented in time as well as space, across the virtues (faculties) of thinking, willing, imagining. Here is one justification for consulting as interface metaphor: the scene of instruction must be a projection in time (this is also a condition of Prudence).

The scenario of the birth of Venus (Roman instantiation of Greek Aphrodite) is a touchstone for annotating this dis/continuity of epochs and apparati. As noted in the *New World Encyclopedia*, the name "Venus" is associated etymologically with the Sanskrit *vanas*, referring to loveliness, longing, desire. It is important to keep in mind the network of stories surrounding this "birth" (generation, genesis).

The story of Venus' birth, borrowed directly from the Greeks, explains that she arose from the foam of the sea shore. This miraculous creation resulted after Saturn castrated his tyrant father, the supreme sky god Caelus (equivalent to the Greek Uranus). After Saturn had sliced off Caelus' genitals, he promptly threw them into the sea. As the genitals drifted over the water, the blood and (or, in some versions, the semen) that issued forth from the severed flesh mixed with the sea water to foment the growth of the child who would become Venus.

The *sea foam* is the active image, a figure capable of movement across the levels and dimensions of the allegory, to which we will return in other contexts.

WELL-BEING

Well-being is the primary concern, a boundary object of the metaphysics emerging within the apparatus of electracy, to complement the priorities of the previous apparati (Orality = Religion, Right; Literacy = Science, Truth). Well-being is understood dynamically, in tension dialectically with disaster. Our project to invent an electrate Justice, that is, to design an equivalent for electracy of the concept form—Idea—invented by Plato to support understanding, imagining, and acting relative to justice. Pope Francis, with his recent encyclical *Praise Be to You*, identified climate change as a threat to humanity and especially the world's poor, adding a moral imperative to the argument, placing religion and science on the same side in addressing this emergency. At the same time the encyclical explicitly rejects the market (the primary force of the corporation as metaphysical institution) as offering a solution to the crisis. In the context of apparatus theory, we recognize that the market is fundamental to electracy and must be included in the new syncretism of civilizations. Climate change (global warming) may be a default aporia for konsult, to hold the place for any disaster egents wish to address. Timothy Morton identified climate change as the prototype hyperobject. A hyperobject is sublime, meaning that it exceeds human capacity in all three dimensions of virtue. It is "object" in a condition of sprawl, overwhelming all orders and measures of address and apprehension. "Object" here is a misnomer, or at best a catachresis, for lack of a term to name what is better accounted for within modernist ontology of relations and systems.

EmerAgency konsulting as the means for invention introduces Arts and Letters research into the public sphere in the context of democratic policy formation. In an EmerAgency konsult our point of departure specifies well-being as problematic, according to the arguments of Amartya Sen, winner of the 1998 Nobel Prize in Economics. A first step is to outline briefly Sen's thought-provoking vision, followed (in subsequent topics) by a review of this vision in the context of contemporary art and philosophy. The question for Sen concerns how a free democratic society measures the in/justice of its policies, relative to the well-being of individuals and communities affected. He admits that public reason (deliberative or practical reason) has its limits, but he insists that it is imperative to apply reason to problems to the extent possible. Sen's position offers a benchmark for electracy, whose metaphysics precisely departs from "reason" as the primary guide of thought, learning, and action. Sen continues to address Justice as "Idea." Referring to both the Enlightenment tradition in Philosophy, and a tradition of jurisprudence in his native India, Sen identifies two overall approaches to social justice (each identified by the Indian terms): *niti*—organizational or institutional propriety and ideals; *nyaya*—the actual lives that people are able to lead. The philosophical division is between contractual approaches (Hobbes, Rousseau) or comparative approaches (Bentham, Marx) (Sen, *The Idea of Justice*).

What recommends Sen's vision as transition into electracy is his focus on capability or capacity. Well-being, quality of life, is relative to an ability (power, virtue) to reason and choose, with freedom to decide according to one's values and preferences, the kind of life (life-style) one lives. Every term in this summary statement is problematic in a positive sense, meaning that this vision helps organize our konsultation. The caveat is that Sen's commitment to reason and logic as the dimension of persuasion means that he remains within the metaphysics of literacy. Our argument is that electracy accesses a dimension beyond the reach of orality and literacy, even while learning from these previous apparati the questions to ask. Sen rejects the Kantian deontological ethics that judges according to principle, regardless of outcomes. Sen clarifies that his approach differs also from utilitarian wellfare economics, or approaches that center on resources, happiness, or fairness. He claims that examination of the actual lives people live indicates that the best measure of thriving is neither principles nor outcomes, not accomplishment or achievements, but conditions in which citizens have both the capability and the opportunity to act upon their preferences, and this is an electrate condition (attraction-repulsion). One of his most telling points, made while observing the lack of correlation between the wealth of a society and its measurable happiness, is that there is precisely a capacity for happiness. An implication is that it might be useful to revise the United States Declaration of Independence to identify the inalienable right not as the "pursuit of" but "capacity for" happiness. Sen's argument raises the possibility that a society or culture may be set up in a way that renders citizens incapable of satisfaction. In Aristotle's terms, we could say our capacity for happiness is in a privative state (*steresis*), potential only, not actual (Greek "steresis" from *steresthai*, to lack or be deprived of). Egent, they lack.

There are four terms structuring Sen's measure, constituting a dynamic tension that contextualizes well-being against disaster: agency and freedom on one side; well-being and achievement on the other. Sen acknowledges that Martha Nussbaum noted the relevance of Aristotle's ethics to the capability approach, and this context is indeed the one that we will explore, by adding another pair of terms to Sen's dichotomy: potentiality/actuality. This context references the entire tradition of Western Philosophy, from Aristotle to Deleuze, a tradition that has undergone a fundamental change in modernity: not only a change of epoch, but a change of apparatus. Electracy opens a new dimension of this question, to carry it beyond the confines of pure and practical reason, into the seemingly irrational passions that engage the dynamic of disaster against well-being, beyond the resources of thought and will. This third dimension of desire involves imagination as power. Konsult augments the virtue of imagination.

SEN MYSTORY

Egents appropriate the functionality of descent (avatar), representing Absolute (measure, limit of world), to reoccupy the questions developed within religious and scientific metaphysics, to discover new answers specific to electracy. The compass of existential positioning is constructed by composition of a genre called mystory, mapping your place in the popcycle (Ulmer, *Teletheory*). As a reminder of the operations of the popcycle, it is useful to apply it analytically (if only superficially) to a figure such as Amartya Sen, especially in this context, given his Indian and Hindu background. Sen discusses the *Bhagavad Gita* in several of his books, which contextualizes its use here as the document representing his historical Community. Sen's commentary takes a fresh look at the traditional tale (a point of departure for Avatar *Emergency* also). The circumstance is the beginning of a civil war. Arjuna, the hero warrior of one side, arrives at the battlefield in his chariot, driven by his closest friend, Krishna. Arjuna hesitates to give the command that will start the battle. He expresses his doubts to Krishna, who reveals himself at that moment as Avatar, god on earth. The *Bhagavad Gita* consists of Krishna's explanation of the metaphysics of that world order. Arjuna's duty (Dharma) as warrior is to fight, which includes much killing, but none of that is his concern, but rather is for the gods alone (death being an illusion). Such is ethos and destiny. Sen today takes Arjuna's side against the deontological principle of duty, to suggest that Arjuna was right to consider the consequences of his action. Krishna persuades Arjuna to fight. "But was Arjuna really mistaken?" Sen asks. "Why should we want only to 'fare forward' and not also 'fare well'?" (Sen, *The Idea of Justice* 210). Sen's rereading of a classic of his civilization demonstrates Blumenberg's reoccupation. The invention of electracy includes the reoccupation of significant positions of orality and literacy, as generative templates for innovation, as in our reoccupation of the allegory of the cave. The conversation between Krishna and Arjuna is an allegory for you in your situation. Konsult as genre is designed to receive address from Absolute.

Identity formation (individual and collective) is one of the three registers of an apparatus, invented just as much as are the technologies and institutional practices. The new identity experience of electracy is generating a collective subject. This subject is to electracy what self is to literacy or spirit to orality. Our approach to imagining and constructing electrate identity is through the new functionality assigned to the term and history of "avatar" in digital culture. The popcycle provides an analytical matrix for documenting your place with respect to the avatar function (the forces of ethos and destiny), keeping in mind that pop culture usage confuses "avatar" with "brand." This confusion shows that cyberfiction appropriations of "avatar" are constructed from within the selfhood of literacy, such that the protagonist's position is as if that of Krishna in the prototype, when in reality (apparatus metaphysics) it is that of Arjuna. One must be capable of receiving communication with Absolute. The original Avatar is a representative of the Hindu deity Vishnu, who descends into the world in a time of crisis. Avatar is an actant position, in that historically it is performed by ten different gods. The protagonist in this scene of instruction today modeling comportment in an image culture is not "warrior" but "rock star." "Pretty much anyone can be a 'rock star' today," one commentator noted recently, "except actual rock stars, who are encouraged to think of themselves as brands" (Chocano, "Revolution Blues" 34).

The equivalent in Sufi gnosis is the encounter with the Angel, establishing an individuated cosmology of macrocosm-microcosm. Islam and the West took different paths, emblematized in the difference between Avicenna and Averroes (a theme developed by Henry Corbin). Islam retained the personal connection with the archetype, the Angel, maintaining angelology, which was abandoned in the West, which is to say that Islamic metaphysics is fundamentally that of the oral apparatus. To attain the status of Face or Person, one must create a place for the encounter. The figure is called *Fravarti*, which we may use as another reference for avatar functionality (Cheetham 92). Heidegger's "bethinking" similarly accesses this "giving" of Being (*Seyn*) as the opening of a "momentous site" (Polt, *Emergency of Being*). The functionality concerns orientation, direction on behalf of well-being in reality (EPS), through opening correspondence between microcosm and macrocosm. Blanchot alludes to the consequences of the "decision" for secularization in *The Writing of the Disaster*, marking "disaster" as separation from the star. Socrates's relation with his Daimon expressed his status as transitional figure, syncretic man possessing qualities of both orality (personal Daimon) and literacy (critical thinking Self). The Latin translation of "Daimon" is "Genius," with this translation (in Heidegger's reading) already marking the dissipation of the power. Konsult opens communication with the Angel of disaster.

Meanwhile, the metaphysics of avatar survived in aesthetics, the arts and letters, which is the site of retrieval for our heuretics of electracy. To hold open this place for now we may cite the explicit record of an Event of encounter in Rainer Maria Rilke's *Duino Elegies*.

> Who, if I cried out, would hear me among the Angelic
> Orders? And even if one were to suddenly
> take me to its heart, I would vanish into its
> stronger existence. For beauty is nothing but
> the beginning of terror, that we are still able to bear,
> and we revere it so, because it calmly disdains
> to destroy us. Every Angel is terror.

> And so I hold myself back and swallow the cry
> of a darkened sobbing. Ah, who then can
> we make use of? Not Angels: not men,
> and the resourceful creatures see clearly
> that we are not really at home
> in the interpreted world. Perhaps there remains
> some tree on a slope, that we can see
> again each day: there remains to us yesterday's street,
> and the thinned-out loyalty of a habit
> that liked us, and so stayed, and never departed.
>
> (Rilke, "The First Elegy")

Does this experience of "terror" resonate with the physical violence of warfare among the apparati? A preliminary insight into the formal operation of konsult is found in Rilke's inventory here of what remains (a tree on a slope, yesterday's street), which is to say, the most ordinary features of quotidian environment. These background settings of everyday life are the foundation for moving from fourth estate journalism of literacy, to fifth estate sharing of social media, reserve of a new global public sphere. Angus Fletcher's environmental theory for American poetry calls for "diurnal knowledge" to be described no longer in the clichés of news, but the observations of immediate experience, reinforcing Sen's attention to the life one actually lives (*nyaya*).

> For the poet, dilating his diurnal perspective, significant long-term thinking is primarily never one of politics, despite appearances, since the poetry has to come from a source deeper and more personal than the group thinking defined in political terms. Justice is not a forbidden subject for this poetry; however, the poetry must first discover the living moment in which questions of social justice are embedded for actual human beings. In this sense poetry cannot proceed from the Platonic position, but instead must heed Hart Crane's call for a "poetic logic" (Fletcher, *A New Theory for American Poetry* 80).

This poetic logic, alternative to Platonic conceptual universals, is put to work in konsult as genre of invention. Here is a key to the transition into electracy: poetic logic displacing Idea as the primary organizer of education. Konsult appropriates the practices of arts for heuretics education. The instruction is to compose your diurnal (and nocturnal) quotidian circumstance as scenario of Justice. In what follows, "justice" proper is in suspense, while we develop the aesthetic poetics required for designing the momentous site (time-space) wherein electrate Justice may emerge.

Freedom and Identity

To continue with Amartya Sen's mystory, the device constructing the place of encounter (momentous site), his Family story may be represented by an incident he repeated in several books.

> I end this list of illustrations with another that draws directly on a personal recollection from my own childhood. I was playing one afternoon—I must have been around ten or so—in the garden in our family home in the city of Dhaka, now the capital of Bangladesh, when a man came through the gate screaming pitifully and bleeding profusely; he had been knifed in the back. Those were the days of communal riots (with Hindus and Muslims killing each other), which preceded the independence and partitioning of India and Pakistan. The knifed man, called Kader Mia, was a Muslim daily laborer who had come for work in a neighboring house—for a tiny reward and had been knifed on the street by some communal thugs in our largely Hindu area. As I gave him water while also crying for help from adults in the house, and moments later, as he was rushed to the hospital by my father, Kader Mia went on telling us that his wife had told him not to go into a hostile area in such troubled times. But Kader Mia had to go out in search of work and a bit of earning because his family had nothing to eat. The penalty of his economic unfreedom turned out to be death, which occurred later on in the hospital.
>
> The experience was devastating for me. It made me reflect, later on, on the terrible burden of narrowly defined identities, including those firmly based on communities and groups (I shall have occasion to discuss that issue in this book). But more immediately, it also pointed to the remarkable fact that economic unfreedom, in the form of extreme poverty, can make a person a helpless prey in the violation of other kinds of freedom. Kader Mia need not have come to a hostile area

in search of a little income in those terrible times had his family been able to survive without it. Economic unfreedom can breed social unfreedom, just as social or political unfreedom can also foster economic unfreedom (Sen, *Development as Freedom* 8).

The point Sen argues here and elsewhere, relevant to our project of identity invention and construction, is that identity is not destiny, and that persons belong to numerous categories of identity. Identity formation necessarily is both individual and collective. The formations invented within orality and literacy persist in electracy, reconfigured within the new formations of electracy. Sen attributes many of the problems of violence today to the reification of just one (collective) identity category (ethnicity, religion, race, nationality). An implication of his argument concerns the obsolescence or even crudeness of the ideological categories existing within literate critique, along with the ideals and values relative to them appropriated as values by individuals. Such ideals, categories, and values are leftovers of oral and literate metaphysics, universal forms, concepts, ideals, to be displaced through supplementation in electracy. However speculative, the heuretics of electrate identity offers a new possibility of finding alternatives to mass murder motivated by religion and nation. The crucial point is that the identity dimension of an apparatus is reified in institutions—institutions that regulate and augment nearly all behavior. A further practical point is that Sen argues as an economist against the use of market measures alone to assess well-being or success of a society or state, in favor of an expanded field, a holistic assemblage of freedoms, requiring a holistic category formation. Unlike the Pope, Sen begins with the market as site of institutional invention.

UPDATING THE ALLEGORY

Writing *Avatar Emergency* (AE), approaching electracy through the virtue of Prudence, I learned that the tradition of Descent (Avatar) continued in the work of Ralph Waldo Emerson, in an American version. Emerson condensed into his *Self-Reliance* (Transcendentalism) a syncretic tradition of communication between God and man, between Being and thought, drawing on both Eastern and Western variations. My guide in AE was Nietzsche, who adopted his motto from Pindar—*become what you are*. I had not appreciated the extent to which Nietzsche relied on Emerson. A reason for noting the relativity of our pedagogy for a global apparatus, then, is just this local character of our scene of instruction.

There is a scenario (and obscenario) under construction here for an electrate education, but you have to design and test it for yourself, for your own place and time. Mystory is a genre for the construction of the Place of Encounter, the Event of orientation, momentous site, revelation of direction (sens in French: sense and direction). Electracy responds to the affordances of Real Time digital connectivity by retrieving the epiphanic scene of revelation, understood as mise-en-scene of one's mental model, a modeling of the interface scene supporting individualized learning, mediating the egent's personal experience with the ecology of world knowledge and power. For the circuit of correspondence to be opened, making a place for Avatar (reception of Absolute), the ground must be prepared, that is, put into the scenes of mystory (and these scenes to be networked via konsult). Such is the key to heuretic learning: when the Philosopher proposes that the emergency of being requires opening a *momentous site*, we take it personally, and test it in our own case. The theories reviewed in this book should be understood not as information, but instructions for konsult experiment.

This book and its related online context offer testimony, even testimonial, to describe a particular engagement with the Emersonian prototype, my striving to persevere in my own being, to become what I (already) will have been (monad, conatus, Dasein). The claim is that creative invention within disciplinary sciences, and effective action relative to power, require orientation within this scene of instruction (Avatar, Fravarti). Pedagogy has its own parameters and conditions, separate from personal life and career discipline alike, which is why learning requires theopraxesis (syncretism of all capabilities—virtues—relative to the institutions constructing world). Here is a fundamental insight: the capabilities of the human body (its powers, virtues) are projected into the world and reified as institutions. The learning begins when you undertake to configure this relationship in your own case, to review the process of becoming what you are (Prudence). The contemporary twist on this ancient imperative concerns the direction of this movement. Ancient versions of becoming imagined fate or destiny in the pattern, teleology, a purposeful end. In electracy telos is replaced with emergence (as in complexity theory). The French homophone *sens*, which means both sense (meaning) and direction, names the abstracted vectorial nature of becoming that is fundamental to this identity register of apparatus invention. What persists across the apparati is the assumption that what is accessed within metaphysics is the movement of (one's own) life (Protevi, *Time and Exteriority*).

Emerson leads us to an appropriate guide for understanding identity as vector. Stanley Cavell (working in the tradition of Emerson as an American philosopher) joins William Kentridge in exploiting Plato's *Republic*, and the allegory of the cave as a scene of education. Cavell's book *Cities of Words* is a record and review of a course Cavell taught at Harvard for many years. What is the *Cave* today? Plato already challenged his contemporaries by declaring that the "Hades" of Orphic Descent was their own everyday life world. Today the Cave is the illusion or even delusion of everyday life: "Conformity" for Emerson; "Inauthenticity" for Heidegger (the "They" of *das Man*); "Ideology" or "Doxa" for critical theory. The scene of instruction relevant to the educational model we seek happens by means of a conversation, dramatized in the dialogues. The conversation for the Classical Greeks is between or among friends, as in *Symposium*, exploring who is the best lover. Cavell proposes that today the therapeutic dialogue remains valid, with metaphysical friendship modeled in the film genre he identifies as the "Remarriage Comedy." Following upon the individuation of the individual out of the mass or crowd accomplished in literacy (self), electracy pushes singularity into the dimension of they, the crowd. Needless to say, cinema is the commonplace default medium for any updating of Cave.

The first lesson from Cavell is that cinema, even Hollywood popular culture, in a genre of "women's films" that may be unique to the United States, is adequate to conducting the work of philosophy in transition from one apparatus to the other (just as tragedy provided transition from orality to literacy). Cavell's insight is that these film romances perform "the philosopher's journey" or path out of the Cave, out of the dark into the light, the path from enthrallment to conformity and expectations of others (they), to discover and act upon one's own desire, to become what one is (to fulfill one's potential or capacity for experience). Heidegger's "they" in this context helps us recognize what is at stake in egency ("they lack"). Heidegger himself shifted his attention from individual (Dasein) to collective (Ereignis). In electracy They (the collective) must undergo passage between cave and sunlight (between They and We). The capacity in question is change, to turn (con/vert, or a/vert as Emerson says), to remain open to a further, better version of oneself. In electracy this "vert" or "turn" is generalized, opened up to all possibilities of tropological movement (the figures of rhetoric). Learning in essence is change, capability of change and actually changing. This journey requires a guide, a friend with moral standing, to whom one is vulnerable, open (it is a reciprocal openness).

There is a choice, a decision, at the core of identity, dependent upon *phronesis*, the virtue of Prudence (the theme of *Avatar Emergency*). The choice is between life or death. What does this mean? It may be seen in the difference between the genre of romantic comedy and melodrama. In melodrama there is an internal obstacle, something that resists, chains and freezes or fixes the subject (an aporia) in the cave, as in *Letter from an Unknown Woman* (Max Ophuls). Cavell notes that the romance theme, if not exactly the genre itself, continues in such films as *Moonstruck*, or *Groundhog Day*. The uncanny match with *Avatar Emergency* is that my example of a contemporary version of descent (Daimon in the Western tradition) was *Michael*, directed by Nora Ephron, which falls within Cavell's definition of remarriage comedy. In this story the Angel Michael, played by John Travolta, descends to perform as guardian angel (Daimon, but also Fravarti), to assist a couple in recovering their way into living (into happiness).

The conversation, the friendship, does not happen in melodrama. Or, at best, the realization of possibility comes too late, the encounter with life is missed (as in the short story "The Beast in the Jungle," by Henry James). At the graveside of a companion, the protagonist finally realized that she was the one he was waiting for, the great event of his life yet to come (the missed encounter). To choose life is dramatized today as a couple forming from two individuals at odds, as in *It Happened One Night*, directed by Frank Capra, starring Claudette Colbert and Clark Gable. Cavell proposes one scene, one sequence from the narrative, to emblematize the formation of the couple, their emerging love relationship, entering into life, that is, becoming capable of happiness. The shift from conformity to acting upon one's own desire (the moral imperative) begins with the articulation of experience into public diurnal pretense and intimate nocturnal companionship. The Philosopher Alain Badiou identified four conditions, four "truth procedures" for philosophy: art, love, politics, science. Cavell's use of the romance narrative as a vehicle for philosophy foregrounds love in a way that clarifies what is native to electracy: desire. The premise of popcycle is that some pattern of homology repeats across the four truth procedures (life-death as pattern is consistent).

We already glimpse an instruction for revision (how to exceed this model), to reconsider the importance of night and darkness in this articulation (against the denigration of darkness in the cave). The couple negotiate their mutual transformation from isolated manipulation of circumstances to authentic experience (love) through conversation (dialogue). Cavell selects as emblematic of this burgeoning intimacy, emblematic of the genre, a scene on the road (the journey, the way). There are four parts to the emblem: the pair are 1) on the road; 2) walking; 3) together; 4) moving away from the camera. (Cavell, *Cities of Words*). It is a kind of "wedding photo," Cavell suggests, lifting out of ordinary anywhere this achievement of human life, a capacity (without guarantee) for happiness. Cavell's model is relevant to egents of the fifth estate, testifying to the moods of their own diurnal rhythms beyond news. The further proviso is to learn from the new metaphysics of the digital apparatus how to abstract the vector of life from the meaning or content of a particular dramatic scenario (as in the Remarriage Comedy), in order to map the trace of this movement holistically, transversally, across all dimensions of experience.

Moral Perfectionism

We are learning from Sen and Cavell about the current standing of the relation of Justice as capability for well-being (as relays for your own set-up). Cavell reviews a tradition identified as "moral perfectionism" running from Plato's *Republic* to Emerson's "Self-Reliance," that is distinct from the established account of Justice in the dialectical binary opposing deontological (Kant) principle to teleological (Mill) utility: motives versus consequences, right versus good. Moral perfectionism offers a third orientation, focusing on capacity (capability), potentiality of an individual life. To associate "capability" with "potentiality" signals a contemporary shift in metaphysics, away from the actual (present, presence) as what is real, to the possibility and even on into impossibility as ontological. Sen and Cavell take us only part way along this path, but our project for electrate Justice opens with their help.

The initial point is to note the metaphysical status of *everyday life* as the setting for konsult. The scene of the contemporary allegory is domestic (diurnal rhythm), as in the Remarriage Comedies and melodramas described by Cavell. These narratives often find their catalyst in a newspaper story (fourth estate), such as the one at the beginning of

Adam's Rib—an account of a jealous woman shooting her husband caught in adultery—that puts at odds the protagonist couple, both of whom are lawyers. The relevant point is that journalism, known as the fourth estate, is an institution of advanced literacy, essential to the "imagined community" of the literate apparatus. The kind of events and manner of reporting generalize into a cultural practice the categories invented by Aristotle: the ability of propositional statement to distinguish true from false with respect to Who, What, When, Where, Why. Electracy takes up where literacy leaves off, opening the possibility of a fifth estate, even as the fourth estate begins to falter in its function, overwhelmed by the simulacrum circulating through social media as "fake news." The fifth estate must take up the program of the public sphere by doing for ordinary quotidian existence in which "nothing happens" what literacy did for the dimension of extraordinary happenings. Orality addresses right-wrong for salvation; literacy addresses true-false for proof; electracy addresses attraction-repulsion for well-being. Angus Fletcher distinguished two kinds of knowledge, relative to Sen's two modes: acquaintance (news) and description (poetry). Fletcher uses Saint-Simon as journal-keeper, to represent the latter mode of everyday life.

> That events merely happen is the mystery. He establishes the idea of a journalism set free from its compulsion to seek always the newest thing, opting instead for the characteristic thing, the intimate revealing gesture. This is a private journalism, journalism for the family truth. But in this very success the memoir reveals the inherent dilemmas of the journalist, whose yen for public accessibility in fact prevents the new from ever really being new, in the sense that no gesture ever exactly repeats itself, and its deep personal idiosyncrasy has the only newness there ever really exists. The subtlest memoir is journalism saved by privacy. (*A New Theory for American Poetry* 88)

In the context of digital technology, social media become the public sphere, scene of fifth estate gestures, just as the press enabled fourth estate news. "Gesture" is a basic unit of mystory, recording (pre)disposition.

The impetus of Justice as education begins in the contemporary Cave with a feeling of dissatisfaction, an intuition of disparity between outer conditions and inner feeling. This restlessness is possible because of human capacity, the intellectual virtues, the three kinds of knowledge articulated by the tradition, codified in Kant's three critiques, which represent the problematic of theopraxesis. Cavell emphasizes the distinction between Pure and Practical Reason: the first is our ability to understand through our senses the necessity or laws of material existence; the second, using the same "reason," is awareness of our freedom to choose a moral law that contradicts the limitations of nature. Kant initiated the philosophical engagement with electracy when he promoted the third kind of knowing—aesthetic judgment—to equal standing as a fundamental capacity or virtue of intelligence. Konsult takes up the revision of metaphysics needed to include "desire" (appetite, conatus, striving) as ontological, as the order of being. Moral perfectionism is one account of the imperative in this register to act upon one's desire, not to give up on a further version of one's identity, not to accept a life of quiet desperation (as Thoreau put it) or of silent melancholy (Emerson), a challenge addressed to egents.

The educational path we are designing takes us into this order of desire (appetite) understood in this ontological sense of striving to persevere in our own being, to appropriate what is our ownmost, as Heidegger put it, to live and thrive. The rationale for this reflection as the foundation for education across the entire apparatus is that this ownmost engages imagination, and is the basis for creative innovation in the specialized disciplines. Meanwhile, to appreciate the value of film as contemporary allegory, we may take Cavell's point that the marriage dramas are miniaturizations of the possibility, desire, and manner of living together in the city at large, in the society and civilization as a whole. The models of Justice identified so far are recognizable as favoring one of the three intellectual capacities (virtues): constraints of necessity (utilitarian); freedom of right (deontological); desires of potentiality (moral perfectionism). One way to approach electrate Justice is to consider a syncretism of these three stands: is it possible to integrate into one practice what is right, true, and desired (beautiful)—the traditional triple? That is a definition of Absolute, capability of Avatar.

After Gradiva

Cavell's update of Plato's allegory from the Socratic dialogue to the film comedy of remarriage offers a convenient transition for our assignment—to develop an electrate equivalent for the *Republic*, outlining an electrate relation among education, justice, and the city, to be expressed as konsult, just as the *Republic* was expressed as dialogue. The transitional figure is Sigmund Freud, whom Cavell included in his review of the philosophical tradition contributing to moral perfectionism. Cavell's insight into this continuity is based on Freud's appropriation of a novel—*Gradiva*, by Wilhelm Jensen—as an allegory of the analytic method of therapy. Cavell recognizes in the theme and plot of the novel the features of the remarriage comedy. Freud's study of the novel was his first discussion of a literary work. The protagonist, a young archeologist (Norbert Hanold), "who had surrendered his interest in life," in Freud's paraphrase, referring to his aversion to sexuality and incapacity for love, "in exchange for an interest in the remains of classical antiquity and how he is brought back to real life by a roundabout path," a path devised by a girl from his childhood, whom he meets again while visiting the ruins of Pompeii. The story is summarized in an abstract:

> A young archaeologist had discovered in a museum of antiquities in Rome a relief that attracted him. He obtained a plaster cast of it. The sculpture represented a fully-grown girl stepping along, with her flowing dress a little pulled up so as to reveal her sandaled feet. The interest taken by the hero of the story in this relief is the basic psychological fact in the narrative. As an outcome of studies, he was forced to the conclusion that Gradiva's gait was not discoverable in reality; and this filled him with regret and vexation. Soon afterwards he had a terrifying dream, in which he found himself in ancient Pompeii on the day of the eruption of Vesuvius and witnessed the city's destruction. Gradiva disappeared and the hero searched for her. She appeared to come to life in someone else's body. Hanold met her, Zoe Bertgang, and they went away together. With the triumph of love, what was beautiful and precious in the delusion found recognition as well. In his last simile, however, of the childhood friend who had been dug out of the ruins, Jensen presented the key to the symbolism of which the hero's delusion made use in disguising his repressed memory. (Freud, *Abstracts* 187).

Cavell reviews the terms of the analogy of the novel with psychoanalytic therapy, observing that Norbert is the patient, showing that his delusion, "is the state of every human being before discovering the truth or reality of his own experience, namely that it is a life-and-death struggle with unconsciousness, that its unawareness of what it expresses at every moment, despite itself, is a kind of delusion. But a delusion is 'essentially' how Plato in the *Republic* pictures everyday (or 'ordinary') experience in the Allegory of the Cave" (Cavell, 292). The role of a work of art as mediator or go-between is relevant. The bas-relief sculpture referenced in the fiction is historically real, named "Gradiva" ("she who walks") after the Roman god of war striding into battle. This relay was central also in Proust's novel of time regained, the character Swann finally falling in love with the courtesan Odette when he recognized in her face the features of a painting he admired, Botticelli's Zipporah, Jethro's daughter. All the registers of the popcycle are in play in Gradiva: Family (the repressed childhood experience with Zoe); Mythology (the "Gradiva" legend); History (Pompeii); Career: Archaeology.

Because of Freud's attention to Jensen's novel, the Gradiva figure became iconic for Surrealist artists, including Salvador Dali, André Breton, Andre Masson, Michel Leiris. That Cavell's connection falls on the side of literacy, as a service identifying psychoanalysis as transitioning to a new occupation of the educational conversation, may be seen in what André Masson does with the Gradiva icon. Artists in general picked up on the central (fetishistic) detail that fascinated the protagonist in the sculpture, "with her strange walk, one foot held almost perpendicular to the ground." Masson, however, makes explicit the dimension of desire addressed in electrate metaphysics. "The artist transforms this scene [at Pompeii] into an evocation of unbridled libidinal force. The Pygmalion-like motif of stone becoming flesh is here metaphorically extended so that Gradiva's torso becomes a raw steak, while her vagina turns into a gaping shell. A swarm of bees suggests an ambiguous honey sweetness seeping from this half-rotten body." (Mundy, *Surrealism* 64). In this version "desire" is no longer sentimentalized or idealized, but is distorted into anxiety, the modern temperament or attunement. To consider together Botticelli's *Venus* (intended as instruction in Neoplatonic ascent) and Masson's *Gradiva*, shows in a glance the mutation underway in the new apparatus. Our analogy proposes a question: who is the addressee of the educational lesson expressed in Masson's allegory?

The Talking Cure

Jensen's Gradiva as allegory of Freud's analytic therapy clarifies reoccupation as method: The question remains consistent across epochs: education as a lover's discourse. The relays conduct from the Socratic dialogue through the remarriage comedy. When we arrive at the practice and institution of psychoanalysis, created by Sigmund Freud, in a history that coincides with that of cinema, a new answer to the question emerges, a new mode of educational conversation, opening up further dimensions of desire and love that constitute the scene of metaphysics to be designed and tested for electracy. The electrate allegory we seek is proposed within this new kind of conversation that became known as the "talking cure." This appellation was given by the young woman considered to be its first patient (or analysand), known as Anna O., whose real name was Bertha Pappenheim, later an important feminist and founder of social work in Germany. She was originally the patient of Joseph Breuer, to whom Freud gave much credit for the treatment. Freud was trained in neurophysiology, but the mechanist positivism of his day had no answer for the symptoms of hysteria, such as those manifested by Anna O., which had no discernible physical cause. In Cavell's terms, hysteria manifested explicitly the blocked communication of melodrama that imprisoned people in the cave of dissatisfaction, repressed desire, against Eros, fostering Thanatos (Death Drive). In mystical terms, she was separated from the star (dis-aster).

The discovery relevant to the reoccupation of dialogue was that when Anna started saying whatever came to her mind, improvising without reflection, free-associating through a monologue, that this verbalization affected her body, relieved her various forms of paralysis. She called it the talking cure, and also referred to it as "chimney sweeping." The significance of this latter phrase is that it is also the source in French for a slang term, *fumisme*, naming the mocking attitude associated with the "Spirit of Montmartre," the scene of Bohemian Paris in whose cabarets the modernist avant-garde was inventing the logic of electrate metaphysics. A *fumiste* is a chimney sweep, with slang extension to name a joker, crackpot, fraud, and in fact recent commentators on Anna O.'s behavior and symptoms have suggested she might have been "blowing smoke" at the credulous doctors. One of her symptoms that seemed genuine enough was the hysterical pregnancy: she believed she was carrying a child fathered by Breuer.

Love-hate (pathos) aligns the remarriage comedy of Jensen's *Gradiva* with the "transference" relation of Anna O. and Dr. Breuer that arises during therapy. What recommends the psychoanalytic conversation as a relay for inventing electrate education is that through this love-in-effigy the Unconscious appears, and this is the dimension of collective intelligence supported in the electrate apparatus. We might say that the analytic session is for desire what nuclear reactors are for material forces—creating special conditions within which dimensions of unstable elements manifest themselves. Transference is an experience in which the analysand (patient) repeats with the analyst in the present a relationship of dis/satisfaction set in the past, with implications for future well-being. The metaphysics of any apparatus accounts for time-space-cause constituting its reality, and transference is one site for noticing, studying, and gaining access to the time-space-cause of attraction-repulsion native to electracy. Freud's therapy puts into practice (coincidentally) Heidegger's momentous site. We have in mind this difference distinguishing apparati: electracy concerns not right or truth, but jouissance.

We noted at the beginning that the discourse of electrate learning is self-addressed, which does not mean that learning happens in solitude. Socrates practiced dialectic without knowing how to write, and Freud invented psychotherapy without having been analyzed. The other source of access to the Unconscious (egent thought), in addition to the free-associating monologue of the analysand, is dreams. Freud started documenting and interpreting his own dreams, exploring the temporal objects revealed in transference, applying the lessons learned in the clinic to himself, ultimately described and theorized in his monumental *The Interpretation of Dreams*. The self-analysis was carried out in part through correspondence with his friend and colleague, Wilhelm Fliess. Freud himself is a transitional figure between literacy and electracy, in that he was a positivist scientist who reintroduced (reoccupied) into medical and human studies the entire body of cultural creativity—not only dreams but mythology, jokes, literature, arts of all kinds.

Plato at the beginning of literacy famously expelled the poets from his utopian republic, due to their blasphemous irrational representations of the gods. Freud invites this blasphemous irrational version of reality to return, since it models the real forces of desire structuring human reality more accurately than does the propositional logic of pure reason. The logic of the Unconscious (the new register of collective intelligence made accessible to metaphysics in a digital apparatus) is "poetry" (post-medium art). Dream work is tropology. Freud is the true heir of Kant in this respect, following up Kant's promotion of aesthetic judgment to equal standing with pure and practical reason as the intellectual capacities (virtues, powers) of human beings. The challenge of konsult is to design and construct a genre within which literate students convert to electracy. Justice is measured according to the everyday life people actually live.

Figure 3. "Neighbor Roy." Stephen Foster Neighborhood, Gainesville, FL. Photo by Barbara Jo Revelle.

Interlude

Murphy's Well-Being (1)

Pine (Ava)Tar

A wood treatment plant owned by the Cabot-Koppers corporations operated in Gainesville, Florida, for a hundred years. Including in its 140 acres some of the most polluted ground in America, it has been listed as a Superfund Site since 1983. This konsult renders perceptible some of the forces operating in the Koppers slow-motion catastrophe. The konsultation attempts to create an experience for our community not only of understanding but of undergoing that orients citizens to their corporate agency (egents). This concern for well-being, the priority of philosophy since its inception, resonates with one of the threats to the community—the pollution of the Murphy (Murphree) Well-field that supplies the drinking water for the region. This instance of pollution is just one of several kinds of contamination associated with the site. Murphy's Law states that if something can go wrong, it will, and in our case, it did. The danger is not just to the community's well, but its well-being. The well conducts the entropic basins of complexity landscapes, representing attractors or "traps" of our habitus.

The Koppers's dilemma exists within a larger context: it is one of fifty-two Superfund sites in Florida; one of forty-three Koppers sites in the United States; Region 4 is one of ten Regions collecting a multitude of environmental disasters (close to 1300 sites) compromising the well-being of our society. These statistics are familiar and unpersuasive. What needs to be appreciated is the extent to which our disaster is the norm, a system, business model. Or rather, that the cost incurred by our citizens constitutes a sacrifice required to maintain our American way of life. The purpose of "Murphy's Well-Being" (MWB) is to locate this sacrifice in a discursive imagined matrix, in order that it may become a category of electrate theopraxesis (convergence and integration of knowing doing and making). Thus the goal of the konsultation is to pose the disaster as an opportunity for a metaphysical check-up, to measure thriving within an existential positioning system (EPS).

The structure organizing the project design is in the family of cognitive maps and memory palaces: the popcycle, an updated version of the four-part allegory (reflecting the metaphysics of religion) by which pre-modern society made sense of the world. Dante described the four levels in his book, *The Banquet*, and they are recognized still today in typology (visual arts) or figuralism (literary criticism). Northrop Frye pointed out that Hegel's *Phenomenology of Spirit* appropriated the Dantean four-part allegory to structure the dialectical journey of consciousness from individual awareness to absolute knowledge of the whole, a modern version of Neoplatonic ascent. Our invention of an equivalent for konsult of Plato's Allegory of the Cave works with this convention.

The MWB popcycle brings into relationship the following discourses:

1. Family: the Family narrative documents stories of Gainesville citizens most affected by Koppers, such as those living in the Stephen Foster neighborhood adjacent to the site. Denizen testimonials narrate immediate concerns in the context of life stories.

2. Mythology: Hollywood cinema has developed a genre of disaster films, specifically stories in which individual citizens confront and (usually) triumph over corporations or other institutions violating the public trust. *Erin Brockovich* may be the most familiar instance, and James Cameron's *Avatar* is also an example. Such films illustrate the mythology of individual agency informing American values, but belied by events. Contemporary mythology lives through Entertainment.

3. History: Documentaries such as James Burke's *Connections* remind us that the production of pine tar for wood treatment is as old as the Colonies themselves, since wood treatment was a necessary technology for the maintenance of ship hulls. The larger narrative of our crisis includes the entire history of European colonial expansion, all the way back to the original spice trade in ancient times. When Columbus bumped into "America" he thought he had arrived in the Indies. Temporality escapes us.

4. Philosophy: arts and letters disciplines have developed a set of practices within the framework of modernism for transforming immediate embodied experience of pleasure/pain (attraction/repulsion) into a logic for conducting practical reason necessary for ethics and politics in a democratic society. With these devices, the Koppers site is configured as a microcosm for understanding the threat posed by the Superfund phenomenon to the well-being of the macrocosm. The chief insight is that these dilemmas are not anomalies, but the result of a habitus, an ethos, a collective way of life. The disaster expresses egency, that is, the collective (if not individual) behavior of citizens. The question posed is: what is to be done? Ereignis (Heidegger) is the relevant philosophical notion: Enowning. Event, Appropriation, relative to the motto of the EmerAgency: *Problems B Us*. Individual lives incarnate collective forces and histories, whose vectors are mapped by konsult. The Well takes in individual cases and returns a community fable.

Region

Cabot-Koppers Superfund disaster is located for administrative purposes within Region 4. Konsult theorizes region in terms of the metaphysical notion of chora. Chora (space, region) was introduced in Plato's *Timaeus* as a third dimension interface relating Being and Becoming. Derrida repurposed Chora in his collaboration with Peter Eisenman on a design for *Parc de la Villette* in Paris. *Heuretics* (Ulmer, 1994) introduced chorography as the rhetoric of electracy, replacing literate "topics" with choral imaging. *Murphy* konsult is chorographic. Chora produces coherence in a holistic manner, appropriating modernist imaging, as exemplified by Pound's vortex (*Cantos*), Benjamin's constellation (*Arcades*), Situationist hubs (Debord). The sense of chora emerges as pattern, through juxtaposition, repetition, intensification, distortion. The compositional structure borrows from allegory, using the device of miniaturization (*mise en abyme*, play within a play), through which a manifest partial property is made to evoke the (concealed) whole.

To say that Cabot-Koppers is choral means that the geographical place includes several cultural strata (plateaus). The Stephen Foster neighborhood, and the region served by Murphy Wellfield in general, are shaped by cultural forces, and choral mapping (in the tradition of the original chorography dating back to Ptolemy) is cultural (psycho-) geography (partly mimetic, partly geometric). The implication for *Murphy* (MWB) is that our map represents or registers in some manner the composite nature of the region. The supplemental places include the ones noted in a preliminary outline of the allegory (the four-place popcycle of discourses).

Retrieving (reoccupying) an assumption of theology (that nature is God's book), konsult operates as if the disaster (accident) addresses us in a peculiar kind of discourse. Egents are Technics-Whisperers, scenario diviners. "Technics" refers to the autonomous but interdependent ontologies of tools and humans. Technics reoccupies in a secularized metaphysics the old position of "god." Orality as a metaphysics was constructed in order to communicate with and even manipulate to the extent possible divine power. Electrate metaphysics similarly emerges as communication with and manipulation of the machinic, and one of the most direct expressions on the part of technics is the accident (the disaster). In our case, we ask: what is the Cabot-Koppers Superfund intimating? We are seeking (inventing) the electrate equivalent of the propositional statement in literacy, received (if not sent) through disaster, Avatar of Absolute.

The vocabulary and related documentation associated with descriptions of the event (disaster) are expressive, read as "choral words" (taking terms and signs in all their meanings). Several keywords appeared in accounts of the disaster. The first term that connected with our larger context is "Region." Gainesville is in "Region Four" according to EPA classifications, for example. Although some commentators find this terminology alienating, associated with "District Nine," "Region" has a positive connotation in our context. It is a translation of

Chora, the term Plato introduced into Western metaphysics to name the dimension of interface between Being and Becoming.

Images of Wide Scope

Scholarly inquiry is conducted in at least two modes of thought: the high focus of specific questions, guided by methodological presuppositions, and low focus browsing, relying on intuition and associative or lateral thinking. Intuition is the default mode, in research and quotidian thought alike, in conditions of massive complexity with rich redundancy in the information. It is also the mode in which fields of knowledge are invented, and sometimes transformed (creative discovery, sudden insight). If Kant were alive today, his example for the "sublime" might be "information" rather than "ocean storm," with the important difference that the revelation in electracy is of Second Phusis (human artefactual expropriating creative Nature). The information overload of contemporary digital civilization motivates us to adapt the orientation and attitude of intuitive inquiry to database and interface design. The design issue for konsult is how citizens may overcome reification and receive the holisitic pattern locating them in their ecosystem.

The analogy with sublime experience is apt, since, as Kant explained, in those conditions the site of world measure shifts from the objective order of things (the order of beauty), to personal embodied experience. Kant's Copernican revolution in metaphysics (shifting the locus of categories from the world to the transcendental subject) was the point of departure for what has evolved into a new ontology of experience, made viable by digital imaging technologies. The notion of "experience ontology" is proposed by analogy with the invention of semantic ontology by the Classical Greeks at the beginnings of literacy.

Being (ontology) is not in the world, but is a classification system emergent within alphabetic writing (it is metaphysics). Semantic ontology, based on categories invented by Aristotle (substance and accidents), uses rules of definition to extract essential features from observed entities. The salient features that count as "essence" are those manifesting function (purpose, end): "form follows function" was in Greek metaphysics before it became a commonplace of modern architecture and design. Certainly things had functions before literacy, but literacy put this quality of experience into a tool and institutionalized it. In recent decades these ancient categories have been made more flexible, but are no match for the information sublime.

Similarly, experience ontology (visceral design) is relative to the apparatus (social machine) that makes it possible or functional (digital imaging). The quality of experience made accessible to ontology now is that of affective memory in the individual body. Affective memory is the deepest order of memory, existing as somatic markers informing kinesthetic intelligence. It is "enactive," resulting from the accumulation of routines, habitus, acquired through daily life, and carrying emotional charges associated in idiosyncratic (singular) ways with individual enculturation. Anyone who has reacted "automatically" in an emergency situation of instant reflex has drawn on this kind of experience (blink).

More immediately relevant is the fact that this dimension of emotionally cathected sensori-motor enaction is also the source of coherence for intuition and creative insight. This affective network does not depend on specific image representations, but is encoded across the senses, multimodally. The event of insight, in which irrelevant semantic domains are superimposed, yielding eureka moments, is due to an affective match that is not in the semantics of the domains but in the idiosyncratic experience of the egent. The most extensive analysis of these sorts of matches is by Gerald Holton, historian of science, who introduced the phrase "image of wide scope" (wide image) to account for his observations. A fundamental insight into creativity as the mode of thought natively supported by electracy occurs in relating Holton's studies with Heidegger's thought. To study individual cretivity in science, Holton observed, it was necessary to add a third register to the two conventionally used.

> In addition to the empirical or phenomenic (x) dimension and the heuristic analytic (y) dimension, we can define a third, or z-axis. This third dimension is the dimension of fundamental presuppositions, notions, terms, methodological judgments and decision—in short, of themata or themes—which are themselves neither directly evolved from, nor resolvable into, objective observation on the one hard or logical, mathematical, and other formal analytic ratiocination on the other hand. ("Presuppositions" 251)

This z-axis dimension of presuppositions is precisely the dimension of *disposition* that Heidegger theorizes as the Thrownness (*Befindlichkeit*) of Dasein, such that the whole of existential phenomenology could be read as an unpacking of this dimension from which are born the judgments learners make to formulate *hypotheses* relative to problems without known solutions. The best access we have to the source of the principle of action, for the feeling a person has of capability, the "I can" (*possum*) of being able, Heidegger argues, is through this experience of disposition. (Chernyakov, *The Ontology of Time* 187).

Although Holton and others using his methods have studied hundreds of cases of the most productive people across the full range of sciences, arts, and society, the prototype is Albert Einstein. Einstein himself mentioned in his autobiography the importance of the memory of a gift from his father of a compass when Albert was four years old. Albert was fascinated by the fixity of the arrow regardless of the movements of the compass. The attunement of Albert's disposition or temperament was manifested in this fixity, which Holton abstracts as the "invariant principle." This disposition found a match with "speed of light" in the physics problem set Albert addressed as an adult. Holton's argument is that this affective trace is the reason Einstein and not Poincaré or some other equally well-prepared scientist solved the problem of electromagnetism.

I have confirmed the image of wide scope as operative in cases not covered by Holton, such as that of Frank Gehry, designer of the Guggenheim museum in Bilbao. Gehry reported that one of his most vivid memories was of the carp that his grandmother would bring home live from the market. Frank loved to watch the carp swimming in the bathtub, before it was served for Sabbath supper. The movements of this fish are now observed in the sweeping curved geometries of Gehry's designs. The *wide image* accounts for Gehry's recognition of this feeling in the geometries, which he began to use even before he had access to the computers that made them practical.

In these abbreviated examples we jump from a personally memorable childhood experience to a breakthrough accomplishment in a profession, leaving out the complexity of the lived process within which this pattern emerges. The pattern has been observed in so many cases of individual sustained creativity that it has been generalized into a generative principle of heuretics. (Briggs, *Fire in the Crucible*). The immediate point of relevance is to note the interface feature, equivalent in experience ontology of essence in semantic metaphysics. This feature is the kinetic gesture, the motion charged with affect, in the scene (e-motion). Such is the basic unit of rhythm, constituting a vectoral metaphysics for electracy. For Einstein it was the one fixed feature within a turning frame; for Gehry it was the undulations of a swimming fish. Commentators from a diversity of fields have made similar observations of this feature as the appropriate interface between the affective body and the archive of documents.

Gelernter, arguing for adding intuition and poetry to the AI model, used a reading of *Genesis* to show the feature: a series of stories, whose coherence was provided by scenes of Moses making a certain gesture of "a powerful arm outstretched." Deleuze and Guattari, in their study of Kafka, similarly opened a new network of intertext within the oeuvre, a system consisting of an oppositional pair: bent head + portrait photo / straightened head + musical sound. The implication is that the phrases expressing such patterns are present in the surface text, and may be extracted as features, designed as hooks or attractors addressing potential matches in the idiosyncratic backstories of researchers, supporting browsing or low-focus inquiry. *Trace* names the patterns of such vectors forming transversal networks across the popcycle.

The further implication is that experience ontology is inherently supported in audiovisual media. The fact that filmic representation actually simulates the presentation of the world to perception enables it to record the event situations that trigger the somatic markers of enactive memory, which is how catalysis operates. Digital simulations of lens photography further enhance the ability of audiovisualization to enhance, augment, and bring into awareness and articulation this dimension of feeling that until now has remained unmarked (or consigned to art). Digital Humanities as a discipline addresses the possibility that database simulation allows reflection upon the dispositions that are a primary source of judgments and decisions in theopraxesis.

After the Greeks spent time with their epics in written form they began to notice some clustering and patterns emerging within the words, the phenomenon of *paronomasia*, with a variety of words formed out of shared or similar roots. "Dike" (justice) was studied systematically for these patterns, and became the first concept constructed in philosophy (in Plato's *Republic*). Similarly, commentators today are noticing the presence of affective intensities emerging within image work. The next step is to do for these image patterns what the

Greeks did for word patterns: put them into an ontology, metaphysics, that is, a system for storage and retrieval of information within an operating system for a civilization.

The implication is that the steps of our project, joining data extraction, visualization, and collaboration tools, integrate data and interface design. Virtual world presentations, that is, may be designed to support experience ontology, both for pedagogy and research (not to mention entertainment) by addressing the somatic markers of affective memory, enhanced by information retrieval. Trigger warning: *Murphy* may catalyze your sense of responsibility. The promise is that experience ontology, while enhancing text-based inquiry, may in addition be to creative discovery what semantic ontologies have been to scientific method. Literacy perfected the education of empirical experiment and logical analysis. Electracy takes up the third dimension of knowing—(pre)disposition, fundamental to creative invention. The application concerns the capacity of the collective subject (egents) to experience and undergo the consequences of its (their) actions. When our collective foot is in the fire, we need to know it!

2 Allegory

ALLEGORY OF THE WAVE

Our heuretic project is to do for Electracy what Plato's dialogue did for Literacy. The relay exercise is selective in that context: to propose a "text" to function as an allegory that figures our metaphysics, the way the Allegory of the Cave functioned in Plato's *Republic*. Which came first? Perhaps we are reverse engineering a metaphysics. The proposed electrate allegory is by Jana Sterbak (http://www.janasterbak.com/catalog.html). It is a found (appropriated) allegory: a video installation, based on one created for the Canadian exposition at the Venice Biennale (2003), made with Stanley the dog. Sterbak gained international recognition with her *Flesh Dress* (a dress made of meat). Franc Fernandez, who designed the meat dress worn by Lady Gaga in 2010, perhaps got the idea from Sterbak. The Canadian installation was entitled "From Here to There." She fitted her Jack Russell Terrier puppy, Stanley, with a miniature video camera (attached to his head), then took him for a walk at two locations: a trail along the St. Lawrence River in Canada; Venice in winter. In the first version Stanley was allowed to explore on his own. The original idea to have Stanley play guide animal to the blindfolded artist was abandoned. The low POV shot recorded whatever attracted the terrier's attention, which had everything to do with smell and nothing to do with tourism or history. The footage was heavily treated in post-production. *Waiting for High Water* is the title of a sequel, 2004, a French exhibition. Stanley, this time with three head-mounted mini-cams, was walked on a leash during the winter *acqua alta* period in Venice. The exhibition included a catalog essay by Hubert Damisch (Damisch, *Jana Sterbak*).

The Allegory of the Cave is a *mise-en-abyme* (miniaturization) embedded within an expanding series of settings that must also be invented for konsult. *The Allegory of the Wave* functions as the device that in Shakespeare's *Hamlet* is called "the mouse trap" — the play presented to the King performing the murder scene as the ghost described it to Hamlet, to probe for guilt. Miniaturization as a formal device is in the family of related cinematic devices: mise-en-scene (framing), montage (editing). These devices are generalized to image rhetoric for everyday use. The challenge is to construct the correspondences, from the microcosm to the macrocosm, to provide a guide for electrate Justice, and beyond that, for the new thinking, doing, and making relevant to the virtues of global education and citizenship (theopraxesis).

The Emblem City

Venice Image-Sign (Pasolini): a feature of the lifeworld appropriated as a sign (semantic aura). Plato described an ideal city in the *Republic*. We appropriate an historical city. What may Venice express (what is its aura)? Here is a small sample of the archive.

The Stones of Venice, John Ruskin:
> The Quarry
> Since first the dominion of men was asserted over the ocean, three thrones, of mark beyond all others have been set upon its sands: the thrones of Tyre, Venice, and England. Of the First of these great powers only the memory remains; of the Second, the ruin; the Third, which inherits their greatness, if it forget their example, may be led through prouder eminence to less pitied destruction.

Invisible Cities, Italo Calvino:
> Dawn had broken when he said: "Sire, now I have told you about all the cities I know."
> "There is still one of which you never speak."
> Marco Polo bowed his head.
> "Venice," the Khan said.

> Marco smiled. "What else do you believe I have been talking to you about?"
>
> The emperor did not turn a hair. "And yet I have never heard you mention that name."
>
> And Polo said: "Every time I describe a city I am saying something about Venice."
>
> "When I ask you about other cities, I want to hear about them. And about Venice, when I ask you about Venice."
>
> "To distinguish the other cities' qualities, I must speak of a first city that remains implicit. For me it is Venice."
>
> "You should then begin each tale of your travels from the departure, describing Venice as it is, all of it, not omitting anything you remember of it."
>
> The lake's surface was barely wrinkled; the copper reflection of the ancient palace of the Sung was shattered into sparkling glints like floating leaves.
>
> "Memory's images, once they are fixed in words, are erased," Polo said. "Perhaps I am afraid of losing Venice all at once, if I speak of it. Or perhaps, speaking of other cities, I have already lost it, little by little."

Jeanette Winterson:

> Venice has not disappeared under the pressure of mass tourism—it has dissolved. It is no longer possible to look at the buildings and see anything of value. The only way to get at Venice is to use the water- its refractions, reflections, the play of light and shadow, and to re-create Venice where it has always been strongest—in the imagination.

Time Regained, Marcel Proust:

> Revolving the gloomy thoughts which I have just recorded, I had entered the courtyard of the Guermantes mansion and in my absent-minded state I had failed to see a car which was coming towards me; the chauffeur gave a shout and I just had time to step out of the way, but as I moved sharply backwards I tripped against the uneven paving-stones in front of the coach-house. And at the moment when, recovering my balance, I put my foot

on a stone which was slightly lower than its neighbor, all my discouragement vanished and in its place was that same happiness which at various epochs of my life had been given to me by the sight of trees which I had thought I recognised in the course of a drive near Balbec, by the sight of the twin steeples of Martinville, by the flavour of a madeleine dipped in tea, and by all those last works of Vinteuil had seemed to me to combine the quintessential character. Just as, at the moment when I tasted the madeleine, all anxiety about the future, all intellectual doubts had disappeared, so now those that a few seconds ago had assailed me on the subject of the reality of my literary gifts, the reality even of literature, were removed as if by magic. . . . Every time that I merely repeated this physical movement, I achieved nothing; but if I succeeded, forgetting the Guermantes party, in recapturing what I had felt when I first placed my feet on the ground in this way, again the dazzling and indistinct vision fluttered near me, as if to say: "Seize me as I pass if you can, and try to solve the riddle of happiness which I set you." and almost at once I recognized the vision: it was Venice, of which my efforts to describe it and the supposed snapshots taken by my memory had never told me anything, but which the sensation which I had once experienced as I stood upon the two uneven stones in the baptistery of St Marks's had , recurring a moment ago, restored to me complete with all the other sensations linked on that day to that particular sensation, all of which had been waiting in their place–from which with imperious suddenness a chance happening had caused them to emerge–in the series of forgotten days.

We are reverse-engineering a "Republic" for electracy, using as template Plato's version to propose an allegory of our own, but you are not bound by our example; use it as a relay. The proposal is not to compose a new version of the Cave, but to find a new scene evoking the qualities of electrate metaphysics. We continue to work within the frame of literacy for now, using heuretics to generate a plan that models the education we already are performing. A device of philosophy is to create a "conceptual persona," a person in a situation, to dramatize how to live according to the speculative theory. "Socrates" is the conceptual persona created by Plato, based on the figure of his mentor, whose historical life was appropriated and fictionalized to represent the interrogative critical worldview being invented in the Academy. Stanley the dog connotes "appetite," but that does not suffice. Our candidate for an electrate conceptual persona should be an artist, in principle (such as Jana Sterbak), but since the purpose is to demonstrate theopraxesis as electrate "thought," we need an exemplar that integrates knowing and making with living itself, as already recorded in our mise-en-abyme, Sterbak's installation.

Joseph Brodsky is our candidate for electrate conceptual persona, since his relationship with Venice expands upon Sterbak's high water installation. As was the case with Socrates, the persona is not a figure simply to observe, but to emulate. Needless to say, this emulation is not mimicry but provocation. The practices of an apparatus are for everyone, and we study the persona to learn how to generalize his or her conduct into a figure of learning. Poetry as concrete logic is for everyone, not only those who win the Nobel Prize. It will not be a written dialogue defining the properties of an ideal city, however, demonstrating along the way a particular form of argumentation and logic, as in the case of the *Republic*. Those features, rather, supply the slots of a template, whose equivalent for electracy must be identified. In our heuretic method of reoccupation, then, Brodsky is Analogy, just as Socrates is Contrast. We are not saying that electrate people must be poets or tourists, but that poetry (art in general) and tourism (entertainment or leisure travel) model performances relevant to digital education. "Poetry" (post-medium version) is the "critical thinking" of electracy.

How will we encounter our paragon in an electrate way? Plato's purpose was not necessarily to have students write dialogues (although some did), but to learn dialectic (the new logic made possible by alphabetic writing). The equivalent of the dialogue interface that brought students into relation with "Socrates" for us is a filmic treatment of Joseph Brodsky in Venice, perhaps a screenplay adaptation of *Watermark*, the lyric prose autobiographical portrait Brodsky wrote in the latter part of his life. Brodsky was born (1940) and raised in Leningrad, later St Petersburg. In 1964 his poetry got him convicted of "social parasitism," and sentenced to five years "internal exile" to a village in the far north. In 1972 he was exiled out of Russia. It is appropriate in our context to pick up the transformation from literacy to electracy with an exiled poet, considering Plato's exclusion of poets from his ideal city. An ironic connection is that Socrates was executed by Athens for "corrupting the youth." The scenario of Brodsky in Venice, in other words, functions for us in the way that Socrates in Athens functioned for Plato — as an interface figure by means of which we encounter and experience the craft of learning native to our apparatus. It goes without saying that this book is not yet konsult, but a preface to konsult. We may learn from Brodsky something about the comportment of theopraxesis.

Once settled in the United States, where he found work teaching, Brodsky visited Venice nearly every year, going in the month of December, the winter, time of high water. He went there simply "to be" for a time, and (if fortunate) to write a few poems. "And I vowed to myself that should I ever get out of my empire, should this eel ever escape the Baltic, the first thing I would do would be to come to Venice, rent a room on the ground floor of some palazzo so that the waves raised by passing boats would splash against my window, write a couple of elegies while extinguishing my cigarettes on the damp stony floor, cough and drink, and, when the money got short, instead of boarding a train, buy myself a little Browning and blow my brains out on the spot, unable to die in Venice of natural causes" (Brodsky, *Watermark* 41). The tone and sentiment at once express the fantasy, romance and irony of his state of mind. In Sterbak's "High Water" we saw an instance of syncretized knowing-doing-making. *Watermark* expands upon that performance: everyday actions given aesthetic shape, recorded and published, giving reflexively self-knowledge as testimony to the problematic of well-being against disaster. Such is the condition of fifth estate enabled by electracy: my dirunal round appears in the public sphere (my living is telling): it is "liked" (or not) — extended into egency.

The Allegory of the Wave invokes the aura of Venice. Why Venice? Brodsky reported a childhood memory (Family register of mystory) of receiving a gift of a copper gondola, brought back by his father from a trip to China. As a child Brodsky dreamed of traveling to Venice. In exile, the resemblance between the cities — their geographical situation in marshland, the presence of canals — made Venice a place of "rememoration." Rememoration, or "arbitrage," is a condition in which the object itself is not remembered, but the memory of it, applied when the place or thing remembered is a composite (Boym, *The Future of Nostalgia* 303). This composite memory is fostered in mystory (the electrate genre organizing konsult as place of encounter with

Avatar), to access not only the GPS of our physical navigation, but also the EPS or existential positioning system of diurnal/nocturnal living.

A source of Venice as mythology (narrative fiction) for Brodsky was a novel (a series of three novels in fact) by Henri de Régnier, published in the later 1930s, with one entitled *Provincial Entertainments*, set in Venice in the winter. Brodsky read these books, characterized as picaresque detective stories, with the usual plot of love and betrayal, in his early twenties. They were not great literature, but he learned from them that what makes a good narrative is "what follows what." For some reason, he adds, he came to associate this sequence with Venice (38). He leaves unspoken his own experience of a broken heart, betrayed by his beloved with his best friend. The point for now is to note how Brodsky imagines his experience through the frame of a certain kind of B movie, even classifying its genre as "melodrama," with the overtones that this classification carries for us from Cavell. The scene includes a Proustian involuntary memory, triggered by a smell that Brodsky identified as that of frozen seaweed, reminding him of his childhood home on the Baltic, and despite admitting that his childhood was not happy, the sensation at that moment gave him a feeling of utter happiness (the happiness experienced biting into a tea biscuit started Proust on his search for lost time). In any case, Brodsky on his first visit to Venice imagined himself in an adventure narrative.

> So I lifted my bags and stepped outside. In the unlikely event that someone's eye followed my white London Fog and dark brown Borsalino, they should have cut a familiar silhouette. The night itself, to be sure, would have had no difficulty absorbing it. Mimicry, I believe, is high on the list of every traveler, and the Italy I had in mind at the moment was a fusion of black-and-white movies of the fifties and the equally monochrome medium of my métier. Winter thus was my season; the only thing I lacked, I thought, to look like a local rake or [carbonaro] was a scarf. Other than that, I felt inconspicuous and fit to merge into the background or fill the frame of a low-budget whodunit or, more likely, melodrama (*Watermark* 4).

ANALOGOS

Plato makes explicit the structure organizing his Allegory of the Cave by supplementing it with the "analogy of the divided line." The figure in the allegory—the distinction between the condition of the cave and that of the great outdoors—uses experience of the sensory sensible perceptible world to show the difference between ignorance and knowledge in the intelligible conceptual world of ideas. The rhetorical figure is hypotyposis, proportional analogy—A is to B as C is to D. The eye-sun relationship is in perception what the soul-good relationship is in thought. This ratio underlies Justice as Idea in Greek metaphysics: understanding ratio, proportion, as the rule of order, constitutes reason according to what is fitting. The explanation in the dialogue indicates the point of departure for our reoccupation of the *Republic*, moving into the old program, reconfigured for a new apparatus.

> Now take a line which has been cut into two unequal parts, and divide each of them again in the same proportion, and suppose the two main divisions to answer, one to the visible and the other to the intelligible, and then compare the subdivisions in respect of their clearness and want of clearness, and you will find that the first section in the sphere of the visible consists of images. And by images I mean, in the first place, shadows, and in the second place, reflections in water and in solid, smooth and polished bodies and the like. (509D)

This realm of images is the lowest of the four levels of the line, representing conjecture only. The upper half of visibility consists of physical things themselves, representing belief (opinion, doxa). The intelligible invisible realm relates knowledge, especially knowledge of mathematics, to the highest level of intelligence which is understanding of Ideas recording truth, grounded in the Good as first principle.

The electrate allegory also includes four levels (the popcycle, discovered through the practice of mystory, whose operations we are assuming throughout this chapter), but without the dualism or hierarchy of reality asserted in Plato's metaphysics. "No ideas but in things," the poet William Carlos Williams wrote, and that is what we find in Brodsky's *Watermark*: a metaphysics of immanence, an affective engagement with the material perceptible city of Venice. A few citations indicate the association of Brodsky's experience with the lowest realm of reflection. The poet confirms the power of sunlight and shadow constituting the visible half of Plato's ratio, but then remains within it to articulate further tropes.

> The upright lace of Venetian facades is the best line time-alias-water has left on terra firma anywhere. Plus, there is no doubt a correspondence between—if not an outright dependence on—the rectangular nature of that lace's displays—i.e., local buildings—and the anarchy of water that spurns the notion of shape. It is as though space, cognizant here more than anyplace else of its inferiority to time, answers it with the only property time doesn't possess: with beauty. And that's why water takes this answer, twists it, wallops and shreds it, but ultimately carries it by and large intact off into the Adriatic. (*Watermark* 43–44)

Water as element of thought is alternative to Plato's emphasis on shape (eidos, idea). We are proposing a means to support Justice beyond and without Idea, in a more liquid manner. "Element" is the basis for a category system native to Electracy.

> Should the world be designated a genre, its main stylistic device would no doubt be water. If that doesn't happen, it is either because the Almighty, too, doesn't seem to have much in the way of alternatives, or because a thought itself possesses a water pattern. So does one's handwriting; so do one's emotions; so does blood. Reflection is the property of liquid substances, and even on a rainy day one can always prove the superiority of one's fidelity to that of glass by positioning oneself behind it. This city takes one's breath away in every weather, the variety of which, at any rate, is somewhat limited. And if we are indeed partly synonymous with water, which is fully synonymous with time, then one's sentiment toward this place improves the future, contributes to that Adriatic or Atlantic of time which stores our reflections for when we are long gone. Out of them, as out of frayed sepia pictures, time will perhaps be able to fashion, in a collage-like manner, a version of the future better than it would be without them. This way one is a Venetian by definition, because out there, in its equivalent of the Adriatic or Atlantic or Baltic, time-alias-water crochets or weaves our reflections—alias love for this place—into unrepeatable patterns, much like the withered old women dressed in black all over this littoral's islands,

forever absorbed in their eye-wrecking lacework. Admittedly, they go blind or mad before they reach the age of fifty, but then they get replaced by their daughters and nieces. Among fishermen's wives, the Parcae never have to advertise for an opening .(*Watermark* 124)

Time, space, and cause are categories of metaphysics, investigated as concepts for universal essences in literacy. In electracy these same dimensions of reality are described instead in terms of material and even secondary qualities of sensory experience, in order to access the dimension of desire determining digital Being.

THEOPRAXESIS (THEORIA-PRAXIS-POIESIS)

Our generative template is Plato's dialogue, with Socrates as persona dramatizing literate metaphysics through his conversations with friends. Luce Irigaray is a precedent for remaking Plato's allegory in *Speculum of the Other Woman*, including her device of weaving a sequence of puns, as the translator points out, "based on homonyms and rhymes of the word *antre*—cave, or den. The most prominent rhyme is *ventre*—womb. Another important one is *entre*—between." (243). Our license to invent continues from her insight that metaphysics is gendered. We reoccupy the dialogue's question and strategy, but seek something different (not necessarily something "opposite"). The invention of new methods throughout the history of literacy drew upon an implicit CATTt. Four inputs for a tale output, from whose intertextual constellation emerges a set of instructions for the new practice. We call upon this proven device of literacy to bootstrap ourselves into electracy. We don't yet have the complete coming institution, but we have some of the parts, and you are learning electracy by experimenting with design and testing in your own case. Analogy is "art" in a postmedium sense, with the exemplars of Sterbak and Brodsky already being reviewed for instructions. Theory is philosophy again in a general sense, drawing upon the work of Continental Poststructuralism primarily. Target is the Internet, the emergent institution in need of a compositional practice. Tale for now is our lessons and exercises, but what we seek is a genre for EmerAgency consulting, to support participation in a fifth estate. This fifth estate is to a global political order what journalism as fourth estate has been to the order of nation states. We need names for our distinctive processes, forms, and practices, to facilitate discussion, to clarify and direct our collaboration in this invention. Our genre is not dialogue but konsult, rhetorical interface app (cross-platform) for a "smart" device with Internet connectivity, in order to contribute to social media and their database resources, including "surveillance" conditions in intelligent environments.

The fifth estate does for everyday life—ordinary habitus, quotidian routines—what the fourth estate does for newsworthy happenings, "all the news that is fit to print." In everyday life "nothing happens," or rather, everything "else" goes on in our getting by and passing through, all that goes without saying (classified as ideology or ethos). As William Carlos Williams wrote, "It is difficult to get the news from poems, yet men die miserably every day for lack of what is found there." (9). Emerson referred to the "silent melancholy" of routine living, that Thoreau called "quiet desperation." This dimension of everyday experience is registered in "Waiting for High Water," our temporary allegory. Sterbak takes her dog Stanley for a walk on a winter day in Venice. Most people who have a dog take it for a walk every day (the dog insists upon it). Here is an action, Doing—Praxis. At the same time the walk is recorded in video (cameras attached to Stanley's head). This is Making—Poiesis. Thinking frames the performances at several levels, in the interaction between the scene of high water and the manner in which it is experienced, both live and recorded. The fate of Venice evoked in the defamiliarized video clips figures that of the planet. Our city (like Atlantis) is sinking. "City overboard!" Sterbak as exemplary artist developed the footage for an installation, but you and I post our videos online. The archive of recordings is available for further processing, to support a collective experience. These terms signal that our allegory is reconfiguring the relationship among the three intellectual virtues (capacities) identified in literacy from Aristotle to Kant: Theoria (Knowledge of what is necessary), Praxis (taking Action in a particular situation), Poiesis (making an aesthetic product). Kant's three critiques formulate the limits of these faculties—Pure, Practical, and Aesthetic Reason. The most satisfying human experience is when these three capacities function together in harmonious interplay, Kant maintained, although the analytical procedures of literacy have worked to separate, isolate, and put the three in conflict.

It is not difficult to sort out the different emphases of the fourth and fifth estates. My local newspaper reported recently the rape and murder of two teenage girls in rural India. The girls of a lower caste were attacked, raped, murdered, and their bodies hung from a mango tree in the village. The murders were exceptional, as distinct from the quotidian routine context. The context shifts to the concerns of the fifth estate (figure/ground reversal): the girls had walked into a field some fifteen minutes from the village in the dark of night to relieve themselves. Women usually go in larger groups for protection, wary of just such attacks. U. N. figures show that half of India's population of 1.2 billion people have no toilets. "From villages in Nepal to the urban slums of Cape Town, South Africa, women say that lack of safe access to toilets often puts them at risk of sexual violence and harassment" (*Gainesville Sun*, June 4, 2014). The fifth-estate event is not the murders, but the toilets. (Ulmer, *Electronic Monuments*).

Well-being seeks a justice of toilets, and proposes a measure to secure it. One of the classical quarrels in the tradition is among the three crafts of history, literature, and philosophy, concerning the hierarchy of truth. Aristotle ordered the hierarchy with history the lowest, concerned with the past of particular actions; poetry next, imagining the possibilities of what might be; philosophy the highest, articulating what ought to be in eternal truth. Three transcendental categories are invoked—the Good (enacted by Statesmen), the Beautiful (produced by artists), the True (defined by Philosophers). This troika extends from Aristotle through Francis Bacon to the Encyclopedia and beyond. Human understanding has three dimensions, Bacon wrote in *The Advancement of Learning*: "History to his Memory, Poesy to his Imagination, and Philosophy to his Reason." (Bacon). The goal of our konsult genre is to design and test theopraxesis, a performance engaging all three capacities simultaneously. Manifesting the principle of reoccupation, the integration we propose also informs Islamic metaphysics, in the unity known as tawhid. "The three guiding concepts of the religion are Islam, Iman, and Ihsan. Islam is submission to God's will. This is the realm of action. Iman is faith in God, His Angels. His Books, His Prophets, and the Last Day. This is the realm of understanding. Ihsan is doing what is beautiful. This is the realm of intention, of bringing the soul into harmony with action and understanding." (Cheetham 34).

The value of reoccupation is to suggest a certain underlying continuity transversing the discontinuities of apparatus shift, capable perhaps of overcoming the differend of metaphysics. The common measure is found in the capabilities of the embodied person, understood as unifying the three institutionalized metaphysics of three apparati (religion, science, entertainment). The integration of the three faculties requires and enables a reconfiguration of Justice as capability, to enable participation in a fifth estate, working for well-being against disaster. Each apparatus promotes well-being in its own (incommensurable) way.

Category

Literate metaphysics invented a measure of Justice different from the standard functioning in orality. It is important to keep in mind that to invent a measure of Justice involves an entire metaphysics (and this measure is our theme). As Lévi-Strauss once said about language, it must have come into being whole (synchrony), even while it also developed historically (diachrony). As was recently dramatized in the popular television series, *Game of Thrones*, in an oral metaphysics the truth of an event (who murdered the King?) may be decided by combat. Of course, that measure still exists collectively in our civilization, in the form of war: Jihad vs. McWorld. Our interest in Plato's Justice is not only in its measure of that condition, but in the concept as such. Orality institutionalized Justice as action. Literacy institutionalized Justice as knowledge (concept). Electracy will have institutionalized Justice as affect. Plato asked not for this or that example of justice or injustice, but what is Justice itself, the pure form. The verb "to be" was put to work beyond its function as copula in Indo-European grammar (linking subject with predicate), to pose the question of Being proper, the nature of what is real. The written word "Justice" (*Dike*) is a recording device, and the practice of definition was devised to determine and state those features or properties of "Justice" that constituted its function and purpose. The term *eidos* (shape) was promoted from everyday usage to name the Idea, the Form of Justice as it appeared and manifested itself to the senses (to vision). The Academy began the project of recording reality in this way, and the dictionary and encyclopedia today are the fruits of this program (along with nearly everything else in our civilization). Definition of terms plays an important role in many dialogues, such as in *Euthyphro*. On his way to prosecute his own father for the crime of impiety, Euthyphro encountered Socrates and is asked to explain what he means by "piety" and "impiety." Euthyphro contradicted himself repeatedly, since he was not literate, and Socrates demonstrated that his interlocutor did not really know what he was doing. Unfortunately, this proof often was not appreciated, resulting in Socrates' reputation as gadfly.

Aristotle continued the invention of literate metaphysics by creating the Categories of what it is possible to say (or write) about anything that may be proven either true or false. Here is the fundamental invention of literacy, putting civilization on the path to science, materialism, empiricism, evidence-based thinking and behavior. Aristotle singled out the declarative proposition, a statement such as "Socrates is a man." The term "category" in ordinary Greek means "indictment," as used in jurisprudence. Definition as practice was modeled on accusation, charging an entity with being what it is, and proving or disproving it by inventory of attributes, differentiating essence from accident. It is relevant that the corresponding term for "defense" against an accusation (category) is "apology," recalling the title of the dialogue dramatizing Socrates' unsuccessful attempt to defend himself against the charge of corrupting the youth. There are ten categories itemizing this dimension of saying: Substance (Socrates, to cite the conventional example); Quality (a philosopher); Quantity (5' 8" tall); Relation (friend of Plato); Time (noon); Position (standing); Place (the public square); State (ill-clothed); Action (talking); Affection (being taunted).

This categorial system enhanced a particular institution shared by numerous cultures that the Greeks called Theoria. An individual such as Solon (reputed to have preserved Greek democracy by introducing the principle of equal protection under the law) or any wise elder trusted by the community was a theoros, and a group of such individuals was a Theoria. Information management was important to the thriving of a community, and Theoria was used for rumor control. When some piece of information circulated widely enough to cause disturbance, a Theoria was dispatched to investigate. The importance of sight and seeing to this metaphysics is registered in the names, with "Theoria" in Greek meaning "contemplation, speculation, a looking at, viewing, a sight, show, spectacle." The most famous Theoria in Western Christendom is the Magi (the three wise men), who visited the baby Jesus in Bethlehem, to determine the truth of the rumors that a new king was born. Plato reports in *Timaeus* about Solon's travels and his return to Greece with the story of Atlantis. Theory in its early form was as much tourism as it was investigation, and this aspect of knowing as travel is part of the relevance of *Watermark* as reoccupation of dialogue for konsult. The sages arrived at the site, met their local counterparts, toured the shrines. When Theoria returned they reported in the public square of their city what they had learned, and that became truth (and no other version of the case was permitted). It is not difficult to discern in Aristotle's categories the guiding questions of the fourth estate, modern journalism, reporting (ideally) the Who What When Where Why of any event (the attempted assassination of Malala Yousafzai for example).

When we say that literacy is metaphysical—as manifested in its practices such as the categories and propositional logic—we mean that every facet of alphabetic civilization is organized according to this apparatus (set-up, framing, dispositif). (Agamben, *What Is an Apparatus?*). In School one learns the craft of propositional thinking. Konsult must be designed to support a different mode of thought, not opposed to concept or totem, but extended into a dimension beyond the range of propositional logic or ritual magic. The saturation of reality by a set-up (Gestell, enframing) may be observed in other practices structured by discourse. Kenneth Burke, the American rhetorician, developed "dramatism" as a way to describe the practices of our institutions through the filter of Theoria: Act (What); Scene (Where-When); Agent (Who); Agency (How- What Means); Purpose (Why). His notion of "symbolic action" is a version of theopraxesis, anticipating the emergence of "media events" in electracy. Any Hollywood screenplay casts our world into this frame, and provides a transition in this mode, with entertainment movies having undertaken the process during the past century to translate our novels and stories into film versions. The scenario is an appropriate interface metaphor for encountering electracy, just as Plato used a dramatized conversation in the dialogue for encountering dialectic. For konsult we appropriate the scenario form originating in theater and used by consultants to project possible future situations for client enterprises (the performance of tale as scenario must wait for online experiments with our CATTt). Meanwhile, we recognize the completion or final cause of Aristotle's metaphysics in the genesis of computing. Propositional topics were put into truth tables in modern philosophy, where this system was recognized as *fitting* (a guideword for our project) the capacities of electric switches, true/false, on/off, and 1/0. A "bachelor machine" description of "computation" is: the meeting of Aristotle's truth tables and Leibniz's binary numbers in Tesla's logic gate. What happens when literate metaphysics is put into a machine and fully automated? It is the point of departure for a new apparatus, just as happened when the oral epics were transcribed in writing at the beginnings of literacy.

Writing was invented within oral civilization; computing was invented in literate civilization. The lesson is that as important as computing is for science (literacy), nonetheless the metaphysics of electrate computation is something other. The function of this review of concept and category in literacy is to ask: what is the equivalent for electracy? The institutions and practices of orality and literacy continue today, and are being supplemented now relative to a new measure, produced within a digital apparatus. We propose to learn from a poet's visit to Venice a metaphysics of well-being against disaster. Brodsky and Sterbak are in Venice (and me in my place, you in yours) konsulting for the fifth estate. What is their process, their operating rhetoric, equivalent of "dialectic" for electracy?

Deconstruction

In *Avatar Emergency* I attempted to reoccupy Prudence as a means of bootstrapping into electrate education. Our entry into electracy (to the design of metaphysics for a digital apparatus) continues this reoccupation of Classical Virtues (Ulmer, *Miami Virtue*) through reoccupying Justice (theopraxesis of measure). Our models so far are of the artists Jana Sterbak and Joseph Brodsky in Venice during the winter season of high water. In seminar we will have devoted considerable time discussing the implications of this relay. We extrapolate to our own case, FRE in Gainesville, Florida, you in your place. The instruction we are testing is theopraxesis (unified thinking-acting-making). The poetic method is that of troping the existing form of virtue. John Hollander proposed this poetics, applied by Angus Fletcher to read Walt Whitman. A succint example is Cervantes in Don Quixote troping the entire genre of romance. Fletcher's citation of Hollander on Whitman is especially relevant to our experiment.

> A map of the "greatest poem," the United States themselves, shows us shapes formed by natural contours—seacoasts and lake shores, demarcating rivers and so forth—and, by surveyed boundary lines, geometric, unyielding, and ignorant of what the eye of the airborne might perceive. Whitman's poem of America purported to have dispensed with all surveyors, with arbitrary strokes of a mental knife that score our legal

fictions like state boundaries or city limits. It declared that all its component lines, stanzas, and strutures sould be shaped only by the natural forms they exuded. Which meant, as in every great poet's high ulterior mode, that the art that shaped them would teach older formal paradigms and patterns to dance, rather than negate them utterly. (Hollander, in Fletcher, *A New Theory of American Poetry* 150).

"America" itself becomes metaphor in the imaginal world of *Leaves of Grass*. Our heuretics of Justice tropes the received history of Justice (the archive as figure), to displace concept into *felt*. Martin Heidegger is a resource for learning how to undertake this correlation of philosophy with poetry and politics, in the transition from literacy to electracy. His misjudgment of Nazism in politics is a reminder that there are no guarantees in practice with any metaphysics. The challenge is to design the digital equivalent for desire of alphabetic logic for reason, in order to "think-act-make" through appetite. The project proposes an alternative and supplement for Justice as concept and ritual, by identifying the fundamental orientation of electrate reality. Heidegger undertakes "destruction" (or deconstruction in the version developed by Jacques Derrida), remotivating Husserl's *Rückfrage*, of the tradition of Western Philosophy, a return back to the beginning and inception of philosophy, to the Greek invention of literacy. The first instruction is: trope tradition (reoccupy archive). Heidegger recovers the first experience of Being at the origins of writing. He observed that Plato in the Academy made a decision, actualizing one possibility modeled in the life of Socrates, relative to the affordances of alphabetic writing and the institutional requirements of school. There was, however, another possibility also available in pre-Socratic writing, another beginning (inception), that was neglected and then forgotten (archived). Heidegger's insight into this other beginning is our point of departure for electrate metaphysics.

The original experience at the origins of Western literacy Heidegger recovered in the Greek word for "truth" — *aletheia* (suggested initially by its German translation) — noting "lethe," such that an (invented) etymology hears "unconcealment." "Truth" is a disclosive concealment: beings or ontic things appear here and now (space and time), are present in an opening cleared by an unnoticed withdrawal of presencing, the happening event of appearance (a double process, an oscillation). The original meaning of Being is rooted in Sanskrit *asti*: is, of itself, maintaining itself, an act in which a thing holds itself erect. It is as well a radiant thrust of life that the Greeks termed *Phusis* (Nature)—that which emerges or arises, the act of coming forth into the light, as happens with seeds, eggs, a fetus (natality). The invention of literate metaphysics is traced in a certain genealogy of terms, beginning with *Phusis* (or *Physis*) noticed in a declarative—*that it is, this!*—recorded in the Presocratic writings. The fatal decision, Heidegger explains, happened when Plato took the path into concept by asking "this what?" crafting the Idea (from the word *Eidos*, shape). The showing of what is, Heidegger states, is not a matter of the eye, vision or sight only, but of coming out of the dark and obscure into the light, a gleam of sun shining on a surface, the Gestalt of light and shade. Emergence (emergency). *Eidos* or Idea happens in three ways: Phusis (standing in the light); Non-being, a mere aspect or accident of what appears; Glory, celebrity, regard (esteem), appearing with respect to praise or blame in a community. (Brogan, *Heidegger and Aristotle*).

Heidegger's deconstruction returns to the academic concern with logos, to statements addressing Being as Idea in its visible aspect or properties, to point out that this analysis of what appears in being forgets about the opening or unconcealment, the Being itself of beings (which he calls the ontological difference). The academic tradition unfolded with the invention of several more terms to name the inventions of literacy, taken up after Plato's Idea in Aristotle's categories (as noted previously). From Nature and Idea followed Form (Morphe, arranging the parts of matter), Entelechy (Being immanent in matter, such that a thing becomes what it already is through growth); Substance (the primary category establishing the unity of a thing); Soul (Psyche, the dynamic causal principle of life); First Cause (the Prime Mover, God, intelligence at work) (Emonet, *The Dearest Freshness Deep Down Things*). This matrix of terms set Western literate metaphysics on its way, by means of a particular manner of gathering (logos), bringing order out of chaos by means of conceptual invented within alphabetic writing.

Heidegger's project of deconstruction returns to the beginnings of the evolution in Presocratic philosophy, to the first experience of Being as Phusis (Nature), the registration of life emerging into appearance, the clearing or opening that shows, and to find another path from this opening, other than the way of Idea, concept, correctness, calculation, taken in alphabetic writing invented in the Academy, in a project that is the prototype of the modernist program more generally. This way is modeled in poetry, and Heidegger devoted much of his later career to extracting from the art of a few exemplary poets (as well as from other arts such as painting and architecture) a new practice of thinking that is a relay for our design of electracy. We are following Heidegger's lead, proposing to learn from the poet Brodsky in Venice an electrate (post-conceptual) manner of undergoing Phusis (disclosive withdrawal of Being), the movement of life. One important update within apparatus theory is that our encounter is with Second Phusis, to receive now the revelation of Technics, with techne and artefact appropriating the creative power of Nature, producing in electracy the condition known as the Anthropocene.

JOINTURE

Heidegger's method is to return to the writings of the Presocratics, providing a clue to the original experience of Being at the beginnings of literacy. The case most immediately relevant is Heidegger's translation and commentary on the one surviving fragment by Anaximander. This discussion defines precisely the fundamental turn and return guiding our design of electrate Justice. The standard translation of the fragment is: "... according to necessity; for they pay one another recompense and penalty for their injustice" (Heidegger, *Early Greek Thinking* 40). Heidegger offers his own translation, based on an assessment of each word, in order to bring out the potential of the other beginning: " ... along the lines of usage; for they let order and thereby also reck belong to one another (in the surmounting) of disorder" (57).

Heidegger's other beginning (inception) focuses on the experience of Phusis as an emergence from the hidden (unconcealment), shifting away from Plato's Techne and Logos (craft and plan). Heidegger poses a different question that does not depend on building or looking, but rather that which concerns limit, and here is the opening towards another metaphysics, another Justice. Entelechy was the term Aristotle coined to name the immanent relationship of form and matter, of actuality (energeia) developing out of potentiality (dunamis). Aristotle interpreted Plato's question about the relationship between Being and Becoming (of permanence and change) in terms of biological development: an acorn becomes what it is over time (an oak). There is an internal limit; an entity holds itself in its ending. This end (purpose, final cause) is present in its idea, in what it looks like (it has a face). Substance is what is available for view or action in an object (the categories). Heidegger's focus is rather on the original power of emergence, the force of Being that is not a thing but a process of relation, as he explains. The issue is not correctness (true or false), but apprehension or experience of being (felt). The emphasis is not on the permanent or eternal, nor that which persists through all change, but rather precisely on the transcience of matter, the arriving and departing, ebb and flow, birth and death: in short, time. Heidegger learned from Aristotle that there is more than one way to say Being, and poetry (arts) offers another kind of relation, another way to understand ordering, of how parts gather and separate, converge and disperse, come into appearance and disappear again. His test case is not biological growth but the art of tragedy, and the limit that it dramatizes, specifically the strangeness of human encounter with the Overpowering (called *Deinon*), the fundamental limit of finitude, mortality, disaster, death, as effects of behavior. Human beings are uncanny, inherently exiled from hearth and home, in confrontation with the irreducible aporia—death—as we learn from the destiny of Antigone.

Heidegger's method adheres to literate metaphysics in recognizing that ontology—the science of being—is a capability of alphabetic writing. His turn to poetry as the model of inquiry liberates him from the jurisprudence of category, to exploit polysemy rather than definition as a resource for thinking. He examines the term Deinon (Overpowering) and finds two senses with respect to confrontation. One involves Techne as a violence of laying down a way or path, and that is the way taken by literacy. The second sense is the source of Heidegger's innovation, establishing the basis for creating a new Justice thought beyond Idea. This other power is revealed in the German term *Fug*: *der Fug* (what is fitting, just, right); *die Fuge* (joint, seam, gap, space, suture); *fugen* (to join, fit together). One says, *Die Zeit ist aus den fugen* (the times are out of joint). Figurative usage of the verb *fügen* gives "fitting arrangement" explicitly concerning justice. There is even the homonym "fugue," referring to the musical form, relevant as a figure of counterpoint in this context. Heidegger developed this semantic field relative to "injustice" and "necessity" in Anaximander's fragment. Heidegger unpacks *Fug* relative to Justice (Dike) as jointing, jointure, a framework (set-up) determining what is fitting, thus merging the two senses (Techne, Dike): confronting the Overpowering, men search for order (*Fug*) yet cannot master it. The Overpowering requires a place, a scene of disclosure. This scene of joining and breaking is humanity itself: Dasein (there-being). In his later period Heidegger shifted the point of view of this breach from individual to collective, replacing Dasein with Ereignis (Event). Man (humankind) is a breach into which and through which being bursts forth to appear as event (not thing) (Janicaud, *Heidegger from Metaphysics to Thought*). This account approaches well-being and Phusis from the side of aporia or impasse: death, disaster, catastrophe not as "accident" but "necessity."

The risk Heidegger took in generating this reading of the fragment enables a leap out of literacy into electracy, for in searching for *le mot juste* for the truth of Being he articulates exactly the reality addressed in the new apparatus. His strategy is to rethink the sense of category as "indictment" (the handing down—or up—of accusation, from jurisprudence), to hear this handing over and exchange as the coming into presence of Being as a certain enjoining, and finally, enjoyment. "Necessity" becomes "Usage" (*der Brauch*). "Justice" in this reading enjoins each epoch to bring about what is fitting, appropriate, in the manner in which what is given belongs together (appropriation).

> "Usage" should not be understood in these current derived senses. We should rather keep to the root-meaning: to use is to brook [*bruchen*], in Latin *frui*, in German *fruchten*, *Frucht*. We translate this freely as "to enjoy," which originally means to be pleased with something and so to have it in use. Only in its derived senses does "enjoy" mean simply to consume or gobble up. . . ."To use" accordingly suggests: to let something present come to presence as such; *frui*, to brook, to use, usage, means to hand something over to its own essence and to keep it in hand, preserving it as something present. . . ."To brook," *frui*, is no longer merely predicated of enjoyment as a form of human behavior; nor is it said in relation to any being whatsoever, even the highest (*fruitio Dei* as the *beatitudo hominis*); rather, usage now designates the manner in which Being itself presences as the relation to what is present, approaching and becoming involved with what is present as present. (Heidegger, *Early Greek Thinking* 53).

Enjoyment is to electracy what Truth is to literacy or Right to orality, shifting ontology from object or thing to relation. There are as many versions of "relation" as there are ontologists today, but they share a consensus.

Heidegger's inventive translation developed the rich semantic field of this name. The manner of accomplishing enjoyment, however, turns out to be as troubled as were the primary purposes of the previous apparati. We shall return to this guideword of Being in later chapters.

DAIDALA

Heidegger turned to the Presocratic philosophers such as Anaximander to find clues regarding Phusis prior to Idea and Concept. We are taking up Heidegger's promotion of this other beginning as a guide for the design of electrate encounter with Second Phusis. Heidegger acknowledged that his method uses literacy to bootstrap into this other "way." His "way" resonates with Asian Tao, as the family of his Event [Ereignis], replacing object in his new ontology. Literate conceptual thinking reduces everything finally to rational "calculation," whereas thinking Event is like following a path, even what Heidegger calls *Holzwege* or forest paths, often overgrown, that come to an abrupt stop or dead end. The path may (or not) connect one location with another, not without errancy or wandering. The "forest" in *Holzweg* as a figure of method refers to any craft, such as the craft of poetry, and the "path" refers to the internal relationships and affordances of the material and practices that a craftsman learns and uses in making. What Heidegger wants to learn from poets (arts) is how to receive from language and the formal conventions of art direction for the creation of sense and significance (*signifiance*) relative to the new power of artefacts in industrialized techne. Calculation (literate science) produced our contemporary GPS systems. The task of electracy is to supplement GPS with EPS—Existential Positioning System—capable of wayfinding relevant to *Holzwege* or movement as electrate logic. The wayfinding of Ereignis concerns what is one's own (ownmost), the feeling (felt) of "belonging to me." The compass is personal, the path invented, but the cardinal and ordinal orientation is measured relative to situation, environment of correspondences historical and cultural as well as physical and material.

Heidegger's "path" repeats Anaximander's own move in the invention of Philosophy, which was to find an equivalent in the new apparatus of alphabetic writing for the craftwork of well-made objects (craft as Analogy). Anaximander modeled his cosmology on the architecture of the Ionic temples whose construction he witnessed. The decision that sent literacy on its way into Idea and Category is recorded in the drama of Socrates, who began his career as gadfly in the city when the Oracle at Delphi declared that no one was wiser than Socrates. Refusing to accept this assertion, Socrates set out to question craftsmen of every sort, experts in all the important specializations of the day, from shipbuilders to generals. As the dialogues demonstrate, he found that, however seasoned in their craft, none of his interlocutors possessed wisdom (knowledge of universal principles, the forms, the true nature of reality). They lacked the Idea of knowledge, of course, because it was only then being invented. Heidegger returns to the Presocratics whose cosmology records precisely what he wants to understand—the emergence of Being, not the properties of extant beings. "Emergence" is the event, natality, genesis, generation (genos). Anaximander is a transitional figure (just as was Socrates after him), being himself a craftsman. The "emergence" in question is that of order and its measure of beings (the elements) out of chaos, their ebb and flow, coming and going, upsurge and destruction, through time—oscillation. The manner of this emergence makes present the potentiality of Justice in the expanded field of terms naming usage, usufruct, joining, enjoining, fitting, enjoyment. Justice means finding the ratio of proportion for civilization as a whole.

The truth that Anaximander expressed in his written text he also modeled with three inventions, three *daidala*—representations of cosmos relevant to the work or craft of theory. Theoria involved travel, journeys both literal and figurative, undertaking investigation and speculation. In support of this work Anaximander designed the first celestial sphere, a map of the world, and a gnomon (as sundial to track time) (McEwen, *Socrates' Ancestor* 17). Well-made crafts (an excellent ship or poem) had a double function: they physically gathered and arranged material into function and service, and through the beauty of the well-made object order showed itself and appeared. This production of cosmos (world) through making applies to every dimension: not only objects but also moral ethos, the city as place and as political order (Justice). Adornment reveals nature, cosmetics show beauty of face, clothing shows body, and revelation through craft is what Heidegger took as his point of departure for the other inception leading to our digital metaphysics (incepts rather than concepts).

The legendary figure most associated with cosmological craft is Daedalus, who fled Athens (went into exile) to the court of King Minos in Crete. The emergence of order that models our instructions is expressed in this legend, whose terms are clarified by their usage in Homer's epics, especially the *Odyssey* (hence the connection with the cleverness of Odysseus/Ulysses). The ambiguity or double nature of emergence is documented in the daidala credited to Daedalus: both Labyrinth and Choros (dance floor). In craft making, dead-end wandering transforms into dance, just as cosmos emerges from chaos. "Diodorus Siculus uses the same adjective, apeiros, to describe the tortuous dead-end passages of Daedalus' Labyrinth, for apeiros means not only boundless but also, like aporia, without escape, which is also to say unmeasured, or immeasurable. It is the measure of Ariadne's dance, the confused regularity of the 'moving maze' traced by the passage of 'well-taught feet,' which spins the thread that leads out of the Labyrinth, and goes on to weave another. In the still-living imagery of Minoan murals, slim Cretan youths leap over the horns of death-dealing bulls in order to dance with them. For the early Greeks, the dangers of aporia were not problems to be solved but the basic precondition for artifice" (*Socrates' Ancestor* 59).

We are reminded by this vocabulary of the novel *Gradiva*, that Freud adopted as allegory of psychoanalytic pedagogy, including the peculiar gait that identified the historical, mythological, and actual women for the protagonist. "The feet of the dancers in Ariadne's dance are *epistamenoisi*, knowing feet, and one cannot claim to have knowledge of dancing until one can, in fact, dance" (126). The fundamental difference between literate Idea and inception is this role of experience, the participation in the craft, savoir-faire as distinct from pure knowledge, of having seen what is already given, not literally for us, but retreived as relay. The separation of the virtues of capability into knowing doing making, characteristic of literacy, is reversed in theopraxesis: the dancer, dance, and dance floor that make cosmos appear. Such is Walt Whitman's poetics, to set the forms dancing.

Here is our question, opening an opportunity for invention, taking up in our turn the confrontation between human power (virtue, capacity) and Deinon. We understand that Justice is a certain kind of relation, a jointure to create order, limit, well-being against violent disaster in the breach opened by humankind (Problems B Us). Literacy took the way of Idea and conceptual logic with which we are familiar, with extraordinary success. And yet today Deinon reigns, going by the name Anthropocene. It is Second Phusis in that it generates out of itself, beyond human intention, manifesting its own ontology

(Mark Hansen, *Embodying Technesis*). Heidegger opens the possibility of jointure or ratio between techne and Dike (Justice). The relay from First to Second Phusis reveals the other side of Life, or the oscillating dynamic life-death. Our assignment is to develop for and through postmedia arts and digital technology a new operating logic, another way of dis/joining, different from the analogy of the line, the allegory of the cave, the ratio of proportion structuring Plato's metaphysics (and Western thought after him): to find and construct another ratio, another line. It is important to note, in this context, that Heidegger's Open (Breach), the gap of dis/joining, explicitly refers to one of Plato's most important innovations, offered in *Timaeus* (a companion dialogue with the *Republic*). Plato took up in turn the gap or joint broached in the Presocratics. To solve the problem of how Being and Becoming (the Intelligible and the Sensible) interact (how pure eternal forms somehow participate in the changing transcience of matter), Plato introduced a third dimension that he called "chora," borrowing from ordinary Greek the term for region, space, receptacle, and evoking the legendary daidala such as choros (dance floor) and chorus (in tragedy). Our entire enterprise comes out of this hypothesis: Chora.

In *Timaeus* there is a first attempt to account for cosmos (joining into relation) strictly through Intelligible Form (Idea), but the account breaks off and its inadequacy acknowledged. A second account begins, that introduces between Being and Becoming, on the cusp or threshold of passage between the two orders (the location of hinge or joint), this event of inmixing, jointure, emergence: Chora. Since Chora is neither intelligible nor sensible, it may only be discussed in poetic allusive terms (muthos, the mythology that Plato had hoped to avoid). The Theory (Pythagoras) directing Plato's heuristic CATTt held that world order emerges from chaos, disorder, obscurity. Chora is how Plato includes the event of emergence in his metaphysics, and Heidegger's aletheia and jointure return to it, privilege it as an augmentation of the other beginning, neglected by tradition. Derrida's reading of Chora associates this second beginning in *Timaeus* with Heidegger's other beginning. (Derrida et al., *Chora L Works*). Chorography (Ulmer, *Heuretics*), names the designing of relations, of jointure or ratio of what is fitting, appropriation. Although forgotten by the institution of schooling, Chora persisted inevitably, producing an interdependence of Idea and Receptacle throughout the Western tradition, with Kant's third Critique assigning to imagination the functioning of Chora, bridge between Pure and Practical Reason, between Necessity and Freedom.

The larger implications of this genealogy become clear when we recognize the Unconscious as the most recent treatment of the primordial gap. It is important to note in the context of the global syncretism involved with electracy, that *Timaeus* and Chora played a major role in the formation of Sufi and Islamic cosmologies. "This space, which is the location of visionary events, is called the 'alam al-mithal in Arabic, which Corbin has translated into Latin as the mundus imaginalis, or the imaginal world" (Cheetham 67). "Yet the fact remains that between the sense perceptions and the intuitions or categories of the intellect there has remained a void. That which ought to have taken its place between the two, and which in other times and places did occupy this intermediate space, that is to say, the Active Imagination, has been left to the poets" (Henry Corbin, cited in Cheetham 69).

This third power specifically is that of the Imagination, similar to the three powers articulated in Kant's critiques, constituting the virtues of theopraxesis. The poets are the default caretakers of this capability, which concerns the operations of "symbol," the concrete universal where spirit and body conjoin. "The Burning Bush is only a brushwood fire if it is merely perceived by the sensory organs. In order that Moses may perceive the Burning Bush and hear the Voice calling him 'from the right side of the valley'—in short, in order that there may be a theophany—an organ of trans-sensory perception is needed" (Corbin qtd. in Cheetham 71). In the West this third dimension or capability was reduced to fantasy, lost its ontological foundation, but then was retrieved by Nietzsche and Freud. Henry Corbin argued that active imagination has its own laws, characteristics, and must be educated just as are the other two human cognitive capabilities in order to accomplish the visionary dimension of intelligence. Konsult reoccupies Chora, to recover the functionality of Active Imagination for electrate metaphysics, which is to say that electracy syncretizes the previous apparati, reoccupying the questions of religion as well as of science, each recognized in its fullest sense as metaphysics of an apparatus (orality and literacy).

Fouring

An introduction to electrate learning assigns egents responsibility for an event of Being, mediated within poetic form. We are prepared now to appreciate the value of allegory provided by Sterbak and Brodsky, as instructions for theopraxesis. Brodsky fits well with the Theory relay from Anaximander/Heidegger, given his late poem, "Daedalus in Sicily" (1993). "Here, in Sicily, stiff on its scorching sand,/ sits a very old man, capable of transporting/ himself through the air, if robbed of other means of passage./ All his life he was building something, inventing something./ All his life from those clear constructions, from those inventions,/ he had to flee. . . . Yet he had already invented, when he was young, the seesaw,/ using the strong resemblance between motion and stasis./ The old man bends down, ties to his brittle ankle/ (so as not to get lost) a lengthy thread,/ straightens up with a grunt, and heads out for Hades" (*Collected Poems in English* 404).

David MacFadyen noted "Daedalus in Sicily" as the signature text of late Brodsky (1990–96), in part because the organizing conceit of *Watermark*, the image used to express the feeling or experience of Venice for Brodsky, is that of the Daedalian Labyrinth.

> The whole business is Daedalus' brain child, the labyrinth especially, as it resembles a brain. In a manner of speaking, everybody is related to everybody, the pursuer to the pursued, at least. Small wonder, then, that one's meanderings through the streets of this city, whose biggest colony for nearly three centuries was the island of Crete, feels somewhat tautological, especially as light fades—that is, especially as its pasiphaian, ariadnan, and phaedran properties fail. In other words, especially in the evening, when one loses oneself to self-deprecation. (*Watermark* 87).

MacFayden's reading superimposes the Daedalus poem on *Watermark*, identifying "nomadism" as the trope gathering "the maze of fifty-one prose vignettes" into formal coherence, felting into one digressive portrait events dispersed through nearly twenty years of visits. Brodsky as poet Theoros. "The metaphysical potential of Venice's dignity in decay is investigated *a posteriori* by Brodsky, so that he might later advocate it to others as a rule, a priori. Like Daedalus setting off towards an empirical investigation of death, with a thread trailing behind him in the hope that he might return from oblivion, the poet sets off into the labyrinthine streets of Venice, leaving a meandering narrative behind him of his findings, (heuretes: one who finds), which urge their reader to overcome the danger of vanishing unnoticed into physical or metaphysical death. *Watermark* reflects this deliberate meandering or nomadism both in form, with its multiple vignettes and in content, with its tale of a maximally devolved poet going the final few steps, back into the muddy, alluvial source from which all life and language once sprang" (MacFadyen, *Joseph Brodsky and the Baroque* 175).

The basis for MacFadyen's classification of Brodsky as exemplary of a contemporary "neo-baroque" aesthetic is his use of the conceit in a style he learned from the English Metaphysical poet, John Donne, among others. The conceit yokes together the disparate, the unlike, known as *discordia concors*, hence its association with wit, considered as a mode of perception (Ruthven, *The Conceit*). The conceit anticipates surrealist dissociation, disjuncture, which is the mode of dis/jointure required for designing assesmblages in electracy. Heidegger's poetics of the fourfold, *das Geviert*—his replacement for the proportional analogy structuring Plato's Line—extends the range of the conceit to gather microcosm-macrocosm relationships. He demonstrates the poetic manner of jointure precisely with reference to a potter's jug as "thing." His fouring distances itself also from the four-square of Aristotle's categories. Aristotle continued the decision of Idea that forgot about emergence (presencing and withdrawal) to focus on beings as object, substance. He accepted the inheritance of Presocratic kosmoi, of craft as what makes order appear, and in fact adopts it as his own analogy to explain causality. In the case of a bronze statue, for example, the material cause is "that out of which" (the bronze); formal cause (the shape or design of the statue); efficient cause (the source of change: the artisan and the art of casting); final cause, that for the sake of which a thing is done, the purpose. Aristotle promotes fabrication to universal status as his creation story, achieving closure, Heidegger says, in our modern condition of capitalist commodities: *reality is a product*. Within the field of "usage," we can anticipate the shift in electracy from use value to exchange value in commodity form. The irony of this analogy is that artefacts produced through techne lacked being in Aristotle's metaphysics, or represented second nature (produced through external power). In electracy, Second Phusis (Technics) expropriates Nature itself.

As alternative to metaphysics of fabrication, of techne (of product and object), Heidegger places the jug within a narrative of event, of action and praxis. It is a holistic regioning (Chora) in which the nature of the jug in its capacity as vessel (receptacle), a void capable of holding, is revealed in the context of its ritual usage, the pouring of a libation of wine, a sacrifice to the divine. The jug as conceit fits the act of pouring out wine with the relation of gift between gods and mortals, in a performance that is for itself. This terminology is appropriated from Heidegger's poet-guide, Hölderlin. "The gift of the outpouring is a gift because it stays earth and sky, divinities and mortals. Yet staying is now no longer the mere persisting of something that is here. Staying appropriates. It brings the four into the light of their mutual belonging. From out of staying's simple onefoldness they are betrothed, entrusted to one another. The gift of the outpouring stays the onefold of the fourfold of the four. And in the poured gift the jug presences as jug" (Heidegger, "The Thing" 173). The performative ritual indicates circumspectly the metaphysical "gift" of be-ing (Seyn, archaic spelling of Sein), upsurging presencing of presence. The alliance of philosophy and poetry is demonstrated here: the abstraction of Seyn is accounted for in the scenario of the jug. The fouring is a poetics of theopraxesis that calls attention to the possibility of EPS for a digital apparatus. Heidegger discusses the question in terms of the transformation of what is meant by neighborhood now, the turning of what is near and far. Jointure in the other inception requires fouring.

Heidegger borrowed vocabulary from the poets, Hölderlin and Rilke for example, in an effort to avoid the "white mythology" of concepts. While sympathizing with Heidegger's other beginning, Hannah Arendt recognized that he remained caught in the production-centered hierarchy, so her revision emphasized the need to distinguish among the three capabilities, to clearly recognize the distinct functions of *theoria, praxis*, and *poiesis*.

> Arendt's theory of political action departs from the conviction that the current "oblivion of praxis" is, in fact, firmly rooted in the Platonic-Aristotelian conceptualization of action. This conceptualization submits *praxis* to the dominance of *poiesis* (overtly in Plato, more insidiously in Aristotle), the better to curtail plurality, drain action of ambiguity, and assert the supremacy of *theoria*. The bottom line is that the (philosophic) constitution of "the political" in the West coincides with the erection of a

teleocratic conept of action, a concept that submits action to the rule of a goal-representing reason and a commanding, sovereign will (Dana Villa, *Arendt and Heidegger* 244).

The challenge of Konsult precisely is to reconfigure Reason and Will through mediation of Imagination, the capability being institutionalized in electracy. Arendt took up Kant's *Critique of Judgment* (aesthetic capability and reflective judgment without concept) as relay for a better fit among the capabilities (theopraxesis). The danger of *Gestell* (Age of the World Picture) was that the political would be reduced to a technocratic implementation of calculating knowledge. At the same time, she felt Heidegger risked reinventing a Platonic ideal in which the political sphere could be shaped in the manner of the plastic arts. Arendt's insight is that media support the emergence of *Phusis* in ethics and politics as well as in nature, the disclosive emergence into appearance, to one another and to oneself. Appearing in the public sphere included narrative shaping (*Erfahrung* for Benjamin), *mise-en-scene* of Konsult scenario, testifying agonistically to the condition of wellbeing against disaster. Julia Kristeva reads Arendt in similar terms, as achieving a synergy among the three virtues. She describes Arendt's proposal for community thriving as performing political action revealed through the language of story and history. All Arendt is a defense of narrative, Kristeva says, lamenting only that Arendt showed little interest in the poetry and vanguard arts important to Tel Quel theory (Julia Kristeva, *Hannah Arendt* 69).

Dana Villa finds Arendt's history has more in common with Walter Benjamin's "fragmentary history" than with Heidegger, finally.

> It is the spirit of Benjamin, not Heidegger, that informs her search for hidden treasures—moments of pure initiatory action—covered in wreckage by the "angel of history." . . . We cannot make this critique of her story about the fate of political action itself, for this is a story not of structural possibilities or unfolding inner logics but of moments and events; of spontaneous resistance, revolution, and disobedience; of heroic yet failed causes. It is, in short, a very un-Heideggerian history, in which every moment is the strait gate through which the Messiah might enter' (Dana Villa, *Arendt and Heidegger* 267).

Theopraxesis as reception of Second Phusis engages with such moment and events as correlation among the virtues, rather than the superordination of any one capability over the others. The temporality specific to electracy is "moment" (*Augenblick, Kairos*).

Popcycle

Geographical location is just one dimension of four in an electrate cosmology, or five, if you count the emergence of Being (Gift dimension) resulting from their jointure. Brodsky's world demonstrates the fourfold as relay for determining our own EPS. We have extrapolated from these four-square systems our own relational ratio. Where is Joseph Brodsky EPS when he is in Venice, Italy GPS? Brodsky wrote an essay, reflecting on his experience of extensive travel, commenting on how memory makes a composite collage, retaining not actual places and events but postcard icons.

> The composite city of your subconscious sojourn—nay! return—will therefore permanently sport a golden cupola; several bell towers; an opera house *'a la Fenice* in Venice; a park with gloom-laden chestnuts and poplars, incomprehensible in their post-Romantic swaying grandeur, as in Graz; a wide, melancholy river spanned by a minimum of six well-wrought bridges; a skyscraper or two. . . . In other words, regardless of what it says on your ticket, of whether you'll be staying at the Savoy or the Daniela, the moment you open your shutters, you'll see at once Notre-Dame, St. James's, San Giorgio, and Hagia Sophia. (Brodsky, "A Place as Good as Any" 38–39)

Brodsky gestures in this assemblage towards the "mental model" (memory palace) that learners construct in order to consult. Konsult takes up mystory as a genre designed to make the best of this inescapable quality of natural memory. A practical issue of interface design for User of Stack concerns the collapsed quality of dimensions referenced in Brodsky's composite scene. Literacy designated actual presence as Real for a reason. Electracy must commit to bringing into interface these potential dimensions of EPS folding into experience.

Your EPS neighborhood (the popcycle) consists of at least four sites, four dimensions, whose intersection at the crossroads of chiasmus unites four into one. First, Mythology (popular culture): Brodsky fantasized "Venice" before he was exiled, before he ever thought it would be possible to go there, given the confinement of Russians in the Soviet era. The

Venice he visited as soon as it became possible was the one of Visconti's film, *Death in Venice*. Second, Memory (Family): In interviews Brodsky explained part of the attraction of Venice was that it reminded him of his hometown, St Petersburg (formerly Leningrad). His memory of home, recounted in anecdotes, included that of his father returning from one of his trips as a photojournalist for Soviet media with a gift of a toy, a souvenir copper gondola from Venice. This souvenir was still on the adult Brodsky's bookshelf, preserved in a personal memorial exhibit, reconstructed from a photograph of his room the day he suddenly departed for the West.

Third, History (Community): Brodsky was an exile by disposition long before he was exiled by the state. His acknowledgement of his historical community is found in an image he used to explain the experience of exile. The image draws upon the Soviet space program, the experiment of sending dogs into space before risking human passengers. "To be an exiled writer is like being a dog or a man hurtled into outer space in a capsule (more like a dog, of course, than a man, because they will never bother to retrieve you). And your capsule is your language. To finish the metaphor off, it must be added that before long the passenger discovers that the capsule gravitates not earthward but outward in space" (Brodsky, "The Condition We Call Exile" 10). This historical metaphor continues into the final dimension of Career (Craft), which is the anagogy of this allegorical ratio. Describing the style of the novelist Platonov, Brodsky ties together the full conceit of his popcycle. "He [Platonov] will lead the sentence into some kind of logical dead-end. Always. Consequently, in order to comprehend what he is saying, you have to sort of 'back' from the dead-end and then to realize what brought you to that dead-end. And you realize that this is the grammar, the very grammar, of the Russian language itself," (Haven, *Joseph Brodsky: Conversations* 49). The Labyrinth in Brodsky's mystory repeats across all levels, resonating with Heidegger's nearing, neighborhood, *Holzwege*.

"Exile" is the alienated condition of all citizens in secularized modernity. The practices of religious metaphysics are designed to help the exiled sojourner to return "home" (to be with God). As a relay for electracy, however, Brodsky's exile is ontological. As theoros in Venice he is in search neither for god nor information, but for immanent experience, atmosphere as mood and attunement with world, "dwelling." The Konsult interface maps the composite scene of one's existential neighborhood (choragraphy), in order to negotiate the uncanny event. Venice as scene is a palimpsest of dimensions: the meandering streets and canals recall those of St. Petersburg, but also the Labyrinth and Choros of Daedalus, and even the very grammar of the Russian language, all evoking finally the state of mind, the mood of the poet Joseph Brodsky. Such "states" replace "things" in Heidegger's relay for electracy. The city outside gives meaning to his state of being (Heidegger's attunement). His theme he said is what time does to a man. His formula is time equals water; time passing is recorded in the dilapidation of the architecture in Venetian buildings, which decay from the bottom up. Venice as Symbol or concrete logic: metaphysics pursued by other means.

Brodsky offers his own updating of the allegories we have collected.

> I simply think that water is the image of time, and every New Year's Eve, in somewhat pagan fashion, I try to find myself near water, preferably near a sea or an ocean, to watch the emergence of a new helping, a new cupful of time from it. I am not looking for a naked maiden riding on a shell; I am looking for either a cloud or the crest of a wave hitting the shore at midnight. That, to me, is time coming out of water, and I stare at the lace-like pattern it puts on the shore, not with a gypsy-like knowing, but with tenderness and with gratitude. (*Watermark* 43)

Brodsky reoccupies the Neoplatonic scene of instruction, the birth of Venus, to give the figure a further turn. Brodsky's neighborhood may be an emblem of Existential Positioning in general, considering that the concetto concentrating the experience of his disposition is some small vessel—Chora, receptacle—the gondola souvenir, the space capsule, even the room-and-a-half in which his family lived in St Petersburg, where he created for himself a little cubicle, walling himself off from his parents with his bookshelf. These are figures of travel serving as theoros for the fifth estate, referencing his particular power of poetic imagination, his craft.

Each of us may ask: what is that for me, in my own place? What belongs to me? Where is my own four-fold neighborhood? Venice as allegory and symbol offers a figure in concrete logic of time and space as constituents of Being. Here is the matter of our konsult, the project for the invention of electrate education: Konsult is a composite scenario, a mental model, cognitive map, choragraphy, supporting the Active Imagination as interface relating the singular individual's life experience with the disciplines of knowledge and powers of the public sphere. As such it functions as Interface for the position of User in the digital apparatus that Benjamin Bratton named Stack. How may Absolute (total information) encounter Deinon? They meet in your neighborhood, through you (you are the opening). The lesson extrapolated from Avatar (Fravarti) reoccupied for electracy is that creative invention may be included in disciplinary learning by designing a personal relationship with disaster on behalf of well-being. The proposal is that disciplinary invention (theoria) and public policy effectiveness (praxis) pass through imagination (poiesis), with mystory as the genre recording correspondences. What remains for later (Konsult Experiment) is correlation of theopraxesis with the affordances of digital technologies.

Figure 4: "Halloween House," Stephen Foster Neighborhood, Gainesville, FL. Photo by Barbara Jo Revelle.

Interlude

Murphy's Well-Being (2)

SOLIDIFICATION

Inventional konsulting, disaster whispering, includes reviewing the lexicon of conventional consulting for egent terms, pivot or switch features in the expository field of documentation (applied to all documentation of the site) that expose otherwise unnoticed networks of operation. An example of evocative vocabulary is the term *solidification*, proposed by engineers as primary remediation, to prevent the creosote pollution from the waste lagoons on the Koppers site reaching the Murphy (Murphree) Wellfield that supplies the drinking water for my region. The procedure involves creating a *corral* for the pollutant, itself a term that resonates with the lexicon of Chora activated in deconstructive architecture, in the collaboration of Jacques Derrida and Peter Eisenman on *Parc de la Villette*.

The Record of Decision (ROD), calls for the use of remediation technology known as solidification, as treatment for the polluted lagoons on the Koppers grounds—sites of creosote leaching into the acquifer, and moving towards the Murphy Wellfield, northeast of the property. The application of this process is so common that it has its own page in Wikipedia, listing a variety of contaminated places to which it has been used. Solidification refers to the physical changes in the contaminated material when a certain binding agent is added. These changes include an increase in compressive strength, a decrease in permeability, and condensing of hazardous materials. Stabilization refers to the chemical changes between the stabilizing agent (binding agent) and the hazardous constituent. These changes should include a less soluble, less toxic constituent with hindered mobility.

One of the challenges facing the designers of metaphysics is to bind together the dimensions of the apparatus into working coherence (*logos* is the name for this binding). The choral method notices and maps these repetitions of function transversally across all levels. The "trace" in electracy, for example, references an irreducible *contamination* between Being and Becoming, transcendental and empirical. Konsult alerts egents to this rhythm, the structural irreducibility of contamination against purity in every order (contamination is physical and metaphysical). One recommendation for solidification in this transversal register is that it is the procedure God used to bind Satan in Hell, according to Dante's authoritative account known as the *Divine Comedy*, in the part covering the *Inferno*. Dante's eye-for-an-eye Justice suggests a moral remediation procedure that might be part of an overall clean-up policy: let the punishment fit the crime. Here is the Sparknotes summary of the relevant Canto. Note the reference to a "well" as passage.

> Virgil and Dante proceed to the Ninth Circle of Hell through the Giants' Well, which leads to a massive drop to Cocytus, a great frozen lake. The giant Antaeus picks Virgil and Dante up and sets them down at the bottom of the well, in the lowest region of Hell. In Caina, the First Ring of the Ninth Circle of Hell, those who betrayed their kin stand frozen up to their necks in the lake's ice. In Antenora, the Second Ring, those who betrayed their country and party stand frozen up to their heads; here Dante meets Count Ugolino, who spends eternity gnawing on the head of the man who imprisoned him in life. In Ptolomea, the Third Ring, those who betrayed their guests spend eternity lying on their backs in the frozen lake, their tears making blocks of ice over their eyes. Dante next follows Virgil into Judecca, the Fourth Ring of the Ninth Circle of Hell and the lowest depth. Here, those who betrayed their benefactors spend eternity in complete icy submersion.
>
> A huge, mist-shrouded form lurks ahead, and Dante approaches it. It is the three-headed giant Lucifer, plunged

waist-deep into the ice. His body pierces the center of the Earth, where he fell when God hurled him down from Heaven. Each of Lucifer's mouths chews one of history's three greatest sinners: Judas, the betrayer of Christ, and Cassius and Brutus, the betrayers of Julius Caesar. Virgil leads Dante on a climb down Lucifer's massive form, holding on to his frozen tufts of hair. Eventually, the poets reach the Lethe, the river of forgetfulness, and travel from there out of Hell and back onto Earth. They emerge from Hell on Easter morning, just before sunrise. (http://www.sparknotes.com/poetry/inferno/)

Part of the interest of contemplating Dante as a context for our own project is that many of the characters the protagonist visits during his descent (avatar) with Virgil are people Dante knew personally from his hometown of Florence, Italy. The heuretic principle is to ask: what is that for us, in Gainesville, Florida, present day? Cosmology is local. The most striking resonance in Dante's representation is the hierarchy of sins, the vices and their punishments. Treason is the worst offense. We may suspend judgment for the moment, especially since the EmerAgency motto is *Problems B Us*. In this framework, we suspect that civilization is an opportunity to design one's own *Comedy*. There is at the outset, however, at least one traitor to the community who could be identified in this specific case: the man who deliberately breached the berm that allowed the festering lagoon on Koppers property to spill into and pollute the local creek system (Hogtown Creek). His corporate rationale: it was cheaper to pay the fine for pollution than to bear the costs of cleanup.

The reference to "descent" activates the category of "avatar" that we are retrieving for collective identity formation, documenting instances found in the Western tradition, to correlate with the version passed through Hindu culture. The *Inferno* is one of the most famous examples of catabasis in the Western Tradition. Catabasis refers to descent into Hades (or any region deemed infernal or other). Every novel dramatizes a catabasis into an Other world. The significance of descent is made explicit when it is recognized as a translation of the Sanskrit word *avatar*. In the dualist metaphysics inherited from Plato, life on earth is itself a catabasis of the soul into embodiment. One's descent may be *vicious* (if given over to indulgence of the body) or *virtuous* (if ascetic and committed to return to spirit). Here might be the makings of an Augmented Reality project: to visualize our Chora (region 4) through the frame of old-school virtue and vice, using conventions of iconography to register the measure of behaviors in process. In electracy "emergence" replaces "descent" with respect to our understanding of how life comes to matter, invoking (after Heidegger) upsurging and urgency. The more fundamental challenge is the necessity to flip the valency of "vicious" avatar: electracy is *vicious* metaphysics.

The remediation plan for the Koppers Superfund cleanup is not to remove the contaminated soil but to treat it on-site (by means of solidification and related chemical neutralization technologies considered to be "experimental"). The most polluted soil will be consolidated in a mound feature, capped to prevent further seepage due to rain. The resulting look architecturally may be classified as a ziggurat, (step pyramid), a structural design dating back at least to Ancient Mesopotamia. Google search produces a list of modern designs inspired by this form. One of these instances is the Gold Vault in Fort Knox, Kentucky. The Mound plus Enhancement. This fact suggests a possible Augmented Reality project, to add to the Koppers Toxic Mound an image (for mobile devices) of Fort Knox. The juxtaposition of a Toxic Waste Mound with the Gold Vault creates a provocative conceit, whose signification is open, indeterminate, or whose pragmatics is left to the viewers' discretion. Freud already established a vector joining excrement with money.

MURPHY EMERGENCY

We depend upon a choral domain classified as *Murphy*. What is the writing of this disaster? A choral device attends to any semantic domain associated with the disaster condition. Murphy's Wellfield gives us a generative term for a series (keeping in mind that this name is a slippage from the historical "Murphree"). Most people are familiar with "Murphy's Law" (if something can go wrong, it will). Evidence for this law accumulates around disaster. There is a confidence game known as the "Murphy game": To deceive or swindle by means of the Murphy game (to be murphied). There are many confidence (con) games and get-rich-quick schemes recorded in folklore and that have found new marks through the Internet. Perhaps the industrial revolution is a murphy, that is, what it promised humanity is too good to be true. Another slang meaning of "Murphy" is "potato," used in England as a disparaging reference to an Irishman (the associative slide: "Murphy" a common Irish name; the Irish live on potatoes). Samuel Beckett's novel *Murphy* is worth recalling in our context (describing the efforts of an Irishman to overcome Cartesian dualism). "The sun shone, having no alternative, on the nothing new" (the first sentence).

The *Murphy* Konsult invites egents to compose a fable in need of a moral; it is didactic, with a lesson to impart. But what lesson, what is the moral of the story? What do we know, what disciplinary knowledge guides communication within the community? The assumption of this experiment is that we are testing disciplinary knowledge and personal memory relative to the reality manifested in the disaster. Blanchot's title was "the writing of the disaster," suggesting that what we want the community to receive is "what the disaster (itself) writes." The key to this service is to understand who or what speaks or writes in the event. Event replaces Idea or projects order apart from and beyond Idea. Or rather, it may be that event is a message without sender (trace), or konsult is a way to "divine" an event as message (for sensible ones). Trace retrieves divination. It is a gift trace in Derrida's sense. Theory tells us that the experience of the Industrial Revolution (the epochal origin of electracy) is alienation, reification, objectification. These terms name the loss of agency in the industrial city, such that our own actions return to us (like the repressed) as if originating elsewhere, from some external power, thus separating us (traumatically) from responsibility. The feedback loops of digital technology now recirculate the return of the repressed at light speed: the recursive Unconscious. What rhetorical practice may harness this condition for well-being?

Egency invokes systems theory to recover feedback enactment: theopraxesis as savoir-faire. This effect in the frame of electracy is due to the emergence of a new identity formation, a group subject, actantial (Greimas and Bratton), whose institutional instantiation is the corporation. "Incorporation" reoccupies the metaphysics of incarnation (descent emergence). Konsult in general has the task and opportunity to bring into appearance this event as such, that in the drama of modern disaster we are witnessing the equivalent of Thespis stepping forward out of the Chorus, to speak as an individual actor, on behalf of a new subject (after selfhood). The corporation is a collective Thespis.

Just here is the crucial opportunity for intervention. Corporations already walk among us, have donned a mask in order to appear, and this mask is Brand (Logo as logos). *Frankenstein* evokes a hostile view of this creation of Second Phusis. The history of the corporation foregrounds the event of collective personhood, since that status is precisely what defines the institutional nature of this entity: a company or group of people authorized to act as a single entity (legally a person), whose speech is money, recognized as such in law (new Leviathan). Recent decisions by the US Supreme Court, such as the "Citizens United" case, have extended this legal standing of personhood even further, recognizing the first amendment rights of this entity. So much attention given to "animal" these days, when the real news is the animation of corporation. Comedians have enjoyed mocking the implications of this development, proposing that corporations could run for president or date our children. From the point of view of electracy, corporations are the institutional order within which the digital apparatus appears, just as school and science nurtured literacy, or church and religion organized orality.

What is the immediate point of relevance for the design of *Murphy*? *Pine Tar is a commodity*. We know that corporations communicate with society by means of commodity signs (this sign is one of the fundamental innovations of electracy). As Marx noted in his revolutionary analysis of commodity fetishism, if commodities could speak, they would be the most ingratiating, lovable, obsequious, pet-like creatures imaginable, for they see every passerby as a potential customer. Theory picked up this insight and developed it extensively, realizing that commodities do speak a kind of pure language, consisting entirely of exchange as such, pure relational circulation. Here is the discourse of desire emergent from appetite: the circulation of part-objects outside language, as a logos of Bodies Without Organs (BWO). Each apparatus requires adaptation of the human sensorium, which the Philosophers reference as "innervation" (facilitation). The commodity performs innervation on behalf of the newly reordered sensorium, now within the hegemony of the "lamella" (mythical organ libidinally synthesizing the body's orifices). There are positive opportunities offered by this circulation, but the immediate point for konsult is that the commodity operates a con game, specifically the game known as a "Murphy": bait and switch, offering an opportunity too good to be true and fleecing the suckers who bite (one born every minute). It is the lesson of conduction, of electrate flash reason: the secret is hidden in plain sight. Why did the vulgate translate "Murphree's Well-Field" into "Murphy"? Oracle: a fable with as many morals as buyers.

3 Enjoyment

JOUISSANCE

This apprenticeship in electrate education includes participation in the design and testing of metaphysics for a digital apparatus, using "metaphysics" to name the operating rhetorics invented relative to the affordances of technology. Part of the experiment is this process of invention itself, within the practice of heuretics. Our method is to adopt Plato's *Republic* as template, as a prototype of genre, and also as Contrast in a heuretic CATTt, in that everything we are proposing for the template is different relative to Platonism and Neoplatonism. Plato's Idea continues in electracy, but enframed now by Event. The procedure is that of reoccupation or retrieval of the invention of literacy as metaphysics, in order to generate an electrate equivalent (there is no apparatus without metaphysics). The conceit of this book as pedagogy is that you are using our descriptions to translate exercises into your own case. The pedagogy remains within school, in other words, exploiting theoretical resources to bootstrap into what Heidegger called the other beginning, into electracy. In the future, egents will encounter not this written argument, but an image event (a post-medium app, game, mixed reality encounter, New Wave interactive social medium), just as students of the academy encountered the written dialogues, rather than a religious ritual, presented within the context of esoteric conversation. So far we have the Allegory of the Wave (High Water in Venice), embedded (mise en abyme) within the drama of a conceptual persona, the poet Joseph Brodsky, visiting Venice every December, as relays for theorpraxesis capable of generating the experience of Second Phusis. Now we need to consider the next step, our equivalent of the encompassing dialogue genre itself, and its logic of dialectic performed by Socrates with his interlocutors.

We have identified our genre as konsult, through which egents undergo education as participation in a fifth estate, appearing to one another in social media, konsulting on Justice for a global digital society relative to a specific scene of disaster (policy problem in the public sphere). Egent is the collective-in-me, Ereignis, Avatar, Person in the imaginal world. What does an egent do in the service of konsult? We see at once the relevance of theopraxesis: how may egents think-act-make? We learned from Philosophy (Theory of our heuretic CATTt) that the real of Being in a post-literate metaphysics, directing the discovery of a new Justice, is *Enjoyment*. Heidegger proposed this word (understood in its fullest etymological and semantic range) to summarize his translation and update of the original experience of Being (Phusis) at the origins of literacy. It is important to note these definitions—concepts, ideas—as points of departure for our transitional project. The Greek word Heidegger identifies as primal is "necessity." He translates it as "usage," including a broad etymological semantic field. "We should keep to the root-meaning: to use is to brook [*bruchen*], in Latin *frui*, in German *fruchten*, *Frucht*. We translate this freely as 'to enjoy,' which originally means to be pleased with something and so to have it in use" (*Early Greek Thinking* 53). A footnote references the archaic sense of German *brauchen* as: "to make use of, to have the enjoyment of, to bear or hold, to possess the right of usufruct—i.e., the right to cultivate and use land one does not own, and to enjoy its fruits" (53).

We do not have to invent konsult ex nihilo. Our CATTt supplies us with several resources: image arts as Analogy; Internet as Target; consultant scenario as tale. We stay with Theory in this book (since that is the strength of academic literacy) to take up psychoanalysis as relay for our digital pedagogy. We have established that electracy as apparatus is concerned with well-being (against disaster), complementing the concern of literacy with truth (science), and orality with salvation (religion). Enjoyment is the force of electracy, and psychoanalysis has done the most to open this dimension for metaphysics (the construction of reality). Psychoanalysis articulates a materialism of enjoyment. Plato began his education in the universal response to physical beauty, understood as merely the lowest level of the line, the proportional analogy tracking transcendence to intellectual contemplation of Beauty as such, and ultimately the

Good. He believed that this vector of ascent was the propensity of the world. Lacan, after and against Plato (speaking for the new paradigm), remains with material embodied sexual experience (attraction and repulsion), in order to address our fundamental question of well-being against disaster. Platonic transcendentalism becomes sublimation. The question returns: why is human thriving violently destructive?

Electracy is the apparatus of body (appetite, conatus), just as literacy is the apparatus of mind (reason), and orality the apparatus of spirit (belief). It is clear that these apparati complement one another in principle, despite the historical record of hostility and mutual repulsion of the respective institutions, and in fact it is possible to consider Plato's projection of human qualities of mind, heart, viscera into political classes of the Polis as his version of theopraxesis. The important point for our project is that Jacques Lacan (extending Freud's invention) defines the primary experience of enjoyment—*jouissance* (in French)—with explicit reference to Heidegger. His comment foregrounds the original association of "usage" with "right," "law," that motivated Heidegger's translation with respect to Anaximander's invocation of "justice."

> A word here to shed light on the relationship between law (droit) and jouissance. "Usufruct"—that's a legal notion, isn't it?—brings together in one word what I already mentioned in my seminar on ethics, namely, the difference between utility and jouissance. What purpose does utility serve? That has never been well defined owing to the prodigious respect speaking beings have, due to language, for means. "Usufruct" means that you can enjoy (jouir de) your means, but must not waste them. When you have the usufruct of an inheritance, you can enjoy the inheritance (en jouir) as long as you don't use up too much of it. That is clearly the essence of law—to divide up, distribute, or reattribute everything that counts as jouissance. What is jouissance? Here it amounts to no more than a negative instance. Jouissance is what serves no purpose (ne sert 'a rien). I am pointing here to the reservation implied by the field of the right-to-jouissance. Right (droit) is not duty. Nothing forces anyone to enjoy (jouir) except the superego. The superego is the imperative of jouissance—Enjoy! (Lacan, *Encore: The Seminar of Jacques Lacan Book XX* 3)

Lacan's comment participates in the argument we observed previously, in the cases of Sen and Cavell, thinking Justice beyond the terms of utility and duty. Now Lacan introduces the disturbing dimension of usage enjoyment: *waste and loss.* Here we encounter the fundamental character of the coming apparatus, especially that which renders it incommensurable and unacceptable to the institutions established to preserve the previous apparati: *metaphysical waste and loss.* The interest of this attention given to Enjoyment as the guideword of Being (specifically in the context of apparatus formation) is the extent to which it has been appropriated, adapted, and applied in the mainstream Humanities and Arts disciplines, promoted through the transformation of all discourse into "text." Roland Barthes, writing in the context of the Tel Quel group in France (one source of our Theory) promoted this understanding of text as performance of jouissance, translated as "bliss."

> "Signifiance" is a process, in the course of which the "subject" of the text, escaping the logic of the ego-cogito and engaging other logics (that of the signifier and that of contradiction), struggles with meaning and is deconstructed ("is lost"). "Signifiance"—and this is what immediately distinguishes it from signification—is thus work, not the work by which the subject (intact and external) might try to master language (for example the work of style), but that radical work (which leaves nothing intact) through which the subject explores how language works him and undoes him as soon as he stops observing it and enters it. "Signifiance" is "the without-end-ness of the possible operations in a given field of language." "Signifiance," unlike signification, cannot be reduced to communication, to representation to expression: it puts the (writing or reading) subject into the text, not as a projection, not even a fantasmatic one (there is no "transport" of a constituted subject), but as a "loss" (in the sense which the word "perte" can have in speleology); whence its identification with "jouissance": it is through the concept of "signifiance" that the text becomes erotic (and for that it does not have to represent any erotic "scenes") (Barthes, "Theory of the Text" 38).

In our context, it is clear that, despite the success of this vocabulary of "text" (écriture) within the university, the import of what it calls for (the shift "from work to text" in Barthes's phrase), has not been fully understood, let alone implemented. This failure to take up the project of "enjoyment" in its metaphysical sense is not surprising, given what is at stake. The Church managed and resisted the full potential of science (Reason, rational entailment, proof) as long as it could, with Galileo as the symptom, emblematic of the turn into a new hegemony of reason against faith. We are approaching a similar crossroads, of Enjoyment beyond reason and faith, carrier of a coming metaphysics (new orientation to reality). The right of Capability related with electrate Justice must be pursued in this dimension not of signification (meaning) but of *signifiance* (vector). Electracy is felt.

My My

Lacan's materialist framing of enjoyment clarifies the challenge facing our experiment to develop electrate Justice. Law and Justice are not the same thing, which gives rise to certain paradoxes. The theoretical notion of the Unconscious—which names the gap or interval, the open of jointure for which we seek a new ratio—identifies the dimension opened to metaphysics within electracy. Heidegger names it *Riss*, translated as itself a jointure of Rift and Design. Here is a philosophical word, perhaps the equivalent for electracy of Hegel's Aufhebung. Is he suggesting the gap (hole) is open to design? Literacy figured out how to read and write with mind (intellect, reason), just as orality operated spirit by means of ritual, totemism, magic. Neither religion nor science, entertainment supplements these established frameworks with new possibilities for body. Egent (Avatar, Daimon—catachreses for collective identity) is a new identity formation emerging in the digital apparatus, adding to selfhood of literacy and soul of orality. Our term egent clarifies the reoccupation of what Avatar, Daimon, Fravarti named in orality, and which was "obsoleted" (McLuhan) within the hegemony of science (individual selfhood of literacy). This construction of identity is termed "Subject" within our theory. Lacan credits Descartes with the isolation of Subject from within science, expressed as the cogito: "I think therefore I am." Kant completed this invention when he introjected Aristotle's Categories, making them properties of mind that enabled experience as such. Freud's invention appropriates Subject (capitalized for this special usage) for electracy by noticing the gap situated at the hinge of *Ergo* (therefore), splitting thought from being. Lacan codifies Freud's discovery of the Unconscious with a new formula, expressing not cogito but *desidero* (I desire): *I think where I am not, and am not where I think.* Here is the challenge for konsult, for choragraphy, to add to the GPS technology an EPS (Existential Positioning) capable of mapping the movement of this dislocation, disjunction, disjointure of Subject (its dispersal across dimensions and systems of Stack). We know from the impasses of our civilization that the apparatus of literacy does not suffice for well-being (any more than did religion). What is the intelligence of this further dimension of body as excess and waste? How does it work, operate; what is its logic; how do we experience it; what is its truth or its nature?

> To situate psychoanalysis, one could say that it has been constituted everywhere the truth makes itself known only in the fact that it surprises us and imposes itself on us. An example, to illustrate what I have just said. There is no other jouissance given to me, or givable, than that of my body. This does not impose itself immediately, but no one has any doubt about it and there is established, around this jouissance, which is indeed henceforth my only good, this protective grill of a law described as universal and which is called "Human rights." No one can prevent me from disposing as I wish of my own body. The result, at the limit—we put our finger, our foot on it, we analysts—is that jouissance has dried up for everyone! (Jacques Lacan, *Seminar XIV* 2)

The jointure and search for a new ratio of electrate Phusis is found precisely in this register of relations—with one's own body, and between and among bodies: between Subject and Other. Late Heidegger shifted from individual Dasein to collective Ereignis to address this jointure—Ereignis as Event, translated as Enowning, concerning what belongs to me, appropriation and expropriation of what is my own, beginning with owning my mortality (being towards death). Subject is not substance or essence but a collective relational formation, a field theory of identity. We recall the initial framing of our educational mission, the dissatisfaction of Amartya Sen and Stanley Cavell with the options of conventional ethics for Justice as Capability. Both reject the choice between Kant and Mill (or Bentham), between deontological principles versus utilitarian results (amounting to the options for salvation between Protestant and Catholic Christians). Sen and Cavell remain with a Platonist frame of dissatisfaction with given reality, which Nietzsche referred to disparagingly as the ascetic ideal (denial of life). Cavell makes clear, however, that he and Sen are committed to a Justice of life, with Cavell updating the Platonic model, codified in Plato's *Symposium*, with Hollywood romances of remarriage. Lacan agrees that romance is the right place to look for our ethics, with the qualification that we must consider the grounding of Capability and its cognates, such as virtue, and power, in the fundamental reality of im/potence: the male organ in its comings and goings (de/tumescence), and its mark in the Symbolic order—the phallus. The "joint" in this context invokes a pun (a joke), but "gag" is to electracy what non-contradiction is to literacy. So what is this relation of a couple and coupling? "The pure subject is situated at this junction, or to put it better, at the disjunction of the body and jouissance. It is a subject in the measure of this disjunction" (XXII, 6).

We are looking "under the hood" of Enjoyment, which is the contribution that *Theory* makes to konsult. The observation is worth attention, situated as it is at the event of emergence of electrate Being.

> Jouissance as I pointed out, is an ambiguous term. It slides. From something which makes us say that there is no jouissance except that of the body and which opens the field of the substance in which there comes to be inscribed the severe limits in which the subject contains itself from the incidence of pleasure. And then this sense in which to enjoy (jouir), as I said, is to possess, the my. I enjoy something. Which leaves in suspense the question of whether this something, from the fact that I enjoy it, enjoys. There, around the my, there is very precisely this separation between jouissance and the body. Because it is not for nothing that I introduced you to it the last time, with the reminder of this articulation—a fragile one because limited to the traditional field of the genesis of the subject—of the phenomenology of the spirit, of the master and the slave. My . . . Henceforth I enjoy your body, namely, your body becomes the metaphor for my jouissance (XXII, 6).

The functionality that egent extrapolates from Fravarti is how to open a personal relation with the universal whole (Absolute, God). Science required objectivity and accepted alienation as a necessary consequence. Electracy reoccupies the project of a personal experience of Absolute, understood now as the manner in which creativity appropriates total disciplinary knowledge through Symbol. Such is the Desiring Machine emerging in the digital apparatus. The problematic of mystory as pedagogy takes up this transformation of science into Person accessed as My dis/jointure. Lacan shows the complexity of this jointure with the famous argument of identity between Kant's Categorical Imperative of duty, and the Marquis de Sade's radical evil. Sade's maxim, articulated in his prison writings, situated directly in the fundamental metaphysics of usage as usufruct, is to claim that his right of enjoyment extends beyond his own body to that of his neighbor: I have the right to enjoy your body, to say to one and all, without limit. The newspapers carry stories daily documenting events of this sadistic kind. Lacan reminds us of the feudal droits du seigneur, in which any lord might play de Sade with his peasants. Georges Bataille documented the history of Gilles de Rais, field general serving Joan of Arc in her military campaigns, who was just such a monster, torturing and slaughtering hundreds of children for personal gratification. His history is considered to be the source of the tale of Bluebeard (Charles Perrault).

Such is the emblem of the aporia of Justice: *Saint Joan served by Gilles de Rais*. Look for it everywhere. Lacan places Sade's *Philosophy of the Bedroom* in the context of Hegel's Master/Slave dialectic, the struggle for recognition among people, the dynamic of pure prestige, which Heidegger recognized as having a part in Being, to appear by means of glory, public renown, or notoriety. This is the force that generates collectivity, which was why Hannah Arendt insisted on praxis as just this capacity to appear to one another in the public realm as the basis for pluralistic democracy. The Master is willing to die, while the slave relents to preserve life. Such is the power of attraction-repulsion at the core of electrate metaphysics, instantiated in Social Media, which indicates why no apparatus may be apprehended through technology alone. Here also is the paradox and danger of theopraxesis: the media event, some heinous act composed, recorded, published—performed as a "statement." The dialectic clarifies the constitutive reality of electracy: not so much pleasure-pain, but attraction-repulsion, is the register of relevant experience: not beauty but the sublime in Kant's terms, defined as an experience of simultaneous attraction-repulsion. Jouissance (in short).

Alienation

Egents perform konsult by means not of cogito, but desidero (Lacan, *Seminar XI* 154). Each in our own place, learning from Brodsky in Venice how to map Chora: we compose a cosmology of My place (situation), so that they appear within a global economy. Electracy adds EPS to GPS, to include the new dimension of reality under construction, this Unconscious (egency) in which I am not where I think, and think where I am not (either I am not thinking, or I am not). What is the practice adequate to this orientation of the lifeworld, in which My cause and effect circulate through systemic feedback loops consituted by others? In Lacan's terms, the new metaphysics concerns not physical seeing (literacy took care of that), but the gaze (look, regard), which is the electrate reoccupation of the visionary imagination. Konsult must navigate by means of a parallax relating my point of view with the field within which I am seen. The gaze is "seeing" in electracy. What is the look of Venice (of any chora), meaning, where am I in that scene, which is not one, but a complex of intertangled layers (the popcycle)? Subject as collective identity makes available every narrative position in principle (this is the capability of fantasy, whose function is as pedagogy of desire). As Bratton noted, the User position in Stack is not Subject, let alone self or person, but actant (recalling Greimas's semiotic deep structure of narrative), open to occupation by multiple entities, human and non.

> Counterintuitive as it may seem, the design decision should not be to locate sovereignty in the encapsulated person who steps into the *User* position but instead into the position itself. Particular agents may step into or out of composite *User* assemblages (as tangible as a Google Car or as intangible as a trace over time), and their interests do not remain stable as they do so. From the Stack's perspective, the *User* is both the edge-state on the other side of the *Interface* and the agent initiating columns back down into its layers: it is defined by what it connects to, not by who or what it "is." (Bratton 286)

The name of the impasse confronting electracy—motivating the emergence of Subject as a new identity formation—is alienation. Alienation is inherent in human identity formation: one's own sense of self is acquired by identifying with others (the big Other). At the collective level, specifically in the conditions of modernity, we have not just "forgotten" about Being, as Heidegger said, but repressed it (pushed it out of the literate apparatus). Lacan offers a scene to evoke the conditions of Chora today.

> The being of man, in so far as it is fundamental for our anthropology, has a name, in the middle of which the word being (être) is found—it is enough to put it in brackets. And, to find this name and moreover what it designates, it is enough to leave your house one day to go to the country for a little outing and, crossing the road, you will meet a camping site and, on the camping site or more exactly all around it, marking it with a circle of scum, what you will meet up with, is this being of man in so far as—verworfen—it reappears in the real. It has a name. It is called rubbish (*détritus*). It is not today or yesterday that we have known that the being of man, qua rejected, is here what appears in the form of these tiny circles of twisted iron, which, we do not know why, we find a certain accumulation of around the habitual site of campers. (Lacan, *Seminar XIV* vii, 7)

Heidegger spoke of the "thrownness" of Dasein (*Geworfenheit*), the arbitrary contingency of one's individual existence, but Lacan extends this feeling into "thrown away." The rubbish is Symbol of our presence: we litter or abject our own material but don't know it (alienation as estrangement from agency). Our very planet is now just such a camp, with a ring of dead and dying satellites circling it, crashing to earth occasionally, producing a self-made meteor storm. It will be an issue for Science eventually, Lacan observed presciently, in the form of planetary (interplanetary) pollution. Andrei Tarkovsky's film, *Stalker*, dramatizes an allegory of psychoanalysis in this context. Based on the novel *Roadside Picnic*, the film tells the story of a mysterious Zone created in a region that was the site of a rest stop by a spacecraft from another planet. The litter opened a Zone capable of fulfilling a person's innermost wishes. A stalker is one who guides visitors to this site of wishes in the Zone. The wish turns out to come not from conscious will, but from the Unconscious (from desidero, not cogito), resulting in outcomes without relation to the Good. Here is a key to electrate metaphysics: desire has its own condition, its own force, now emerging as hegemonic, not constrained by Right or Truth. The function of theopraxesis is to configure the fit (jointure) among these powers.

We lament the desecration of earth, as if it were happening on its own, not recognizing that it belongs to us. Slavoj Žižek applies Lacan's insight to the ecology crisis, in a way that clarifies the challenge facing konsult.

> If we grasp the ecological crisis as a traumatic kernel to be kept at a distance by obsessive activity, or as the bearer of a message, a call to find new roots in nature, we blind ourselves in both cases to the irreducible gap separating the real from the modes of its symbolization. The only proper attitude is that which fully assumes this gap as something that defines our very condition humaine, without endeavoring to suspend it through fetishistic disavowal, to keep it concealed through obsessive activity, or to reduce the gap between the real and the symbolic by projecting a (symbolic) message into the real. The fact that man is a speaking being means precisely that he is, so to speak, constitutively "derailed," marked by an irreducible fissure that the symbolic edifice attempts in vain to repair. From time to time, this fissure erupts in some spectacular form, reminding us of the frailty of the symbolic edifice—the latest went by the name of Chernobyl. (*Looking Awry* 36).

Žižek warns against reading what the disaster writes, but that is exactly what egents must do. Yes, everyone agrees, the Split or *Riss* is inherent, irreducible, but they forget the intuition of the Great Chain of Being. The old wisdom was, if humans were meant to fly, God would have given them wings. *Yet now we fly*. Apparatus is a *desiring machine*. It is not pragmatic, utilitarian, in its motivation. If humans were intended to coincide with themselves in Absolute self-possession, God would be human. This constitutive split in Subject articulated as Unconscious is not an absolute limit but an edge open to jointure. We are devising machinic self-possession (albeit in the modality of impossible). Here is uncanny logic (dreamwork): *I know I cannot coincide with myself; but still, I believe I may*. Such is the Lacanian version of the Deinon, the Overwhelming, identified as the constitutive aporia that makes humans (speaking beings) uncanny: the tremendous exertions of our enterprise checked by death. Lacan paraphrases Heidegger's famous elaboration of this aporia as coming from the Chorus in the tragedy *Antigone*, by saying that mankind is everywhere "screwed."

EmerAgency konsult will not leave it there, but this aporia clarifies the stakes of invention, and why apparatus mutation is not only a matter of technology.

Lacan invokes Heidegger's image of the jug as event, indicating that he is addressing the same cosmological problematic, offering a more precise version of the fouring that joins the microcosm and macrocosm, Subject and world. The reoccupation of Avatar or Angel is just this endeavor to reestablish the correspondences relating macro- and microcosm (cosmology): to reconnect with the star (aster). Lacan is mindful of the metaphysical import of Heidegger's apologue of the craftsman, concerning the relationship between Being and Becoming, Form and Matter, with making or craft productivity promoted to prototype of Being as such. The new beginning, Heidegger advised, should concern not products but events. "Now if you consider the vase from the point of view I first proposed, as an object made to represent the existence of the emptiness at the center of the real that is called the Thing," Lacan writes, "this emptiness as represented in the representation presents itself as *a nihil*, as nothing. And that is why the potter, just like you to whom I am speaking, creates the vase with his hand around this emptiness, creates it, just like the creator, *ex nihilo*, starting with a hole" (*The Ethics of Psychoanalysis* 121).

Lacan's argument is that this hole is us, as Subject, and the *Geviert* of gods and mortals, heaven and earth, is entirely immanent, mapped using topological geometry, tracing an orbit around this (b/lack) energy. The jug or vase (a "mustard pot" is used in another version of the story), incarnating the receptacle of Chora, as process of hinge, jointure, is modeled in the klein bottle. Heidegger borrowed from Rilke the *Open*, to ground his inquiry into what is specific to human experience, to name the event of Being. At the same time, we should notice Lacan's joke, in that the primordial part object is the breast, lest we forget that we are precisely mammals. The point to keep in mind is that all these theories circulate around the same insight, relating to the dimension of human Capability now accessed directly within a digital apparatus. Electrate Justice requires a new understanding of fit.

TAO

This choral conceit of jointure has global cross-cultural value, signaled by Heidegger's statement that perhaps the only translation for the Event of Ereignis was the Tao of Asian wisdom. Egency requires global education. Since Lacan himself brings in Japanese (and Chinese) examples to explain his theory, it is worth noting an occasion of *japonaiserie*. *The Book of Tea* (1906), written by Tenshin Okakura in the context of his intercultural work, including establishment of the Eastern art section at the Museum of Fine Arts in Boston, explicates the aesthetics of traditional ritual. Okakura references the Chinese philosopher Lao-tse: "The reality of a room . . . was to be found in the vacant space enclosed by the roof and walls, not in the roof and walls themselves. The usefulness of a water pitcher dwelt in the emptiness where water might be put in, not in the forms of the pitcher or the material of which it was made. Vacuum is all-potent because all containing" (cited in Arata Isozaki, *Japan-ness in Architecture* 5). Isozaki's account includes the impact reading *The Book of Tea* had on Frank Lloyd Wright, who recognized in it his own understanding of architectural design. A further loop in the network is the fact that Okakura learned his style of composition in English in part by reading the essays of Emerson, also a major influence on Wright as well as Nietzsche. In electracy the Taoist principle of omnipresent emptiness helps clarify the positive or affirming dimension of Subject as existential Nothing. Or rather, Subject is like zero in mathematics, Lacan explains, which is not nothing, but a relational place (the empty set). Chorography (EPS) maps the vectoral movements (sens as direction) of this place.

Topological geometry comes to play a central role in Lacan's pedagogy, producing his own analogy of the line. What is the relation (the ontological category of electracy) of egent with environment, inside and outside, past and future, or any other binary dynamic? What is the path through the labyrinth of Unconscious, negotiating the divided condition at every level of world? Here is Lacan's updating of the invention of ratio for a digital apparatus. "It is a bottle, it is this one here, a bottle whose neck has entered the interior and has inserted itself onto the bottom of the bottle. And if, in addition, you blow up a little this neck that has gone in, then you have this very pretty schema of a double sphere with one comprehending the other, and this is a particular happy way to make you put your finger on the advantage of this model which man discovered very early, in this double and conjugated image of the microcosm and the macrocosm, for example, the first Chinese astronomy" (Lacan, *Seminar XII* iv: 8). Throughout his seminars Lacan introduces topological figures — moebius strip, torus, cross-cap, as well as klein bottle—to model his description of the relational feedback loops of electrate ontology. Plato's analogy of the line is reoccupied in electracy by topology.

Symptom

Lacan keeps our Theory focused on the other beginning, initiating the invention of a measure and ratio of Justice for electracy (a proper fit ordering an ecology). Logos determines how a cosmos coheres: electracy promotes ethos and pathos to assist with this role. Our template (the *Republic*) shows that we need to design the digital equivalent of the dialogue, including the propositional logic that Socrates used to give his interlocutors some experience with dialectic. We don't have to invent this practice out of whole cloth. On the contrary, it has already been invented in various dispersed institutions, so that our task is to assemble, integrate, correlate, generalize and adapt the prototypes for konsult (global fifth estate egency). Indeed, as we learned from Barthes's explanation of text as creating effects of jouissance (in one's own body) by means of *signifiance*, Konsult is generalizing for a digital apparatus the cumulative inventions of modernism. These inventions are the source of fit, the new ratio of the digital apparatus. It is worth reviewing this genealogy briefly, just to have in mind the conditions in which we find ourselves, to understand the challenges of and resistances to this education.

Konsult takes up disaster as site of education, to learn desire as force, as manifesting what constitutes reality. If the assignment is to witness and compose Second Phusis, the emergence of Being (Life-Death) in my place, my Subject, in order to produce the imaginal world as interface with egent, what do I need to learn? The practical assumption is that neglect of this dimension constitutes the aporia of disaster. "Cause" (that for the sake of which) remains obscure. Symbol today is symptom, and (ultimately), writable as *sinthome* (to anticipate our argument). The detritus (signifier of being as waste; the General Economy) of polluted environment is a symptom of My (of egency). As literate agents we are not able not to pollute, or even recognize pollution as mine. Pollution is egent waste. Egency through collective Subject (Avatar) proposes to address this fatality. Lacan credits Marx with inventing the symptom (the signal received from the real). The argument is relevant in our context, with electracy emerging historically from the inception of the industrial revolution in the late eighteenth century. Industrialization and the related city form are the original conditions of alienation, replacing craft with machine production, capitalization, such that workers and citizens lost any sense of agency in environments of reduced experience, the disenchantment of the world. Marx perhaps did not realize the extent to which his foregrounding of economic productivity reflected the completion, the telos, of Western metaphysics, with capitalist industry embodying fully the model of making first theorized at the beginnings of literacy, with the crucial difference being the shift in techne from craft to machine. Marx described capital as usury, in the phenomenon of surplus value, referring to the value created by workers in excess of the cost of their labor, manifested as profit and appropriated by owners.

Usury we recognize (etymologically) as within the family of terms associated with usage, Brauch, Enjoyment, Jouissance. One of the fundamental inventions of capital, and central to electracy as apparatus introduced as part of the industrial revolution, is the commodity form, and here is one of the pivots of the paradigm. The commodity form is a universal equivalent, with money as its sign, making it possible to bring into relation and exchange incommensurable and heterogeneous products. We are familiar with this story, one of the great if misunderstood and abused inventions of electracy, in which exchange value separates from use value. In a word, this is écriture (Writing, text). As should be expected, given the central role of entertainment and corporations in the institutionalization of electracy, advertisers are electrate, just as sophists were literate. They discovered and fully implemented by the 1920s the insight that marketing concerned not cogito, let alone use value, but desidero, exchange value. The market operated not (only) through supply and demand of needs, but supply and demand of desires. It was not about steak, but sizzle. Commodity exchange writes with part-objects (libidinal sensorium).

Lacan recognized that this separation of exchange value from use value manifested a fundamental principle of language and of being. The prototype, which Lacan adopts as his generator for "letter" as discourse of body, to supplement signifier in language, is the Egyptian hieroglyph. In Egyptian writing there is a pun, homology, such that the word for "scarab" and for "becoming" sound the same. Hence, in the invention of writing, in early pictographs, an image of a scarab (beetle), separated from its literal referent, served as a sign for the abstract notion "to come into being," which is the equivalent of Greek

Phusis. The homophone motivated the image of the scarab or dung beetle rolling its ball of dung as a figure of god moving the sun through the heavens (Symbol). This dung makes detritus ontological already in the origins of civilization. The dream is a rebus, Freud discovered, meaning that it communicates in a pictographic, ideogrammic way. The optimistic aspect of this account is that text functions similarly across all apparati, regardless of technology. This operation expropriating properties of material experience to refunction them as abstractions of thought, whose circulating produces *signifiance*, is a practice of konsult. Egents write emergence, urgency, emergency (EmerAgency).

Lacan's principal invention, fundamental for electrate metaphysics, the digital equivalent of the literate "thing," is the *objet petit a*, the little other, which we write @ for short (as if the "at" sign inscribed autre in object—autre other). Justified by the fact that Freud followed Marx in appropriating the pidgin term "fetish," borrowed from colonial discourse referencing the status of objects in oral (magical) apparatus, Lacan described the libido or sexual energy of the body as functioning in the manner of commodity form, including an experience of surplus enjoyment (libidinal surplus value). Egents are as alienated from the libidinal economy as workers are from the capitalist one. The @ (*objet a* or little other) is a kind of general equivalent, like commodity, a relational figure rather than a classical object of substance and properties, a bit of dung appropriated for higher things. The fundamental importance of psychoanalysis for electracy as apparatus of attraction-repulsion is found in this insight, the opening of a libidinal economy to metaphysics. Electrate reality addresses the body and its sexuation or life energy as the order opened for ontology. The @ is a material fragment operating as a temporal relation, orienting human enjoyment (relative to well-being), to situate the project of gathering within time. The argument is that libidinal energy is a dimension of power operating in the problematic of well-being against disaster thus far neglected by consulting.

Humans (speaking beings) begin life in total dependence (impotence) as infants, and this dependency (impotence) is what recommends the phallus as primal signifier. Our orientation and formatting as subjects are grounded in biological needs, but these needs are precisely not the concern of psychoanalysis as metaphysics, addressing ontology of Enjoyment. The @ is embodied in a potentially infinite series of individual signifiers or products, focus of our actions in a given situation. It is a temporal object in that it manages a relation between our present desires and our originary satisfactions (such as nursing or control of the bowels). Indeed, one of Plato's emblems for Chora was that of (wet) nurse. Here is part of what it means to say I am not thinking or I am not: my present behavior is haunted by a lost and forgotten satisfaction. The perversity of human behavior, as manifestation of libidinal drive, is that maintaining that lost satisfaction from the past takes priority over the accomplishment of some purpose in the present. To be clear: what we are describing is a power, a force in the real that is the equivalent in electracy of nuclear power in nature or God in religion. Desire names metaphysical cause, augmented in the apparatus. The material atom when split generated nuclear energy. The Subject begins split. Libidinal energy already circulates in the world, now to be captured in konsult.

How does libidinal energy circulate? There are at least five partial objects (quasi-objects), grounded in the dynamic relation between need and demand, whose gap generates desire. Here is the waste, the detritus, to which Lacan referred, in that the part objects are experienced as separable from the body, related to their inherent quality as waste (milk, feces, sounds, glances, sperm) as transitional in an intersubjective dimension shared by subject and other: breast (oral, milk), excrement (anus), voice (speak/listen), gaze (see, be seen), phallus (genitals). What is the half-life of this energy waste? This (fantasmatic) mobility of body parts constitutes "castration," in Lacan's version, explaining his formula that Unconscious is structured like a language. Perhaps there would be less confusion if he had said "like a written language," or even more accurately, "like a tropology" (in fact before Subject was constructed as matheme Lacan explored it as trope). The world is a rebus composed by body. McLuhan suggested the apparatus context for this insight when he said that the body constitutes the "etymology" of technology (artefacts are prosthesis of body). Egents learn to read and write in this cosmology, with this etymology.

The conventional account of apparatus shift is that the sensorium of orality is dominated by hearing, and of literacy by seeing. The sensorium of eletracy is organized by the erogenous orifices (the *lamella* in its fantasmatic relation). One can appreciate why this original constitution of jouissance in the body is repressed, necessarily displaced to return in the real. It is scandalous. Human libidinal energy (the fusion power of human life behavior) originates in the drive to recover the satisfaction undergone through embodiment. Desire is defined as a constitutive loss of primordial satisfaction, and the continuing difference or gap between need and demand (I need not only nourishment but care, not only toilet hygiene but control, and so forth).

The part objects are associated with drives, forces of appetite within each person, interacting in a field, such as that of gaze, with circulating @s functioning as "shifters" in the resulting struggle for pure prestige. Usufruct as Enjoyment refers to the necessary interdependence of bodies. Justice manages usufruct. The eye demands to see and be seen, for example. *The organs are appetites, served collectively by institutions.* The commodity sign analogy is that these part objects separate from bodies and circulate through the macrocosm, as libidinal lining of all mediated communication and interaction, a "language" of aesthetic properties carried by global digital technology. This observation is the basis of Tel Quel investment in avant-garde poetics as vehicle of political revolution. Commodity exchange circulates part-objects as its semantics, expressing a visceral discourse functioning by catalysis. One necessity for theopraxesis, is that in electracy My actions are published (surveillance). This is the Unconscious, structured like a language. Unconscious is *chosique*, thing-like, the letter circulates through cultural fields just as the signifier circulates through discourse. The secret of desire is that what resists human satisfaction (happiness, well-being) is just the nature of the drives associated with the part objects, which is to maintain themselves as such, as desiring, and not to find satisfaction in some goal or end. The definition of blues may be generalized as slogan for the human condition: *happy to be feeling sad*. We may want to be happy, but we don't desire it.

Pedagogy

Given this metaphysics (this account of how a cosmos of Enjoyment works), what are the lessons for electrate learning? Psychoanalysis as an institution and clinical practice has lessons for education. Sigmund Freud, who is credited with the "discovery" of the Unconscious, was a medical scientist in the positivistic sense that was the norm in the nineteenth century. Freud's method is a good relay from the Platonic dialogue, in which Socrates led interlocutors through the steps of dialectical reasoning. Psychoanalysis, dubbed the "talking cure" by its first patient (known as Anna O.) inverted the terms of the dialogue: the patient (analysand) talks and the analyst listens, remaining mostly silent. Critical reason (literacy) is suspended, and the patient is instructed to free associate, saying whatever comes to mind without censorship, while the analyst practices a floating attention, scanning for repetitions, patterns, slips, ready to interrupt with an interpretation, monitoring her own desire. Trained in neurophysiology, Freud learned from Anna O. and similar cases that hysterics (the original neurotics) suffer from symptoms that have no physical cause. His research seeking alternative explanations included self-analysis, probing his own desire through memory, dreams, daily encounters, readings, as resources for learning the discourse of symptoms. Like Socrates, who could perform dialectic without benefit of writing, Freud did on his own what became institutionalized as the training analysis. Konsult is not concerned with clinical therapy, but may extract the principles of self-discovery (desidero) from this clinical technique.

Freud's insight (famously) was that neuroses (perversions, obsessions) have their source in sexual life and its repression or denial, leading some to reduce the discovery to a problem specific to bourgeois society with its conservative and hypocritical mores. The difficulties concern "love" (in a word), and to address it Freud reopened metaphysics to the entire archive of cultural materials excluded from the *Republic*. Literacy invented science by focusing on the declarative register of written language concerned with the logic of statements (propositions). The logic of the other beginning is found in dreams, jokes, mythology, literature, and related modes. Patients sought treatment when their symptoms finally made living impossible. They found themselves suffering without knowing why; repeating the same behaviors despite themselves, returning to the same situations from which they intended to depart. They were caught in the uncanny experience of Unconscious, precisely in the interval or gap opened within electracy right at the hinge dimension between Being and Becoming articulated in literacy. Unconscious is not a condition of erasure or elimination, Lacan argued, but of suspension (exploiting the semantics of *souffrance* in French, both "suffering" and "pending"). Between potentiality (dunamis) and actuality (energeia), there is a dimension of unrealized possibility (Chora), identified as the imaginal world. This way of putting it suggests that Unconscious is the scene of Capability, addressed in our invention of electrate Justice. Aristotle had recognized steresis or privation, based in the possibility to "prefer not to," as Bartleby the Scrivener famously put it in Melville's story, as a necessary obverse to choice, to the enacting of a capacity (a power, a virtue).

Lacan's point goes further, to account for steresis beyond choice, outside reason or will. Hysteresis is privation beyond Aristotle (beyond literacy). Here is the aporia, the enigma: our comportment is without why. It is the scene of "can/not" reoccupied by the H'MMM discipliness (Humanities + Movies Media Music, responsible in principle for the economy of the Creative Industries).

Unconscious (imaginal world) locates and opens to invention and management a fundamental division, a split and hole in the real created by language. One way to think about the division relative to the apparatus is by means of the "sign," introduced by structuralist semiotics. A sign is a relation between a signified and signifier, a concept and a sound/letter. In these terms we can say that literacy developed the concept, and this metaphysics persists in the dimension of the signified. Electracy invents metaphysics for the register of the signifier (showing the interdependency of the apparati). This split is further anchored in language in the division between the two subjects operating in any proposition—statement and utterance. In a sentence such as "I think that I doubt" (to use one of Lacan's examples) the "I" of the utterance ("I think") is separate and divided from the statement ("I doubt"). Even in talking about oneself (one's self), this division opens the Unconscious and interrupts introspection. It is impossible to coincide with one's self (no immediate self-presence). Or rather, self-relation is mediated through the discourses of culture, circulates in the double loop of the gaze. I receive it as if from another—from the locus of the Other, in fact, which is the Unconscious. These feedback loops become accessible to technology in the digital apparatus. Klossowski called it simulcrum (Klossowski). Konsult as User and Interface for Stack authors simulacra.

This self-relation that is the impossible digital desiring machine is dramatized in the dialogues as a conversation between (among) friends, updated in Cavell to include the "intercourse" between romantic partners. The premise applied in psychoanalysis is that the analysand is alienated from her experience, and must learn to realize whatever is suspended in limbo (*en souffrance*) by bringing it into representation—learning how to tell a story, for example. What matters in the story is not its historical or biographical accuracy, but its coherence, that it makes sense to the analysand (such is the convention). The anchor of being is just a unary trait, the first mark of pleasure registered in a helpless body. This trait has no meaning, but is in the position of prime mover (Aristotle might say), or proper name, in Lacan's linguistic version. This trait is excluded from, but has representatives in, language, with the proper name as the index of body in language. Identification then enables the emergence of Subject in discourse through the tropes of substitution and displacement, tracing a futile journey in search of lost jouissance. In short, analysis is a school for theopraxesis (my acting is also a making and a knowing). Konsult proposes to accomplish for a fifth estate a generalization of this technique, learning how to bring into *signifiance* this Unconscious knowledge of enjoyment on a collective level. What is it about disaster that we enjoy?

Relay for konsult, Analysis is an apprenticeship in authoring, or in cosmography in our context, or poetry specifically, Lacan says, noting the limitations of narrative and the inadequacy of novels or movies to dramatize what frustrates satisfaction. Novelists, he says, create many variations on ways to get a couple alone together in a chalet, but sexual intercourse is not the primary impasse of souffrance. Tragedy maps the position of "hero," with characters such as Oedipus or Antigone or Hamlet modeling the consequences of becoming trapped in destiny. Lacan calls attention to another position available within the tradition, but left aside during the era of science—that of mystic, even more open to integration into the Outside than are poets. Here is the relevance of the twelfth-century division between Avicenna and Averroes studied by Henry Corbin—the historical moment when the West deleted the imaginal world that continued in Islam. This event perhaps favored the emergence of science in the West, but now the imaginal world must be retreived for electracy as metaphysics of imagination, or even of Fantasy. Psychoanalysis in our context is understood as the scene of this retrieval: school for mystics, in which one learns reception of Avatar.

What is special about Analysis, and why Lacan insists that his seminars have to do with training analysis for prospective psychoanalysts (rather than being merely communications of knowledge or information), is that only in the situation of an analytic session may the Unconscious appear (directly), manifested in the form of "transference." We noted that @ is a temporal object, meaning that it is a relation of past and present experience—the ratio we seek of jointure (Chora, Open, hole). In transference the analysand projects her identifications onto the analyst (mistaken for the Other, the one supposed to know, the Master from whom the analysand demands recognition), and part of the work of therapy is to discover the identity or identities of this Other. This Other retrieves Angel, to form the macrocosmic relation of Fravarti (in our Analogy). What is retreived is not religion (not a personal relation with God), but a personal relation with the causal power native to electracy. In konsult this Person becomes an interface with literate disciplinary knowledge. The wisdom of the endeavor is similar to that described by Cavell in his moral perfectionism: not to give up on one's own desire, apart from any other consideration. But what is this desire? The fundamental point most important to electracy is that desidero is not to be thought intellectually, but must be undergone (felt) in the body as jouissance. This undergoing requires a form, a cosmology, a support, a place (Chora). Konsult designs and constructs this place or momentous site.

Shock

Konsult extrapolates from psychoanalysis as relay a pedagogy of theopraxesis. Our civilization has been tracking for some centuries the perplexing disjunct between human belief and the reality principle. It is the record of the separation of science from religion. Copernicus (earth is not the center of the universe); Darwin (humans are not made in the image of God but ascend from the apes); Marx (fine ideals actually serve only selfish economic interests); Freud (most conscious comportment rationalizes purposes of which one is unaware). Subject emerges in a condition in which our adaptation to two different apparati and their institutionalized metaphysics has left us constitutively divided, committed to what is called fetish logic, whose formula is: *I know, but still . . .* We maintain this contradiction, between fact and value, with the split articulated in various binaries, coming down to a split between being and meaning. It is important for our project to note that these attitudes, supported by fetish logic, are grounded in institutions maintaining distinct metaphysics relative to historical apparati (religion and science). Kant's three Critiques mirror this historical circumstance (Pure Reason = science; Practical Reason = religion; Judgment of Taste = entertainment).

The aporia structuring modern experience has been dramatized in the novel *Nausea* (1938), by the existentialist philosopher, Jean-Paul Sartre. Antoine Roquentin (the protagonist) came to Bouville to research the life of the Marquis de Rollebon, an aristocrat who lived in Bouville during the French Revolution. Seeking the shape of Rollebon's life for a biography prompts Roquentin to notice the lack of meaning in his own life. He desperately searches for some experience that might count as "adventure" (measured by a model internalized from literature). As an historian, Roquentin discovers the double loop that Lacan says analysands must learn, in order to bring into relation being and meaning. For the most banal event to become an adventure, Roquentin reflects, one must simply begin to recount it. The impasse occurs if one attempts to live life as if one were telling a story. It is not possible, according to Roquentin. You have to choose: live or tell.

> *For example, when I was in Hamburg, with that Erna girl whom I didn't trust and who was afraid of me, I led a peculiar sort of life. But I was inside it, I didn't think about it. And then one evening, in a little café at St Pauli, she left me to go to the lavatory. I was left on my own, there was a gramophone playing* Blue Skies. *I started telling myself what had happened since I had landed. I said to myself: "On the third evening, as I was coming into a dance hall called the Blue Grotto, I noticed a tall woman who was half-seas over. And that woman is the one I am waiting for at this moment, listening to* Blue Skies, *and who is going to come back and sit down on my right and put her hands around my neck." Then I had a violent feeling that I was having an adventure. But Erna came back, she sat down beside me, she put her arms around my neck, and I hated her without knowing why. I understand now: it was because I had to begin living again that the impression of having an adventure had just vanished* (Sartre, *Nausea*, 61)

Nausea dramatizes the aporia of theopraxesis. "Live or Tell" is the forced choice. As analysands learn from undergoing transference, speaking beings are temporal, and this time is "out of joint," never synched with itself, such that meaning is necessarily retrospective, governed by the rhetorical figure of metalepsis — mapped by the topology of the klein bottle. Lacan also uses the moebius strip to demonstrate the structure: the single-sided band constructed by putting a twist in a strip of paper that is attached to itself in a loop. This topological figure is Lacan's equivalent of Plato's analogy of the line. Analysands learn that they are constructing the meaning of their being through living, as specified in the notion of "act," which is necessarily a "symbolic action." "This could be sustained and illustrated by reminding you of what I called act, namely, this reduplication of a motor effect as simple as 'I am walking.' This ensures simply that by just being said, with a certain accent, it is repeated, and, from this reduplication, takes on the signifying function that makes it able to be inserted into a certain chain in order to inscribe the subject in it" (Lacan, *Seminar XIV* xvi, 7). The point is made in the context of developing one of Lacan's more controversial observations, that there is no sexual relation, and no sexual act (despite all the screwing going on). Unconscious, that is, knows not of man or woman, and emerges relative not to biology but desire.

Walter Benjamin generalized the individual aporia to the collective level, and proposed the dialectic image, modeled on cinematic collage, as a device capable of documenting this temporality. German vocabulary clarified the choice in the distinction between two kinds of experience: *Erlebnis* (immediately lived) and *Erfahrung* (comprehended through reflection). In his study of Paris as "Capital of the Nineteenth Century," Benjamin discovered in the career of the first modernist poet, Charles Baudelaire, a further dimension of experience produced within the industrial city: *shock*. Freud's work with soldiers suffering from shell-shock during World War I (known today as Post-Traumatic Stress Disorder) led to his theory of the death drive against the pleasure principle. Events undergone in conditions of shock are not registered in experience, remain outside memory, in limbo, "unclaimed," *en souffrance*, and return therefore in the real. Birth and the loss of original satisfaction is a shock in this sense. The goal of therapy (and its value for konsult) is to develop a pedagogy by which subjects learn to bring this shock dimension into some form of representation. The further lesson of modernism is finally that "trauma" is not to be eliminated but captured and managed as a dimension of memory. And trauma as poetics may be learned from the psychoanalytic clinic, as in the example of schizoanalysis (Deleuze and Guattari).

We learn from Sven Spieker, in any case, that Dada photomontage splits between practices of shock and archive, which place discontinuity and rupture as relevant to digital storage and retrieval (Spieker, *The Big Archive* 131). It should be noted meanwhile that the technological dimension of gaze enabling egency in the electrate apparatus is everything to do with "surveillance," including all those interactive video art installations experimenting with shifting and displacing visitors' image feedback loops, to NSA massive collection of communications data. Theopraxesis is the rhetoric of archive surveillance, through which egents learn how to manage this separation, circulation, and return of body (part objects) through the loops of global commodified media. In short, konsult enables Unconscious to appear.

Klossowski clarifies the desiring side of the machine, and the functionality of Daimon or Avatar as intermediary, the mythological expression of the ancient drive to coincide with oneself (to be god). The exemplary case is the story of Actaeon spying on the goddess Diana at her bath. "Argument: Diana makes a pact with a daemon who intercedes between the gods and humanity, in order to appear to Actaeon. Through his airy body, the daemon simulates Diana in her theophany and inspires in Actaeon the desire and mad hope to possess the goddess. He becomes Actaeon's imagination and Diana's mirror" (Klossowski 35). Klossowski generalizes the point: "Thus did the gods teach men to contemplate themselves in the spectacle, just as the gods contemplate themselves in the imaginations of men" (33). The simulacrum function enabling relations in every sense between gods and humans traces the temporality of the imaginal world.

> Diana seems to know no other world than the absolute mythic space in which her chase takes place: hunting, capturing, killing, bathing. Now in Actaeon's adventure, Diana herself is suddenly the hunted one, since the hunter surprises her unarmed and naked. Ths incident still belongs to the world of irreversible and uninterrupted space: the danger, the risk—like that of the hunt and the bath after the hunt—lies in the fact that the sacred grove of Diana's bath is situated in this same space, and that numerous paths which seem to lead nowhere run into that very place. In this same space, Diana seems forever inaccessible to Actaeon; *the next moment*, I defile her—he says secretly to himself. *The next moment*: it is the intermediary daemon who makes him able to have this retrospective experience of time. And the next moment I am dead. But the daemon enables him to see her, beyond death, and to say to himself: "When she is washing herself that is when the hounds devour me." Indeed, Diana does complete her interrupted bath. (Klossowski 46)

The daemonic simulacrum demonstrates the functionality of konsult, as rhetoric managing fantasy-infused (sur)reality. The machine side of "becoming god" in the electrate apparatus is manifested in "new scapes" in which Real Time computation is embedded in the built environment, producing "Liquid Space."

> The new scapes emerge from the interaction and movement of the visitors and vice versa the "dilated and transactive" space created by sensors and controls, sounds and interactive projections in real time, intensifies a phenomenal-phenomenological response that feeds off the virtual dimension. Just as in certain cultures, "walking is not crossing space but pushing space under one's own feet," so the world implemented or poured out in the media representation suggests the idea of a space as a dimension that is internal instead of external to the body, promoting in the interaction the etymoloy of "touch" (from the Latin *tangere*) and more precisely as emphasized by de Kerckhove, "touch from the inside." The space of the virtual disappears as an external realty to reappear as a representation of the world, as the reality of man as intimate reality; or again, as Stephen Perrella believes, it emertges as a "middle-zone" whose "vitality is neither understood solely as architecture nor as subjectivity," since these are both "*de facto* determinants in a co-constitutive dynamics." The co-presence of "embodied experience" and "mediated subjectivity," writes Perrella, produces a hypersurface: this appears when the "superposition" of the electronic images on the topological surface/membrane/substrate reveals new potential relations between form and image without one prevailing over the other, i.e., when the effects slip between reality and hyper-reality, sliding transversally inside a channel of associations. (Gregory, *New Scapes* 83, 86)

Simulacrum (Avatar) is the formal device adequate to the affordances of transarchitecture for which egents design User Interface. A bachelor machine definition of electracy may be: *the meeting of Diana's Bath and Liquid Space in Konsult.*

TROPOLOGY

Roquentin occupies the hero's position, as actant, and his experience of nausea resonates with the spleen documented by Baudelaire in his prose poems of city shock. Roquentin has an epiphany, an event in the city park, when he encounters the void of Unconscious, of alienation, the failure or disappearance of the Other and hence a loss of meaning or significance (the death of God, for short). It is worth citing the material dissolution that is said to provoke the repulsion—a certain viscosity of elemental or primordial life. In our context we recognize it as an event of Phusis, an emergence of Being (his own), but experienced negatively. Roquentin's repulsion is the hero's defense against the absorption into participation that for the mystic position would be undergone as attraction. "It spreads at the bottom of the viscous puddle, at the bottom of out time—the time of purple suspenders, and broken chair seats; it is made of white, soft instants, spreading at the edge, like an oil stain" (Jean-Paul Sartre, *Nausea* 33). Lacan uses a similar image, alluding to Freud's fear that psychoanalysis might be misunderstood as a return to the traditions of mysticism and hermeticism. Freud's shorthand term was "the black tide."

> One of the most essential things to distinguish is the difference between rottenness and shit. For want of making an exact distinction, people do not notice, for example that what Freud designates is this something rotten in jouissance. I am not the one who invented this term. *La terre gaste* is already found in courtly literature, they are the poetic terms used in the romances of the Round Table, and we see them taken up again—we find our good where it is—in the writings of that old reactionary T. S. Eliot under the title, "The Waste Land." . . . What is at stake is nothing else, from one end to the other, than the sexual relation! One of the most useful things, would be, obviously, to decant from this field the rottenness, the shitty coal-tar—I am saying, properly speaking, given the privileged function that the anal object plays in this operation—with which current psychoanalytic theory covers it (Lacan, *Seminar XIV* xviii, 10).

The reference to coal-tar should be marked as anticipation of the FRE Konsult installation, "Murphy's Well-Being," encounter with pine-tar. For now we return to the theme of detritus as the symptom of alienation. Lacan referenced mystics for some years, and by the time of *Seminar XX* (*Encore*), he described a jouissance beyond desire, accessible to women and to mystics of either sex. The mystics' position is the obverse of that of the hero. The hero separates and maintains sharp boundaries of individuation, whereas the mystic attempts to lose the ego, dissolve all boundaries in order to participate in and receive the outside other. One important lesson to be drawn from the increasing importance of "mystics" for Lacan is that Subject opens or reoccupies a position in culture and discourse for a mystic actant (to use the semiotic term). The point for us is to discover the jointure of this dissolution, this breakdown or overflowing of the categorial boundaries of being defined within literacy, to supplement them with a mode for the digital apparatus that gather through pathos rather than logos.

Psychoanalysis applies in a therapeutic context the logic of poetry upon which natural language is founded. *Theory* reminds us that the models of thought activated in electracy are supplied in infinite variation in the practices of aboriginals, children, the mad, as well as artists. Structuralism demonstrated the unity of these modes in tropology. The dream work (joke work) at the core of Freud's logic consists of the cardinal tropes: metaphor (condensation), metonymy (displacement). Jakobson mapped the tropes onto the two axes of language: paradigmatic and syntagmatic axes (selection and combination). Harold Bloom put the whole family together by recognizing that psychological defense follows the same tropological system codified in the tradition of rhetoric. The EPS chorography tracks the vectors of sense as patterns emerging in data following the paths predetermined by the cardinal tropes. In short, konsult is a genre for adapting a general practice for personal, quotidian, and public discourse from creative poetics, to supplement and complement the propositional logic of literacy and mythology of orality. The strategy, against the existential nausea or spleen induced by feeling de trop (superfluous) dramatized by Sartre, is to participate in the movement (the vector) of tropes. Theopraxesis (integrating living and telling) becomes possible when konsult takes the position of mystic actant.

Arthur Koestler "demystifies" the mystic actant by generalizing the positional dynamic in the binary pair of separant-participant. Both are present and engaged in the experience of love, or in the expressions of laughing and crying. "The emotion called 'love'—whether sexual or maternal—usually contains an aggressive or possesive, self-asserting component, and an identificatory or self-transcending component. If emotions were represented by different colors, then the two opposite tendencies would appear as brightness values (black-white mixtures) superimposed on them" (*The Act of Creation* 54–55). Rage and fear predominate on the separant side, joy and sadness on the participant side, anticipating in some respects George Lakoff's assessment of the difference between conservatives and liberals in the United States, or Irigaray's liquefaction of Plato's Idea. For the latter, participation is associated with mysticism but extends to everyday life experience: "The common denominator of these heterogeneous emotions is a feeling of participation, identification, or belonging; in other words, the self is experienced as being a part of a larger whole, a higher unity" (54). Koestler's study of creativity is a classic of heuretics, but the point relevant in this context is his observation that Western modernity favored the separant position, leaving participation to poets and other artists. Poetry is a school for participant experience, the negative capability (Keats) expressed in the poetics of epiphany. Our pop culture narratives are regressive in apparatus terms, dominated by separant heroes. The danger, as Peter Sloterdijk observed, is that the digital apparatus augments thymotic (passional) experience, such that politics today is a projection of resentment (Sloterdijk, *Rage and Time*). Electrate education supports development of a popular culture of participation (beyond self): egency.

Figure 5. "Beware of Dog." Stephen Foster Neighborhood, Gainesville, Florida. Photo by Barbara Jo Revelle.

Interlude

Murphy's Well-Being (3)

Modeling Contamination

Murphy generates fables. How do fables fabulate? Russian semiotics investigated the qualities of pure art: what is the literariness of literature? Jurij Lotman made the point that the art text is *a second-order modeling system*. This fact is a caveat and an opportunity for apparatus invention. The opportunity is that Lotman's analysis suggests a way to access that "mystery" of what makes a construction "art," in a way relevant to all media (post-medial). Testing "emergence" as a boundary process, with a continuity between scientific accounts in complexity theory to effects of connotation in tropology, *Murphy* experiments with interactive design as an art of catalysis. Desiring Machines exploit emergence in the manner of a rhizome, such as the wasp relationship with the orchid. *Murphy* plays orchid to the citizen wasp, eliciting fables. Scientists admit that a wasp experiences interaction with the orchid as a sexual encounter. What experience is accessed through *Murphy*? Egents must receive and undergo feedback loops of behavior. Dante had a similar plan: the person you betrayed will gnaw on your head throughout eternity (for example). The wellfield was polluted on your behalf.

The primary modeling system in our map is natural language itself, which is used to model everyday life. Semantic ontologies (literacy) for the most part work with meaning at this primary level. The dictionary is the archive. Lotman demystifies the aesthetic effect by noting that a work of art creates its particular world (diegesis) by recoding the primary set of semantic equivalences into a secondary set that hold for that world exclusively, and this effect is why poetry is central to Heidegger's other beginning—the transition into electracy. In the world of Lermontov's poetry, for example, a semantic equivalence is established among a wheel of cheese, a particular kind of shield, and the moon. Walt Whitman's *Leaves of Grass* constructs a secondary-modeling system of "America," that Hollander described as "troping" an existing form. Theorists such as Greimas have developed diagrams that map the logical systems relevant to these aesthetic equivalences.

The methodological implication for emergent vectoral sense generated in our interactive archive is to include both the primary and secondary ontologies in our design. The first ontology addresses the natural language lexicon and syntax found in the archive. Could this ontology be used then to produce in the database secondary ontologies for each of the story worlds, across the popcycle? The challenge of electrate metaphysics is to locate a dimension of interface for tracking multimodal post-medial emergence (trace). The design proposes that this dimension is vectoral (playing on French *sens*, as "meaning" and "direction"), which is to say: non-objective movement. Beyond sign, trace names the vectoral markers, the interface between the senses and pressures of force, in a metaphysics organized around desire, which is to say that the archive embodies certain predispositions, inherent propensities.

The first emergent effect to consider is a tertiary modeling system that recodes in turn individual art works in order to produce new signifying modules (in the way that literature recodes natural language). Derrida's trace displaces sign, within a metaphysics in which rhythm displaces structure as the ordinator of force vectors. Meaning as *sens* (nonobjective direction) emerges historically in a passage or movement through epochal stages of tradition, accounting for the importance of pastiche, parody, collage and the like in modernist poetics authorizing simulacra (construction) rather than mimesis. James Joyce's *Ulysses* is an example of this phenomenon, recoding not only natural language, but Homer's *Odyssey* as well. Harold Bloom's "anxiety of influence" describes the experience of literate authors positioned in the electrate archive. Konsult is in the family of "crisis poem," from which it may learn the techniques of metalepsis (troping of form).

NARRATOLGY

Citizens become egents by composing fables of Chora, thus recovering *Erlebnis* through retrospective *Erfahrung*. This collective feedback loop of story generates a virtual (potential) neighborhood. MWB konsult is delivered through an interactive narrative, by means of which a community becomes its own Aesop. The practice is self-parody, to the extent that the ideal citizen evokes associations with the Duchess in Lewis Carroll's Alice in Wonderland. And yet, the effect of pepper on the Duchess (owner of the Cheshire Cat) is ominous.

> The Duchess demonstrates how people can change radically in different environments. When she's in her pepper-filled house with her angry cook and squealing baby, she is rude and violent. But while strolling in the open air with Alice, she is almost too affectionate. She's also ready to assign morals or meanings to anything, even if they don't seem to fit. You can think of the Duchess as a bad literary critic—someone who's trying to slap a trite moral onto the end of everything that happens, as though the world were made of Aesop's fables. Lewis Carroll signals his disapproval of this moralistic attitude by giving the Duchess a sharp chin that she likes to dig into Alice's shoulder—similarly, her boring morals and sayings dig irritatingly into Alice (and the reader) in a metaphorical way. The world of Wonderland resists a moral interpretation; it's really just a fantasy world, and things are neither good nor bad. (https://www.shmoop.com/alice-in-wonderland-looking-glass/duchess.html).

It is true that the Well is a caricature, but with a purpose: to instill a pedagogy of morals. Our context exposes the misunderstanding registered by saying "just a fantasy world." Fantasy (understood in the most general terms as signification constrained only by imagination) is the new dimension supporting electrate metaphysics, with its own institution on a par with orality and literacy before it. Fantasy itself is as old as humanity, so we are familiar with its manifestations. Narrative includes point of view, expresses an attitude with respect to the circumstances in the diegesis (representational world). Care (*Sorge*) transforms contingent circumstances into situation by adding intentionality—project (in the existential sense): egents take ownership of the disaster (Ereignis). *Erlebnis* (immediate experience) being outside thought, *Erfahrung* is foregrounded (event *happens* circumspectly through telling). The konsult experiment tests the extent to which a community might become narrator. Might the community realize it has been *murphied*?

The dimensions of narrative are story and discourse, which MWB supplements with mise-en-scene and the other devices of imaging. "Story" refers to the events (the plot, characters, setting); "discourse" refers to the manner of telling, the style or treatment, and imaging engages with the formal affordances of the medium. The ambition of rhythm as vector is to articulate a ratio relating the forces of desire annotated in the mise-en-scene. The attitude of the narrator/author is expressed primarily indirectly, in the design of story and discourse, with desire triggered through formal attributes. Attitude towards what? The primary guiding force working through narrative is some *value*, a belief or commitment (ethos) fundamental to the culture within which the narrative is composed. This value is often "transcendental"—freedom, justice, beauty—meaning that it is without properties, and must be made particular through examples. Theorists refer to such terms as floating signifiers, or dialogical words, the site of struggle among different factions of a society, directing the dynamics of rhetoric in the public sphere. Politically devisive policies such as Second Amendment rights or the Obamacare mandate hinge upon different understandings of "freedom." The challenge in electracy is to recognize that the debate concerns not logos but pathos, not rational but thymotic force, a condition calling for invention.

What is the value promoted in electracy? *Capability* (modality: to be able). What calls for konsult is that Well-Being (thriving) is in crisis, presents itself to thought as problem, problematic, emergency. *Murphy* does not know what Well-Being is or should be, but that Well-Being is, may be, and must be lived. Well-being is potential (dunamis), virtual (not actual): such is its modality (possible, but not necessary). The metaphysics of electracy shifts construction of value from conceptual levels of abstraction or transcendentals, to a material register of embodiment, manipulated through the circulation of part-objects, investments of libido transported beyond bodies through commodities and commodity signs. In this context we may recognize "audio-visual media" (AV) as a euphemism for "anus-vulva media," acknowledging that the visceral education in body control forming the powers of catalysis occured during weaning and toilet training. Human orientation of embodied mind is not only sensori-motor, but libidinal (and this is the sticking point). The didactic import of the fables emergent from the Well is instruction in Ereignis, event of enownment. The Well maps relevant vectors in the scene—movements of water, infrastructure, demographics, commodities, sense (in every sense). The puncept or hole articulating the groove or rhythm of the disaster finds its emblem in the corporeal senses, synthesized in the sense of taste. The vector (commodity force, rhizome, part object) is *Pepper* (spice). The poetics of MWB tropes spice, beginning with a proposed ritual, an annual visit to the *spice aisle of the nearest market* to check the price of pepper.

Soft Experience

What to call experience looped recursively within the digital apparatus? The challenge is to make available a practice of secondary modeling adequate to thriving in Second Nature. "Artificial Experience" (AE) would resonate with AI, but has negative connotations in the specific usage of "experience," in that we are talking about real experience difficult if not impossible to bring into understanding and reform without medium support. It is precisely the experience of theme parks, themed malls, producct of experience design. The educational issue is that this dimension is "intelligible," and even central to our commercial built environment, but the pedagogy implicit in entertainment as *Erfahrung* is not yet appreciated within school. Here is a site of passage between literacy and electracy. In our experiment it is useful to test this insight: literate metaphysics (the entire orientation to reality of an epochal order) structurally neglects appetite as fundamental to well-being. It does not value it, even when it appears (as it inevitably must), or it is taken for granted. It cannot imagine what a civilization might be in which well-being had an army. The corporation is the army of appetite, so the challenge may be defined as the education of appetite for well-being against disaster.

The position of hero in literate imagination dramatizes conquest, accomplishment, production, individuality, separation (analysis). Beyond conceptual *understanding* and political *undertaking*, there is affective *undergoing*. Part of the invention of electrate education is to supplement literacy and orality by introducing another actant position in our stories, another value, force, vector, orientation, direction. Four dimensions of experience to be identified, instantiated, dramatized, augmented in electracy include:

1. *Other*: Ethical experience involves an encounter with our counterparts in the world. To know people, the wisdom goes, you have to walk a mile in their shoes. Easier said than done, especially when the other is not *mon semblable*, but persons

truly beyond my ethos, not to mention non-human entities. Soft experience enables egents to undergo other encounters.

2. *Collective:* Individuals understand conceptually that their actions have consequences, but it is difficult to change behavior without direct experience of these actions. What can it hurt to throw one plastic bottle into a lake? SE makes it possible to undergo, not just understand, Kant's Categorical Imperative: Act only according to that maxim by which you can at the same time will that it would become a universal law.

3. *Disposition*: The deepest level of memory records the body's accumulated visceral experiences of development within a specific habitus. This experience is preserved by somatic markers that may be triggered in "blink" situations, without passing through any other image or representation. This deep pre-existing emotional investment determines most conscious decision- making but is not itself conscious. SE enables individuals to interact reflectively with the visceral training by means of which they gained control of their bodies in the earliest years of life, now orienting their attitudes as adults and circulating through the formal design of the artefactual environment.

4. *Reenchantment*: One result of modernity (created by the forces of industrialization, rationalization, utilitarianism) has been disenchantment of experience: alienation from one's own everyday behavior. A symptom of this reduction is the Bucket List syndrome, the push to extremity in entertainment and leisure activities: if one has not climbed Mt Everest, one has not lived! SE opens a way to overcome alienation from experience without sacrificing the benefits of enlightenment.

Prosopon

The disenchantment of the world included the disappearance of wisdom (sophia, proverbial common sense) from everyday life, replaced by expert advisors whose specialized knowledge addressed the relocation of reality outside sensory apprehension. An *Analogy* in our heuretic CATTt, generating the design of *Murphy*, is the Aesopian fable and Trickster tales. *Song of the South*—"Way Down on Murphy's Well-Field, far far from home."

Uncle Remus (modern Aesop) and the world of anthropomorphized animals of the sort populating animated films, based on African folklore, is a relay for *Murphy* interface, recommended in part simply because it is ready-made, present in popular culture, but also because of the controversies associated with the troubles of identity politics. User interactivity is culture-specific, catalytic. Our design must trigger the activity of fables already encoded in egent memory. Chorography maps culture and nature together: (Pine)Tar Baby; Koppers Superfund Baby. Uncle Remus tells the story of the Tar Baby

> Is tar baby a racist term? Like most elements of language, that depends on context. Calling the Big Dig a tar baby is a lot different than calling a person one. But sensitivity is not unwarranted. Among etymologists, a slur's validity hangs heavily on history. The concept of tar baby goes way back, according to Words@Random from Random House: "The tar baby is a form of a character widespread in African folklore. In various folktales, gum, wax or other sticky material is used to trap a person." The term itself was popularized by the 19th-century Uncle Remus stories by Joel Chandler Harris, in which the character Br'er Fox makes a doll out of tar to ensnare his nemesis Br'er Rabbit. The Oxford American Dictionary defines tar baby much like Romney used it, "a difficult problem, that is only aggravated by attempts to solve it." But the term also has had racial implications. In his book *Coup*, John Updike says of a white woman who prefers the company of black men, "some questing chromosome within holds her sexually fast to the tar baby." The Oxford English Dictionary (but not the print version of its American counterpart) says that tar baby is a derogatory term used for "a black or a Maori." (Coates)

Tar Baby emerges within the disaster, offering temporary shape for reflection, in the manner of a *sentient doll*. Such is the choral principle: the appearance of any unit activates a relevant set or network. We are learning how to read and write with part objects. The fable relates our local circumstance to the folk tale, and from there to a vector of attractor basins (wells). The sample question for a high-level, focused search (to identify examples of "sentient dolls" as "faces" for part-objects) is a happy choice for designing an archive, a *Murphy* database, since it turns out, upon mapping its context, to be situated at the heart of the problematic of experience ontology. Our design offers a new position in narrative, holding open a place for the coming protagonist of well-being, to shift collective strategy away from con/quest. An inventory of steps (if not the algorithm) connects this immediate short-term question to the long-term ambitions of konsult. These comments draw out the implications of this passage in *The Semiotics of Passions*, by Algirdas Greimas and Jacques Fontanille.

> This theory comes with a more general observation, consisting in noting the instability of actantial roles in passional configurations. In the passion of love, for example, we see the loved object transformed into a subject. This is all the more impressive when the object in question is not an animated being, in the narrative of the fantastic, among others, but also more tritely in fetishistic behavior. Curiosity also tends to transform its object into a subject, even into an antisubject that resists, flees, dissimulates, and so on. There is also no want of misers who treat their "coffers" as subjects, as actual alter egos. In short, in passion the object has a tendency to become the subject-partner of the impassioned subject. Hence the hypothesis that the only generalizable structure to describe passion is an intersubjective structure, or, more precisely, a structure wherein each objectal relation encompasses potential intersubjectivity, a sort of fuzzily contoured interactantiality. (28)

Perhaps the capacity of objects and things to become "sentient" in our stories may set an example for citizens, since passional (thymotic) reality is intersubjective (systemic). Electracy assumes that the human world as a whole functions in passional terms (Heidegger's care). What mathematics is to natural science, aesthetics is to the human sciences. Here is the power: "feeling" (from *sentire*), capability of sensory experience, senses, sensation, capacity for emotion, passion, conscious, aware, living. "Doll," small model of a human figure. A narrow definition of the task is to identify inanimate "dolls" that become animate. The mythological prototype is Galatea, the statue created by Pygmalion, who loved it so intensely that it came to life. *Pinocchio* fits this scenario of doll brought to life by love, as do the Cylons in *Battlestar Galactica*, signaling the relevance of our question to the identity conditions known as the post-human. Cylons lend face (prosopon) to technics as autonomous ontology. The more ambitious version of the challenge is to acknowledge "dolls" as in the family of fetish, extended to any inanimate object or thing that becomes as if self-aware.

Sentient dolls, animate objects, are found in proximity to impassioned subjects. It is this broader relation that opens the path to experience ontology. "Sentient dolls" is a special case of the impassioned object: a subject-object relationship. A sentient doll is a "triple," in a certain manner of speaking. Actor network theory operates with this understanding of system. Sentient dolls are in the tradition of "simulacrum."

> From Plato's time onward, the *eikon* (the copy-image) would be governed by the laws of mimesis and would evolve triumphantly through the history of Western representations, whereas the status of the simulacrum (*phantasma*), image invested with an autonomous existence, would remain fundamentally vague, and full of dark power. The physics of the atomists, which proclaimed the diffuse materiality of all images, rather than contributing a solution to the ambigouous status of the simulacrum, instead acccentuated its highly problematic nature. Lucretius, in *On the Nature of Thimgs*, would be their spokesperson. For Lucretius, the simulacrum is an in-between, an ambigous object between the body and the mind, which "like films drawn from the outermost surface of thngs, flit about hither and thither through the air." A mind-body, a body-mind, therefore. To what degree is of little importance, says Lucretius; what does matter is that "there exist what we call images of things." (Stoichita 1–2).

Stoichita notes that *simulacrum* became one of the key words of modernist and postmodernist theory, source of our CATTt Theory. Winnicott's transitional object may be understood in these terms, as well as Lacan's "lamella" (mythical organ of the unified erogenous zones) organizing the sensorium of electracy. In our terms, egency conjoins persons with objects: pepper for example. Egency retrieves classical emblems, in which figures are identified by their attributes (props). The conventional attributes of Lady Justice, for example, are a set of scales, a blindfold, and a sword. "Guns" are sentient dolls. Anthropomorphism is irreducible.

4 Trace

COURTIERS

Our original question may now be revisited, regarding the particular ratio, the mode of dis/jointure capable of gathering and fitting into coherence the field within which Being (life-death) emerges in a digital apparatus (artefactual being). How may konsult organize learning in a digital apparatus relative to this differently augmented order of reality? A basic principle of heuretics is: invent the genre; test it. In Plato's Academy students acquired literacy through dialogue. Our question in these chapters is: what is the genre of konsult? Each apparatus has its own cosmology, its own metaphysics, its own institutions, accounting for and directing the construction of a native reality: the spiritual order of orality; the material universe of literacy. The reality of electracy concerns libidinal energy, speaking beings as sexed, capable of enjoyment, which in turn participates in a universal rhythm (hysteresis) of generation. *Theory* (Lacan) describes the causality in the human dimension in terms of the object little other (@), cause of desire, around which the body drives circulate in a trajectory mapped by topology. Konsult proposes choragraphy to map egent *neighborhoods* in these terms. The representative of this object is any bit of detritus, a relational stand-in, ambassador, or go-between (marriage-broker in Freud's study of jokes) organizing the field within which Subject emerges as effect (*Phusis*). The object cause is a part object, referring to those experiences of birth, weaning, walking, toilet training, the entry into language mobilizing look and audition, which format the body's orientation relative to Jouissance, just as the mind is formatted to a particular language relative to a culture. Body is the language of language, or the ground of all figures and principle of all institutions, etymology of all artefacts (McLuhan). What dialectic was to dialogue, articulated by means of written logic, part-object is to konsult, articulated in digital imaging. The argument is that the imagination is formatted in infancy and early childhood at the level of biopolitics, to form the primary process layer of egent mental models, which support all subsequent learning; hence the relevance of neuroaesthetics to electrate education.

The @ correlates with "letter"—whose actual incarnation is a substitutable prop, likened to a transitional object, a child's blanket for example, or quasi-object, that circulates within the enjoyment field (emblematic prop). Lacan's emblem for this manifestation of @ in experience is the fort-da game a child played with a reel or bobbin on a string, to manage the experience of the absence and presence of his mother; and the story of the purloined letter, by Edgar Allan Poe (the compromising letter delivered to the Queen, stolen by the Minister looking for advantage, recovered by the detective Dupin). Lacan also used the painting by Diego Velázquez, "Las Meninas" (The Maids of Honor), made famous as a theoretical icon by Michel Foucault, as another exemplar of @ gaze. The juxtaposition of "Las Meninas" with "The Purloined Letter" establishes a scene showing Lacan's idea of how reality is structured by gaze. The dynamic power relations of a court provide an analogy for Subject construction (blind King, devious Queen, scheming Minister, an artist figure, such as the detective Dupin, or the painter Velásquez). Not unlike a game of chess. Another example is the game of Prisoner's Dilemma. The instruction concerns logical time or temporizing: an instant of seeing; the time for understanding; the moment of concluding, which correlate with Pierce's semiotic sequence of firstness, secondness, thirdness, or Derrida's differance. An egent's testimony regarding Phusis discovers one's own version of these scenes and times: where is My detritus? The mapping begins as *felt,* with one's feeling of desire as power, the pull, draw, directedness, oriented flow through one's situation. A shorthand analogy for chorography of Phusis in the spirit of Lacan's models is auteurist cinema: Subject is not only the point of view of the protagonist, but all the positions in play, expressed through the cinematic devices of *mise-en-scene, montage, mise-en-abyme.*

To clarify the status of @ as a relational entity, the electrate ratio, Lacan described it as his equivalent of the golden section or number, associated with the proportions of beauty and harmony in nature, and codified in sacred geometry as a guide to pre-modern art and architecture, but also of humanist proportion in Renaissance perspective, continuing into the present in consumer design. The golden section measures dimensions that are precisely "incommensurable," the scandal of irrational numbers. The phallus as one of the part (separable) objects is designated *Phi* in Lacan's algebra, to play on the signifier of the golden number. This designation is a pun, alluding also to the *phi phenomenon* in perception, identified in Gestalt psychology as early as 1912, describing the optical effect that is the basis for the illusion of movement in cinema. In his later seminars Lacan shifted his models almost entirely to mathemes, drawing on nearly the entire history of modern mathematics as an allegory of Subject (troping the form) to communicate the dynamic logics of coupling, how two become one. This One, vulgarly referred to as "the Beast with Two Backs," is ground zero of Enjoyment, but in turn manifests the rhythm of generation (the illusion of movement). The One is an impossible limit, of course, for which the infinitesimals of calculus provide a relay. It is worth noting that the inventor of French lyrical abstraction in painting, Georges Mathieu, proposed that the equivalent of "proportion" in modernism is "function" as defined in mathematics (215).

The historical setting of the invention of infinitesimals shows that Lacan's scenario extends even to his mathemes. "The idea of the infinitesimal is an intoxicating 'trick': it involves pretense on all sides. But it does seem to resolve something about continuity: gaps can be filled with infinitesimals. Leibniz tired to explain the 'infinitely little' to Queen Sophia Charlotte of Prussia; she said that on that subject she needed no instruction—the behavior of courtiers had made her intimately familiar with it." (Rothstein 54). Rothstein agrees that the analogy is apt. In the early period of calculus, at least, "these odd mathematical creations were used as placeholders, minor functionaries, little more than courtiers in the court of calculation." The icon organizing Lacan's *Seminar XI* in which he most fully introduced gaze is a painting by Hans Holbein the Younger, "The Ambassadors," famous for the vanitas skull included in anamorphic perspective extended across the lower part of the canvas. All those props of our daily life to which we devote so much energy may function as @, stand-ins, representatives of representations as Lacan says (ambassadors of cause of desire, which may not itself appear), in short: Symbol (symptom).

Displaying his characteristic ironic humor, Lacan compares the phallus to the original *gnomon* of Anaximander, the orthogonal upright of the sundial used to measure time. A justification for these associations is the principle of the tradition originating in Anaximander, extending from the legend of Daedalus through Vasari and Alberti to Le Corbusier's Modulor in modernism, is the formula "man is the measure of all things." Lacan updates and transforms this measure (jointure) into electracy by specifying exactly how "man" functions as energy force, beyond biology. This reoccupation of the tradition of "man" as "measure" finds support in recent natural sciences.

> In our time there is a convergence between the new biological science based on cybernetics and information theory, and the mystic doctrine of the Anthropocosm, the evolving universe around and within ourselves can be encountered only through the sensory instrument that we inhabit. Therefore our brains and bodies necessarily shape all our perceptions and have themselves been shaped by the same seen and unseen energies that have shaped every perceivable thing. Body, Mind and Universe must be in a parallel, formative identity. "Man, know thyself" was the principle of ancient science, as it is also coming to be in modern science. To quote the physicist, Robert Dicke: "The right order of ideas may not be, 'Here is the universe, so what must man be?' but instead, 'Here is man, so what must the universe be?'" (Lawlor 92)

Lawlor adds that "the human body contains in its proportions all of the important geometric and geodesic measures and functions," but this confinement of "measure" to the physical body marks the point of departure for Lacan's extension of ratio into libidinal erogenous drives. Calculus provides a relay and symbol of tracking relationships between moving objects, specifically of modeling change. The object @ is a psychic function, with Lacan's shift from proprotion to function reflecting the general shift of the modern noted by Mathieu.

> It is clear that some time after the *Psychoses* seminar, Lacan's analysis of the phallus and the subject shifted from the paradigm of Aristotelian logic dependent upon gramatical predication to that of modern set theory which relies on Frege's and Russell's notions of function and argument. This move allowed Lacan to elimnate any vestige of the idea of the subject

as a substance. In propositionl logic, the subject is merely a variable which may or may not exist, since a universal propositional function may be valid even though in fact no value of x makes the proposition true. (Chaitin 111).

As Chaitin explains, Lacan designates the phallus as function ("phunction" or "phi(x)"). The vectors of desire modeled in Lacan's mathemes represent the reality dimension opened in electracy. Lacan's topology exposes the locus of repression and the inadequacy of religion and science to address well-being against disaster. Religion sanctions sex only in the context of reproduction; science knows everything about cell biology. All the rest (thymotics) is repressed within culture as sentiment or "pornography," and assigned to Entertainment. Literacy metaphysically remains as resistant to sexuation as Orality was to biology.

Montage

The invention of electracy as apparatus of Jouissance begins in the red-light district of bohemian Paris, in nineteenth-century Montmartre, the cabaret scene of vice that evolved from the parodies of all traditions in Dadaist Cabaret Voltaire (Zurich during World War I), to family-friendly vice capital in Las Vegas. Freud raided all the traditions of art and dream to devise his therapeutic techniques, and returned the favor by inspiring Surrealism and related modernist and experimental schools. What is the formal *function* (equivalent of Plato's Analogy of the Line) capable of organizing and bringing into appearance this complex field of desire? Lacan identifies it readily with vanguard assemblage.

> The montage of the drive is a montage which, first, is presented as having neither head nor tail—in the sense in which one speaks of montage in a surrealist collage. If we bring together the paradoxes that we just defined at the level of *Drang*, at that of the object, at that of the aim of the drive, I think that the resulting image would show the working of a dynamo connected up to a gas-tap, a peacock's feather emerges, and tickles the belly of a pretty woman, who is just lying there looking beautiful. Indeed, the thing begins to become interesting from this very fact, that the drive defines, according to Freud, all the forms of which one may reverse such a mechanism. This does not mean that one turns the dynamo upside-down—one unrolls its wires,

it is they that become the peacock's feather, the gas-tap goes into the lady's mouth, and the bird's rump emerges in the middle (*Seminar XI* 169).

Lacan seems to have in mind one of Max Ernst's found collages. Lacan devoted many hours of his seminars creating mathemes from the history of mathematics and logic to formalize the best understanding of how two independent fields or sets are capable of intersecting and interacting, to model the behaviors of attraction-repulsion. His models tend to affiliate human coupling with the history of dissonance and disjunction, the metaphysical import beginning at the moment the phallus fails. The "howling wolf" tritone, domesticated by the well-tempered clavier, and basis of the blues note (updated in Heavy Metal), represents the @ function in the realm of the invocatory drive. The Euler circles, Venn diagrams, and Borromean knots Lacan favored gather within a family used in theology to represent the *vesica pisces*, figure of Mary's womb, a traditional religious instance of Chora (kenosis). The experimental arts tested the limits of concatenation, syntax, tropology, and found that *whatever resembles, assembles*, a logic popularized in advertising. The electrate equivalent of the fundamental rule of non-contradiction organizing literate inference is the "bachelor-machine" (to use the phrase introduced by Marcel Duchamp and promoted through a major art exhibition). The bachelor machine as an inference engine is described as the meeting of a sewing machine and an umbrella on an operating table (the phrase from Lautréamont). Perhaps the most iconic bachelor machine is "The Large Glass" by Marcel Duchamp, "The Bride Stripped Bare by her Bachelors, Even." This work would serve well to support study of the operations of "hinge" or "joint" as function organizing fit and measure in the metaphysics of electracy. What manner of Justice may be articulated within this metaphysics?

An examplar of electrate jointure, also mentioned by Lacan, is Georges Bataille. Bataille enjoyed a combative relationship with Surrealism. He was one of the organizers of the College of Sociology that gathered some of the best-known public intellectuals of Europe in the later 1930s to confront the popularity of fascism at the time. The hypothesis was that the Enlightenment had backfired, and Plato's Cave was taking its revenge (the return of the repressed). Bataille and associates proposed to retrieve "the black tide," to update mysticism and related hermetic modes of experience (alchemy, kabala) as means to explore the General Economy of waste they observed in the cosmos, against the Restricted Economy of growth promoted by industrial capitalism. It is notable that Sufi mysticism belongs in the family of esoterisms consulted by Bataille and company. The General Economy is the death drive manifested in history, using models from ethnography, economies of potlatch, gift exchange, to develop comparative studies of how civilizations expend resources (death is necessary; it is a question of how one spends it). Bataille's cogito, his version of desidero, might be: *depense donc jouis*—"expend therefore enjoy." Against Plato's ideal Forms, Bataille proposed an overflowing of all categories and boundaries of literacy, replaced with Formless (*l'Informe*). (Bois and Kraus, *Formless*). Against Platonic ascendency or transcendence through attraction, Bataille's General Economy investigates the obverse dimension of repulsion, descent into the detritus, everything abjected and abject, expulsed, situated fully within the field of body waste, @ of desire. What Parmenides and Plato after him excluded from Being (spit, mud, hair, and related litter), Bataille promotes as the scene of the other beginning. In the anti-encyclopedia composed by the Documents group (directed by Bataille), one of the entries expounded on "The Big Toe."

> Man is fond of imagining himself to be like the god Neptune, majestically imposing silence upon his own waves: yet the clamorous waves of his viscera, in more or less constant inflation and upheaval, brusquely put an end to his dignity. Blind, yet tranquil and strangely despising his obscure baseness, ready to call to mind the grandeurs of human history, for example when his glance falls upon a monument testifying to the grandeur of his nation, his elation is suddenly pulled up by an atrocious pain in his big toe because, though the most noble of animals, he nevertheless has corns on his feet; in other words he has feet, and these feet lead an ignoble life, completely independently from him. (Bataille 90)

This wave resonates with our Venetian Allegory. To supplement the eye of the soul, from Plato's Allegory, Bataille imagined a pineal eye, pointed downward to contemplate human ignobility. Lacan especially recommended Bataille's pornosophic novel, *The Story of the Eye*, as an example of the gaze or look, the field of libidinal sensorium supplementing the seeing eye of Plato's allegorical light. This other eye configures the dis/jointure of electracy, thus marking the threshold of passage from one apparatus to the other. Here will have been the site of resistance to change. The story narrates the descent into perversion of a teenage boy and Simone, his partner. The novel is part fantasy, and part self-portrait, in that it includes a traumatic memory from childhood, when Bataille watched his blind father use a chamber pot. Georges obsessed about the whites of the father's uprolled eyes. The important aspect in our context is the style of the work, the ordinating role asigned to the signifier, in which the narrative is organized by a bachelor machine system (conduction). The events of the plot (orgiastic or perverse sex acts) are motivated and sequenced not by the mimetic rules of action but by a sliding associative concatenation.

Roland Barthes admired the story and wrote an influential essay analyzing Bataille's device in a way that illustrates function as logic of rule and variable (algorithm). The actions were structured by two series, Barthes observed: first a set of round white shapes—eyeballs, eggs, bull's testicles, the sun; second according to wetness or moisture: milk, egg yolk, urine, sperm. The series were extended into conventional combination: eye weeps, broken egg runs, sunlight spreads (within dramatic scenes). The series finally were submitted to a combinatorial cross, or chiasmatic inversion, as if the plot were a moebius strip, producing the full surrealist effect: breaking an eye; poking out an egg, egg inserted into a vagina. This poetic combinatorial clearly manifests the condensation and displacement of dream work, and even secondary elaboration and considerations of representability. Such is the function ratio of digital jointure, the equivalent of dialectic, logic of sexual energy accessed as causality in electracy. The repeating formal properties of objects and actions present in *The Story of the Eye* join into a vector of movement through the scene, constituting its "melody," or its telos. Such is the logic of konsult, signaling a lack in literate schooling. To gauge the site of resistances differentiating one apparatus from another, we might suppose that Bataille's "eye" is no more acceptable to school than is Darwin's ape to church, and yet each represents the fundamental reality of their respective metaphysics.

WESEN

What instructions are found in the resources gathered in our heuretic CATTt? *Contrast* is Plato's *Republic* (representing metaphysics of literacy); *Analogy* is Brodsky's *Watermark* (along with Sterbak's "Waiting for High Water," representing the arts); *Theory* is Heidegger on Anaximander, and Lacan on Jouissance (representing contemporary philosophy). *Target* is the Internet in general including social media, database surveillance and the like, and specifically such developments as ubiquitous computing, augmented (mixed) reality, smart environments, supporting konsult as education for a fifth estate. Any of the various forms and media used to communicate this CATTt function as *tale*. Tale is post-medium, but its proposed form for konsult is that of New Wave *scenario*. The EmerAgency proposes transmedial implementations in every possible device: app, game, blog, program, database, video, website. The theoretical project of this book is to describe a genre native to electracy as pedagogy for learning and education online. The immediate concern is to summarize the lessons of these introductory chapters for egents, User actants of Stack Interface. The proposal has been to take direction from Philosophy, accepting Heidegger's commitment to the other inception found in the Presocratics as recording an experience of emergent Being (*Phusis*). Heidegger used a fragment by Anaximander, the oldest surviving prose text in the philosophical tradition, to identify the guideword of Being as "usage," specified as "enjoyment." Enjoyment is to electracy what truth is to literacy, or right (righteousness) to orality.

The practical import is that Enjoyment must be embodied and instantiated in institutional practices of jointure, with what is "fitting" for a global society understood in terms of a generalized craft of joining, gathering what is encountered in the Open, hole, gap, interval, Chora, configuring an order for Justice adapted to thymotic complexity and turbulence. Our challenge is to determine the devices of ratio and measure of relationality as such in the apparatus, to enable us to notice and annotate the patterns expressing global causality in our reality, basis for electrate education. A global society coheres in the manner of a dada-surrealist collage, and as such is the basis for coordinating learning across all institutions. It may be useful to repeat the principle that this collage annotates the causal force of Jouissance structuring electracy. Lacan develops and problematizes this directive by placing Jouissance in the context of psychoanalysis and the new emerging identity experience as Subject of Unconscious.

Plato appropriated the verb "to be" in Greek (Indo-European language), its function as copula between subject and predicate, to extend it in writing into ontology, producing a new dimension of reality through discourse. Lacan does something similar for electracy, starting from human copulation and its discontents, appropriating the biological fact to support a further dimension of body in/capacity for desire. Such is the locus of electrate metaphysics: designing the logic of visceral body, equivalent to the system of concepts the Greeks invented for alphabetic writing. Lacan shows that what characterizes the epoch of electracy (of industrial and post-industrial civilization) is a dimension beyond usage and enjoyment, a surplus-enjoyment, separated from use, a formless excess and waste, circulating libidinal energy within and through all the work of civilization in a way that confounds and disturbs, producing turbulence associated with tragedy and destruction as well as romance and well-being. Certainly, the Greeks encountered turbulence, documented as *Até* in tragedy, with Antigone (or Oedipus) as the exemplars. Psychoanalysis appropriates and reoccupies the scenario of tragedy to annotate the dynamics of everyday life. As oppositional partner with well-being, disaster today is nothing exceptional, merely commonplace, and we use our techno-science and bureaucracy against it with an effectiveness similar to that which orality achieved when applying magic to nature. Religion and Science have done their best up to now, and yet *souffrance* and Deinon continue unabated.

Koestler (citing Sidney Hook) summarized well the scale of what konsult undertakes for apparatus invention. "'When Aristotle drew up his table of categories which to him represented the grammar of existence, he was really projecting the grammar of the Greek language on the cosmos. That grammar has kept us to this day ensnared in its paradoxes: it made the grandeur and misery of two millennia of European thought" (176). It is not that Aristotle made a mistake, but, as Heidegger put it, he made a decision that left aside the other possible beginning, which we now retrieve and reoccupy. The heuretic lesson is that any apparatus has powers and limits, and we in our turn may design a new metaphysics by projecting the formal operations of modernism onto the cosmos. This new apparatus does not replace but supplements the existing syncretized apparati.

An example of our equivalent of Indo-European grammar and its writing—everything recordable in digital media—is manifested in "Waiting for High Water" (the Allegory of the Wave). It exemplifies theopraxesis, meaning that it syncretizes in one composition the virtues of knowing (thinking), doing (acting), and making (creating). It proposes writing outside and supplemental to literate discourse, the body sign, what Pier Paolo Pasolini, the Italian poet and cinema auteur, called the image-sign (*imsegno*) (another secondary modeling system). The letter (scarab effect) is generalized in camera work, such that photography does for the part-object what the letter did for phonemes of speech. At the meatphysical level of accessing reality, the camera must use the optics of perception to document apprehension through the pineal eye (so to speak). Pasolini, as a sophisticated theorist of semiotics as well as poet and filmmaker, recognized that the world already is a discourse, confronting us in our situations with a given nature-culture syncretism, such that anything pictured already has a cultural meaning, just as does any word selected include a definition and etymology. Pasolini's films are world poems, so to speak, cinema of Dasein. Egents are auteurs, New Wave consultants, appropriating modernist scenarios for konsult tale.

The further point from Lacan is that the world outside, the given reality of My situation, is the macrocosm of individual microcosm. The event of Second Phusis activated in konsult is a cosmology, meaning that what I experience in the making is the emergence of Subject, My Being—opening the feedback loop of Person (Fravarti). Venice is itself a grand *imsegno*, articulated variously by Sterbak and Brodsky (and many others before and after them), and this historical city and its existence through time is for us what the utopian *Republic* was for Plato. Venice is auratic, so merely designating it evokes significance. The special effects and post-production work of Sterbak's installation are important, as aesthetic intensifiers. Indeed, it is just this intensification that produces the feedback loop of self-knowledge, including the allegorical import of the animal protagonist. Here is the defining shift into fifth estate testimony. Heidegger learned from the arts how to conduct away from literate essence to *Wesen*, translated as "manner." Dennis Schmidt makes the point of how painting functions as "hermeneutic concept" (in the family of Kant's reflective judgment) disclosing presencing of Being by citing Heidegger's discussion of Franz Marc's "Deer in the Forest."

> The photograph of a dog and the image of a dog in a zoological handbook and a painting of "the dog" in each case present someting different and in a different way. The deer in the forest, which, for instance, Franz Marc has painted, are not these deer in a particular forest, but rather 'the deer in the forest.' . . . In artistic presentation a concept is presented which, in this case, presents an understanding of something existing; more precisely, it presents an understanidng of a being and of

its being in the world as a being with me in my environment; namely, the being-in-the-forest is presented (Heidegger, qtd. in Schmidt 71).

The painting is not a copy nor a schema, but an annotation of "firstness" (to use Peirce's terminology): "This was one of the ways in which he spoke of what the word *Wesen* meant: as a presence that is noticed before it is able to be known" (72). In "Waiting for High Water" Sterbak models the *Wesen* of everyday walking-my-dog-in-Venice, which is at once to "have one's cake and eat it too," to live and tell. She produces a feedback loop through recording and exhibiting by means of which she appears in the public sphere as "walking my dog," the whole process constituting an experience of intensified presence. Instagram democratizes *Wesen*, a first step towards a fifth estate for well-being against disaster. The disaster in dynamic dialectic relation with thriving is implicit in the social media environment, represented by the contaminated election of Donald Trump as President of the United States. Virilio might call this event the accident gift of social media invention.

We learn part of the allegorical import of Venice in our project from Lacan's *Seminar XVIII*, in which he introduced his notion of *lituraterre*, to distinguish his appropriation of creative writing from the purposes of literacy. Just as the Academy opened an institution for a practice of pure reason in oral Greece, psychoanalysis as institution fashioned a practice out of the pure aesthetics (pure creativity) emerging in electracy. Lituraterre was inaugurated by the experimental avant-garde arts, Lacan explained, referring to Montmartre cabarets in the space of entertainment opened in nineteenth-century bohemian Paris. The common purpose was the invention of pure art (art for art's sake), a purpose credited historically to Baudelaire, Flaubert, and Manet. (T. J. Clark, *The Painting of Modern Life*). Pure art in our context instantiates more fundamentally a logic of pure creativity. The misreading of the historical moment of pure art is that it constituted the withdrawal of art into itself as institution, when in fact this reformation away from mimesis was preparation for the extension of art as logic of learning through all disciplines and media. The genealogy of "text" tells the story of this commitment to the possibilities of forms apart from (however intertwined with) conceptual literate discourse, concerned with communication and information.

Here we find the project of grammatology undertaken by Jacques Derrida and the Tel Quel School of French theory. French poststructuralism is a continuation of the Parisian avant-garde, with this whole genealogy being central to the invention of electrate metaphysics. The other side of language (the other inception) involves sounds and marks, everything to do with the materiality of inscription, what Julia Kristeva (after Derrida) called Chora. Most importantly, text extends to all semiosis, relative to the historical avant-garde as an investigation of the formal powers of a given medium. The avant-garde invented the grammar of imaging, from which is being projected the metaphysics of a digital apparatus opening a new dimension for civilization governed by Fantasy. In this context Lacan's psychoanalysis proposes Subject as the identity formation emergent within nonobjective arts (text in the broadest sense), isotopic with digital media, just as Self emerged relative to propositional logic within alphabetic writing. The knowledge associated with the productivity of text is that of embodiment, experienced as jouissance. The goal of konsult is to bring these inventions into education, supporting learning as part of a collective global measure, the limit of well-being against disaster ajudicated in a fifth estate.

LITURATERRE

Late in his career Lacan turned to the writings of James Joyce (noting the "joy" in the proper name, in a family with *Freude* in Freud), especially *Finnegans Wake*, the consensus masterpiece of experimental letters, and hence Exhibit One for *lituraterre*. The *Wake* (in which we may hear the waves made by a moving boat, part of our Allegory of the Wave) combines all the resources of the alternative practices of thought contributing to electrate logic (children, aboriginals, the insane, the arts), at least to the limits of writing beyond speech. There is a mythology and epic story related through the *Wake*, expressed in an idiosyncratic style of macaronic puns and portmanteaus drawing upon every language that Joyce knew, creating an effect of controlled psychosis (word salad prepared by a gourmet chef). Lacan recognized and even identified with the *Wake* as a masterpiece of primary process dream work, akin to his own applications of *lalangue* in his lectures. Reading the *Wake* from the position of Analyst, Lacan understood that the breaks, interruptions, obscurities introduced into the epic tale of the Earwicker family constituted symptoms in a clinical sense. Using conventions established by Freud, Lacan offered a clinical interpretation of the symptoms based on a reading of the oeuvre, to pinpoint the foreclosure of the Name of the Father in Joyce's biography, a failure of anchoring point (unary trait) in identity associated with psychosis.

Joyce's achievement, recommending his art as a relay for Analysis, is that his practice of nonobjective *signifiance* transformed the symptom into a *sinthome*. Lacan used an archaic spelling of the word "symptom" to express this difference in function and effect. The import is that Joyce conducted a home remedy, if you like, working through the emotional disturbances of his lifeworld by means of textual play. The lesson: learn the craft of doing something with your symptom, *savoir-y-faire* as Lacan put it, playing on the familiar savoir-faire. "Enjoy your symptom!" is the advice, developed extensively in the theories of Slavoj Žižek. A key feature of this diagnosis relative to theopraxesis is that the therapeutic effect of this textual cure derived from "Joyce" making a name for himself—his recognition through Other as artist (Being through glory or reknown that grants existence). Making a name is to thymos what making a baby is to eros.

It is important to keep in mind that this relay cosmology is not confined to writing, even in this experimental sense, but extends to post-medium composition, using digital annotation to bring desidero into metaphysics. Lacan acknowledged that his theory of the gaze extended Merleau-Ponty's notion of *flesh*, which Merleau-Ponty proposed explicitly as ontology of subject participation in the world (participant actant). Flesh replaces literate substance with "element," Merleau-Ponty proposed, even in the ancient sense of Earth Air Fire and Water. We already observed in *Watermark* a poetics of Water as metaphysical element. Inspired in part by Bachelard's material imagination, Merleau-Ponty also intended his use of "element" to evoke the creative role of the Periodic Table in chemistry. Flesh and its elements were to be developed not only using text, modeled on Proust's "sensible idea" (itself based on the tradition of epiphany in romanticism, exemplifying Kant's reflective judgment), but also in the inventions of modernist painters such as Cézanne and Paul Klee. To clarify that lituraterre is writing with world (cosmology), Lacan in his seminar used some Joycean wordplay of his own to unpack the theory. Here is a summary of word generation (conduction).

> The [seminar] contains a cluster of homophonic puns like litura, terre, letter, literal, litter, littoral etc. The lituraterre is

composed of two parts litura and terre, the first referring to the letter and the second to land. To identify this letter, Lacan borrows Joyce's slip of the letter into litter, and for the meaning of the latter Lacan chooses "refuse." The key to the literary criticism is to locate the littering of the letter in the text and find the root and branch cause of the process. This metaphorical statement means that psychoanalysis finds in literature where the letter is littered. In a topological sense, Lacan rethinks and reiterates that a letter makes a littoral which functions as a border between unconscious knowledge and jouissance. As for the pun on literal and littoral (hence litura-terre), the seminar explains it: Isn't the letter the literal, which grounds itself in the littoral. This littoral, in fact, makes a barrier between jouissance and unconscious knowledge possible, something of which the subject remains unaware. (Azari 67).

The first reminder for the design of EPS is that this littoral zone refers to the mental model interface between the egent and the digital apparatus, grounding the family of "openings" and interval spacings referenced in our discussion. We recognize from the analogy of the camp site and its rubbish the relevance of "litter" as letter, refuse as rubbish as well as refusal, to Lacan's extension of the forgetting of Being into Unconscious, naming detritus the condition of being qua rejected. Our interest in these devices is not that of literary critics, but of inventors of metaphysics. Didactics in electracy exploit these expressive potentialities of discourse and language. The destroyed and threatened condition of our environing world is the return of the repressed, My alienated productivity confronting me. The receiver of konsult is My; composed in the middle voice, following a topological map or feedback loop around the circuit of drives. The perversity of human Enjoyment is that Jouissance is an effect of expenditure in Bataille's sense: waste and death (*Deinon*, the Overwhelming). The appearance of "littoral" in this invention is central to the Allegory of the Wave. "Littoral" names a region of seacoast, the shore area between land and sea. Venice is within such a zone, making it a letter of this other strange area that Lacan calls *demansion*, to mark its Unconscious quality. Venice is mise-en-abyme of electrate cosmography. Konsult constructs a demansion devoted to learning, a Chora within which to encounter Absolute.

Lacan introduces his vocabulary to his seminar with an account of his trip to Japan. He relates a vision he had looking out the window of the plane while flying over Siberia. It is perhaps worth noting that Brodsky was serving his internal exile in a small village in Siberia at the time Lacan passed over (in a film version Brodsky might wave at the contrail of a plane as it passes overhead). Letters and signifiers each function in their own order in Lacan's method, with the letter enabling body inscription in the Real, relative to the signifier in discourse. Here is a passage between electracy and literacy. Not to reject literacy, or any apparatus, but to find the ratio, function, the jointure relating the apparati. Being recordable in digital media, letter traces a hole made in language by Unconscious: Outside, Other: what we don't know and is anyway beyond conceptual representation, unspeakable (in excess of orality and literacy). There is homology across levels (nature, biography, culture, language), creating an isotopy of the void or nothing of subject (refusal), the litter (distribution) of nonobjective signifiers, the littoral region (Venice for example), and the theory of lituraterre. The metaphysical relevance is that in the digital apparatus, via theopraxesis, we write through the Real.

Lacan credits his new ability to read the landscape to his encounter with Japanese arts, especially calligraphy, in its cursive styles, the *kakemono*, in which one cannot mistake the surplus-enjoyment added to a signifier by the sheer play of style and presentation. His route over Siberia allows him to survey the Soviet Empire, he imagines, the industries and military installations that make Siberia important, and so ominous in the Cold War era. Most important, however, is the superimposition of intermittent clouds, rain, and earth with *kakemono* scrolls.

> As appeared to me invincibly, this circumstance is not nothing: the between-the-clouds, the streaming (*ruissellement*), only trace to appear, operating there to do more still than indicate relief in this latitude, in that which of Siberia makes a plain, a plain desolate of any vegetation but reflections, which push into the darkness what does not shimmer. The streaming is the bouquet of a first stroke (trait) and of what effaces it. I have said it: it is from their conjunction that the subject is made, but in that two times are marked there. It is necessary then that the erasure be distinguished there.
>
> Erasure of no trace that might be in advance, this is what makes the shore (terre) of the littoral. Pure Litura, this is the literal. To produce it, is to reproduce that half without

> complement (paire) by which the subject subsists. Such is the exploit of calligraphy. Try to make this horizontal bar which is drawn from left to right to figure with a stroke (trait) the unary one (*l'un unaire*) as character, it will take you a long time to find from what support it is attacked, by what suspense it is arrested. To tell the truth, it is without hope for an occidentalized. It requires a movement (train) which is only captured in being detached from whatever it is that you strike out.
>
> Between center and absence, between knowledge (savoir) and jouissance, there is a littoral which only turns to the literal insofar as this turn, we might take it the same at any instant. It is from this alone that you can take yourself for the agent who sustains it. What is revealed by my vision of the streaming, inasmuch as the erasure dominates it, is that in producing itself from between the clouds, it conjoins itself to its source, that it is indeed in the clouds Aristophanes hails me to find what concerns the signifier: that is, the semblant, par excellence, if it is from its rupture that it rains, the effect inasmuch as is precipitated from it, what was matter in suspension. (Lacan, "Lituraterre")

Lacan is indicating through this analogy of calligraphy and landscape something about how the Real enters into the traces of *signifiance*. Lacan was intimately familiar with the work of Claude Lévi-Strauss, and his prominent reference to calligraphy as a figure of the musical or rhythmic character of pattern in mythopoeic discourse as collective authoring. To construct meaning with the Real involves the operation of the letter (scarab principle).

> It can also be seen why the conparison between painting and music would be acceptable, at a pinch, only if limited to calligraphic painting. Like the latter—but because it is a sort of secondary form of painting—music refers back to a primary level of articulation created by culture; in the one instance, there is a system of ideograms; in the other, a system of musical sounds. But by the mere fact of its creation, the pattern makes explicit certain natural properties: for instance, graphic symbols, particularly those of Chinese writing, display aesthetic properties independent of the intellectual meanings they are intended to convey; and it is these properties that calligraphic art exploits. This is an essential point, because contemporary musical

thought, either formally or tacitly, rejects the hypothesis of the existence of some natural foundation that would objectively justify the stipulated system of relations among the notes of the scale. (Lévi-Strauss, 21)

The issue for electracy is the development out of vanguard arts of a grammar of digital media that in turn is projected into electrate metaphysics, operating logic for the apparatus as a whole (just as the metaphysics of literacy is a projection of Indo-European grammar). Such is the purpose of Lotman's secondary modeling system, or Hollander's troping of form.

The mention of Aristophanes relates Lacan's observation to *The Clouds*, a satire targeting Socrates. Lacan found in Japanese (and Chinese) art a map of lituraterre, not only in the stylistic excess of cursive calligraphy, but also in the landscape aesthetics, in which space empty counts as much as full, and clouds alternate with shapes. Egents learn to read the vectoral patterns of the lifeworld circulating through media as a kind of calligraphy. These features of art are analogies for the holes in the Real, in language, masked by fantasms and @, just as clouds mask the empty in Asian designs, the context recognizing that this void is Chora, functioning as hub of a metaphysical wheel. Literature is an art of these zeros, Gestalts soliciting completion by readers from their own experience. *Seminar XVIII* is full of references to Chinese characters, and to the Chinese Philosopher Mencius. Lacan refers to Ezra Pound at one point, evoking Vortex and the invention of modernist poetics associated with ideograms. Sergei Eisenstein drew upon the ideogram as relay for theorizing his creation of cinematic montage, and Tel Quel in the context of French enthusiasm for Maoism continued this syncretism. Konsult is syncretic.

Konsult consists of several layers, strata, a palimpsest of intertangled systems whose correespondences create egent EPS. The atmosphere of Venice in winter lends itself to this aesthetic of attunement, its littoral geography giving rise to heavy fogs as well as rising waters. The important point is the homology joining the levels and layers of our scene structuring the multiplanar design of the interface. The logic we are learning (inventing) instantiates and opens to design this littoral demansion, adding EPS to GPS. Actual Venice is layered with a topological map of catastrophes (René Thom), of historical events, representation in arts and letters, as scene of micro-macro memory. Lacan's theory orients the conditions of konsult. Our jointure must support a relationship across gap, hole, interval, blind spot called Unconscious (I think where I am not, and am not where I think), at once individual and collective (hence egent). This scene (scenario) hosts an event of Being, put into relation with disciplinary invention in a pedagogy of creativity.

Fouring is a useful general term for the figural rhetoric needed to negotiate this division (*daio* of Daimon) of My, structuring the four-fold of the popcycle. Topology theoretically tracks the division, beginning with the moebius strip as pure edge, augmented by the other topological figures. This graphic edge is the most recent version of an experience of measure beginning with the Greek Daimon (with Socrates the most famous conceptual persona). Heidegger's method of tracking translations shows the Latin word as "Genius." Goethe translated "Genius" as "Grenze" (Limit). Emerson understood this ethics of Daimon as "the god within," in his American update. Lacan's geometric edge is "limit" in this sense, mapped through the mathematics of networks, all in the tradition of measure. Konsult performs in electracy the function of Avatar and Fravarti, returning to Subject a measure of Limit, the ratio of Justice. Electrate education forms around this function as User Interface of Stack.

Differance

There remains one more philosopher to discuss, as *Theory* of our CATTt, enriching the fundamental guideword for electrate metaphysics coming from the other beginning, received from Anaximander. Jacques Derrida takes up the focalizing primary name of Being addressed by Heidegger and Lacan—Enjoyment—to give it one more turn, providing further instructions for the project of inventing a function and measure of Justice. Derrida's variation, *Trace*, is registered within "electracy," naming the theory of *signifiance* functioning in the digital apparatus. "Electricity" plus "trace" gives "electracy," exploiting the conventions of word formation relative to "literacy." That is one reason why we are still in class, performing table work so to speak, and not yet konsulting, in order to encounter this context for understanding Trace as theopraxesis. It is easy enough to reorient or reset ourselves whenever the explanation turns opaque, by remembering that konsult is applied *text* (the entire past century delivered to us this operation), even if "felt" rather than "text" is a more accurate name for the materiality of digital composition.

Digital jointures are not like tightly woven textiles, but more like the fabric felt—a conglomerate mass pressed holistically into any desired shape (eidos, idea) relative to function. We will need this term, since Derrida's trajectory takes him beyond textile.

Derrida supplied a family of names for Trace as supplement for literate sign and signification, thus projecting a quasi-conceptual bridge into the coming apparatus of *signifiance*. The prototype of the family is *différance*, a neologism spelling structuralist semiotic "difference" with an "a," to mark the relational status of the apparatus. This "a" is in a family with Lacan's @ and Joyce's macaronics, among other avant-garde devices. The epochal shift into electracy is invoked in this simple invention (now in the dictionary), the way sense emerges in the silent play produced in writing between one spelling and the other of "difference." The play references the field theory of sense now everywhere assumed, replacing representational reference with network system as the basis for meaning. Trace is the mark of sense created by the vectoral movement from one term to the other. "Now if we consider the chain in which différance lends itself to a certain number of non-synonymous substitutions," Derrida writes in the essay entitled "Différance," "according to the necessity of the context, why have recourse to the 'reserve,' to 'archi-writing,' to the 'archi-trace,' to 'spacing,' that is, to the 'supplement,' or the pharmakon, and soon to the hymen, to the margin-mark-march," offering an inventory of the names he has used in various essays to map this movement (Jacques Derrida, *Margins of Philosophy* 12). Like Lacan, Derrida credits James Joyce with having systematized the linguistics of Trace in *Finnegans Wake*.

The final pages of Derrida's essay are devoted to a discussion of Heidegger's reading and translation of the Anaximander fragment, which he uses in turn to articulate his own project. Derrida accepts Heidegger's translation of the Greek *to khreon* (necessity) as "usage," confirming the nomination of this event as the pivot of a new metaphysics, but he disagrees with Heidegger's assumptions about ratio, that the jointure of the new Justice must be harmony, accord. Derrida's focus is less on "enjoyment" and its discords addressed by Lacan, but something more profoundly amiss, even if less scandalous. Differance alludes to "ontological difference," distinguishing what is present from presencing as such. At issue is how Being is *given* through language, how Phusis or emergence of Being (disclosive withdrawal) may be received and performed, the problem Heidegger took up in *Contribu-*

tions to Philosophy, signaled in the archaic spelling of *Seyn* (translated as Be-ing). Against Heidegger's commitment to one unique word to name Being itself, Derrida quotes Heidegger's own lines to indicate rather the dimension of Trace that made possible Heidegger's creative translation. "And such is the question inscribed in the simulated affirmation of différance," Derrida states at the conclusion of his essay. "'Being / speaks/ always and everywhere / throughout / language.'"

What carries Derrida further into the genesis of a digital apparatus, beyond Heidegger's "destruction" and Lacan's "transference," is the recognition that this giving of Being through language may not be addressed in any conceptual or literate terms. It is not a matter only of bringing a Real into representation, but of developing new modes of annotation generating new orders of meaning. Derrida uses the occasion to articulate his own project, much of which was still ahead of him when he wrote this essay. "And it is at the moment when Heidegger recognizes usage as trace that the question must be asked: can we, and to what extent, think this trace and the dis of différance as *Wesen des Seins*? Does not the dis of différance refer us beyond the history of Being, and also beyond our language, and everything that can be named in it? In the language of Being, does it not call for a necessarily violent transformation of this language by an entirely other language?" (*Margins* 25). The guideword of electrate metaphysics accumulates sense: *necessity, usage, enjoyment, jouissance, trace.*

Chora

Derrida speaks as one of the inventors of the practices of emerging digital metaphysics. He is part of the French Tel Quel school at this period in his career that beginning in the 1960s had taken up the invention process originating in France with the bourgeois revolution, the rise of Paris as industrial city (the industrial revolution begun in England), the emergence of bohemian counter-cultural lifestyle in the vice district of Montmartre. The Cabarets of Paris are to electracy what the Academies in Athens were to literacy: the institutional site opening a place for pure innovation (for Reason [logic] in Athens, for Appetite [aesthetics] in Paris). The logic of electracy in its pure form was created in nineteenth-century Montmartre, culminating in the Dadaism of Cabaret Voltaire in Zurich during the First World War. French theory (Philosophy) took up the project in the twentieth century, providing for pure art (non-objective abstraction as the prototype) what might be called its "secondary elaboration," or extension into a conceptual critique of literacy as metaphysics. The ethics and politics of this commitment to vanguard poetics remains controversial, to the extent that this apparatus framing is not clearly understood. The brilliance of Tel Quel theory was its grasp of experimental arts as a new metaphysics, an essential part of a transformation of civilization. Hence their decision to reject praxis as direct engagement with social themes, and to pursue theopraxesis, in order to access the new demansion of desire, site of value as such.

The flash point was the debate surrounding committed literature, concerning the proper way to promote what we are calling konsult—how to act in the world on behalf of well-being against disaster. The path of committed art, led by Jean-Paul Sartre after the second World War, especially associated with Marxist socialism and Soviet socialist realism, rejected modernist arts as elitist, defeatist, and bourgeois (thus turning away from the direction called for in *Nausea*, written before the war), calling for direct activist intervention in politics and realist naturalism treating progressive themes in the arts. The Tel Quel group, taking up the alternative position represented by such predecessors as Bataille and Blanchot, argued that experimental arts provided the means of a more radical revolutionary politics, when applied as logic to the full range of social institutions. They had it right, within the frame of apparatus genesis, that the more profound possibility for konsult is through the invention of the apparatus itself, rather than the mere appropriation of literate inventions for new themes or agendas. Konsult is not critique, but invention. Konsult does not oppose critique, activist politics, or engineering remedies: may they succeed to the greatest extent possible! Meanwhile, anticipating their limit, konsult takes up the other inception.

Julia Kristeva syncretized for Tel Quel the various sources converging around electracy, drawing the clearest conclusions from the revolutions transforming nearly every discipline across the culture around the turn into the twentieth century. She followed Derrida's lead in designating this new ratio or jointure (disjoining) as Chora. Her version of the other beginning speaks in terms of an alternative economy to the one dominating Western history in the era of literacy, with examples in pre-Socratic Greece, China, and contemporary capitalism. Separating from subject selfhood, including the divided subject of the psychoanalytical clinic (in ego psychology), is a "subject in process" (on trial), which is the formation of identity experience and behavior isomorphic with experimental arts. In this other economy (the General Economy of Bataille), the unitary subject of self-identity is pulverized. The subject of substance is put on trial, into process (it is pure relation). "The process dissolves the linguistic sign and its system (word, syntax) dissolves, that is, even the earliest and most solid guarantee of the unitary subject" (Kristeva, "The Subject in Process" 134). Kristeva's example in this essay is Antonin Artaud.

> This pulsional network, which is readable, for example, in the pulsional roots of the non-semanticized phonemes of Artaud's texts, represents (for theory) the mobile-receptacle site of the process, which takes the place of the unitary subject. Such a site, which we will call the Chora, can suffice as a representation of the subject in process, but it should not be supposed that it is constituted by a break (castration); it is more pertinent to see it as functioning by way of the reiteration of the break or separation, as a multiplicity of ex-pulsions, ensuring its infinite renewal. Expulsion [*rejet*] rejects the discordance between the signifier and signified to the extent of the dissolutions of the subject as signifying subject, but it also rejects any partitions in which the subject might shelter in order to constitute itself . . . As well as being a-subjective, the process, set in movement and renewal by expulsions, is also a-familial, a-filial, a-social. Only movement of social subversion, at times of change or revolution, can offer a field of social action to this process of expulsion. (134)

It is good to recall the functionality of these inventions: *to access and annotate desire circulating through media and the lifeworld as attraction-repulsion*. Kristeva's vocabulary suggests an isotopy in electracy of mobile Chora (psychoanalytic Subject), experimental arts logic, and ubiquitous computing, and this correlation is the very core of konsult invention. Indeed, she asserts that the pulsional drives of the body (alluding to Lacan and the undergoing of Jouissance) produce not signification but *signifiance* (Roland Barthes's pleasure of the text), which enters representation through formal features of the art media (color, gesture, sound). What definition of terms accessing idea was to literacy, high-definition technology accessing felt is to electracy. The nineteenth-century avant-garde, she confirms, was experimenting precisely with the materialism of *signifiance*. Georges Mathieu cited Gestalt psychology as establishing the separability and authomy of pure art features (the scarab principle) and their capacity to address and catalyze corporeal experience (Mathieu 223), thus indicating the practical extension of Kant's reflective judgment into pure art and digital recording on behalf of visceral orientation of the Real.

A useful connection between this mobile Chora authored through experimental styles and Lacan's object @ occurs when Kristeva uses the same example of the child's game of fort-da that Lacan used as an example of @. The bobbin (reel) thrown away and retrieved in the game is a "transitional object" (Winnicott), some bit of the given reality used to articulate the process drives of a body learning to manage itself. This appropriation of some material bit (detritus) manipulated with a bodily gesture is how drive pulsation enters discourse (similar to the way written syntax instantiated the sequence of reasoning). Ultimately the vanguard arts constitute a school of savoir-y-faire, contributing further understanding of the Sinthome recommended also by Lacan. The relevance as felt is that through the gesture and play (the art), the egent experiences Jouissance (through *Erfahrung* or mise-en-scene), just as in literacy Self emerged in the experience and behavior of reason through writing.

> As a topological receptacle of expulsion, artistic production finds its identificatory moment, its "pole of transference," not in the "other" of transference but in the modeling of the receptacle, in the movement of expulsion and its organization, and these aspects can be figured, in inter-subjective relations, by the mother or the nurse. The other subject is pushed out of the movement, and it is the shattered plurality of the same, divided by expulsion, coincident with the plurality of the natural and social world, which intercepts and captures expulsion. This capture is always plural, therefore, but at the same time internal and external to the reversible subject. The fragmented and reorganized chora is best realized in dance, gestural theatre or painting, rather than in words. Artaud's theatrical practice, and perhaps especially the Rodez paintings, or those which accompany the last texts, bear witness to this non-verbal but logical (in the sense of "binding") organization of expulsion. (Kristeva, "The Subject in Process" 165)

Literacy augmented the reasoning mind; electracy augments the desiring body. The lesson inferred from Kristeva's commentaries is that the function of jointure—at least in this epoch of apparatus creation—is dissonant breakup and conflict, rather than harmony or concord. The relevance of Trace as usage, however, is just to notice and experience the logic or means of annotating, gathering, arranging, ordering, relating, composition of Chora as scene of transmedial memory (Chora is to electracy what Topics is to literacy—correlating correspondences across physical, mental, cultural, and technological pleateaus). Such is the support of theopraxesis in electracy. It is worth one more citation of Kristeva to confirm the alignment of this logic of *pulsion* (visceral part objects in psychoanalysis) configuring Jouissance of embodied drives, formal devices of arts constructions, individual and social behaviors, institutional practices, disrupted and reconfigured to bring attraction-repulsion forces into metaphysics. The theme to emphasize is that this connection between embodied Jouissance and formal arts composition is to electracy what analytical reason supported through propositional inference is to literacy. Literacy invents conceptual reasoning. Electracy invents imaged feeling, with the goal of accessing this other demansion of cause operating through desire. The question remains: is the institution of education capable of receiving this history?

> With this practice we are at the most radical site of heterogeneity: on the one hand, struggle against the signifier; on the other, the subtlest differentiations of meaning. If the former, expulsion being maintained, brings us to the heart of jouissance and of death, the latter, through its subtle differentiation (in rhythm, color, vocalization, or even semanticized through laughter or word play), keeps us at the surface of pleasure, in a subtle tension. The most intense struggle towards death, inseparably proximate to the differential binding of its charge in a symbolic tissue which is also, as Freud suggest in *Beyond the Pleasure Principle*, the condition of life: such is how the economy of textual practice appears. Its principal characteristic, distinguishing it from other signifying practices, is precisely to introduce heterogeneous rupture and expulsion, jouissance and death, through the binding and differentiation of life and of meaning. (Kristeva, "The Subject in Process" 160)

Subjectile

Derrida agreed with the status of Artaud as exemplar of the function or dis/jointure of choral logic, using late Artaud productions (works of his madness) to articulate the relation of Chora to Subject as subjectile (Derrida, "To Unsense the Subjectile"). This essay clarifies what is central for designing the logic of konsult, which is the "logos" (pathos, thymos) of digital metaphysics: the use of experimental arts style as cosmology, for constructing the fit of Justice, in a theopraxesis of faring well (against disaster). The metaphysical purpose is to devise a discourse that does for desire (appetite) what grammar and logic in writing did for reason, in order for education to access the same collective dimension industrialized by the corporation as institutionalized appetite. Derrida shows that the instruction to be extracted from Artaud's late works of madness (or from any of the other exemplary resources commonly listed) is not direct imitation of a particular style. Konsult must produce an electrate equivalent for literate categories, to enable thinking beyond and without Idea (Form). Jointure as Justice concerns Limit, Measure, Edge and the arrangement of relations. Subjectile is another name for this dimension of hinge and passage also mapped in Lacan's topology. Subjectile is the interval between (any pair in the metaphysical system of space, time, cause—above and below, inside and out, before and after)—whose function is to gather and relate for theopraxesis the orientations achieved through the visceral body. It is the topological chiasmus inverting or invaginating seeming opposition, contradictions, oxymorons, escaping dialectical symmetry. The logical feature, also observed in Kristeva, is that the formal or dadaist rhetoric is not practiced in pure isolation as it might be within some disciplinary context of art or theory, but functions as Trace, organizing inferential movement through any matter or material (including information) leading to an electrate motto in the spirit of the poet Basho: data is known by dada.

The economy of Artaud as exemplar is extraordinary, in that the works discussed are relevant at numerous levels for theopraxesis. First there is the context, with Artaud identifying in his moments of lucidity with the career and mythology of Vincent Van Gogh. Derrida refers to Artaud's essay, "Van Gogh, the Man Suicided by Society," to notice the effect of "haunting" as Derrida calls it, even proposing hauntology to replace ontology. Time is out of joint, Derrida shows, to explain his turn beyond Heidegger and Lacan, into a further dimension of usage.

Being is given through language in history, and emerges during theopraxesis as gift. The subject is positioned within history, caught up in the movement of archi-writing, archi-trace, that produces through time a passage from individual singular private inventions to universal institutional public truths, as happened in the case of the history of geometry (Derrida's commentary on Husserl's book on the origin of geometry as confirming the historicity of genesis). What we encountered in our other theorists as surplus value or surplus enjoyment, or formally the effect of emergence in complex systems, Derrida addresses as effects of Trace, the movement of sense through the sheer capacity for constellation and configuration of any formal system, the possibility of sense to emerge historically without intention or will, without author: sending without sender, gift without donor, which is why trauma (shock) is accessible to Trace.

This productivity and happening of meaning through historical genesis, through occupying the position of receiver, anticipated in every divination system, is electrate Phusis (revelation of second nature). Derrida's addition to the project of Phusis, beyond the emergence of Being, is to learn how to exploit this extra or surplus sense, a vocabulary he adopts from Marx and Lacan. He was not satisfied with Heidegger's interpretation of Anaximander's other beginning, wanting to focus more on an economy of gift (but this is also Heidegger's ambition in *Contributions* and after). His Joycean surplus is generated through the pun on "present," as presence and gift. It is this birth or natality of sense through chance that Derrida finds in Artaud, extending puncepts beyond language. Elsewhere Derrida located the moment of transition from literacy to electracy in a comment by Mallarmé, regarding his Symbolist poetics as writing without voice, without "self." In literacy Subject is self, with the challenge of literacy being to communicate this original intention of voice through the external memory of writing, resisting all postal vicissitudes. Derrida's critique of phenomenology targets the insistence on intentionality (consciousness). In electracy Subject is egent, and the function of annotation is inventive, to generate and receive (create) an unforeseen significance out of *signifiance* circulating through the collective body. It is Derrida's version of transference operating in history, the way Luther understood his present situation through an appropriation of the example of St. Paul, or the way revolutionaries in France imagined their events through the history of Rome: "as if." Human constructions are metaleptic, haunted by other times, places, events, people, including the future and what remains to come in time (EPS).

The second lesson concerns how mobile Chora or Trace function as inference system, producing a rhythm, constellation, melody, or path through the quantum field of information. Artaud himself learned composition through a conflict between "motif" and its destruction in Van Gogh. "This word motif (how will they translate that?) has the certain advantage of substituting the dynamics and the energy of a motion (movement, mobility, emotion) for the stability of a -ject [jet] which could set itself up in the inertia of a subject or object. When he gives up describing one of van Gogh's canvases, Artaud inscribes the motif in the centre of the 'forces' and the writing forces ('apostrophes,' 'streaks,' 'commas,' 'bars,' etc.), with these acts of 'blocking,' 'repression,' 'the canvas,' and so on as protagonists" (Derrida, "Subjectile" 72). Artaud responds to this force of energy in Van Gogh, a feeling of life upsurging. Part of Artaud's relevance is in the hybrid works he produced in this context—combinations of painting, drawing, and writing—which make them relays for digital composition. Writing and drawing are supplemented with marks and tears, pencil stubbings and related processes of expressive graphic arts. Such composition constitutes an example of what Lacan called Sinthome, and also to Heidegger's *Wesen*, annotating intensity. These areas of "non-sense" exemplify the *littoral demansion*—the rim of drive made accessible and brought into composition, thus establishing a ground for electrate ontology. The purpose of konsult is to bring this demansion to bear on policy invention in the fifth estate.

An instance of the relation of choral logic of force operating within a figural image is Van Gogh's "Sunflowers." The sunflower through the manner of Van Gogh's style is a whirling force of energy. The iconography is appropriated and transformed by the manner. Related to Derrida's discussion of parergon, enframing, by which he problematized all notions of border, the subjectile encompasses the entire experience of making art as living, constituting instructions for theopraxesis. Derrida paraphrases Artaud's description of Van Gogh as "pure art."

> All the heterogeneous categories of "means" are deliberately associated in the same series, and they are means of "pure painting," the thing to represent, the sky and the plain just as much as the body of the artist and the material, that is, the place from which painting spurts forth (the tubes) but also these two supports or receptacles of the spurt projected forth, the "canvases" and this support of the support which is an

easel. As for the color ready to spurt forth, expressed, from the tube, it guarantees in writing a metonymic passing between the red of the hair and the hairs of the brush, between the brushes and the yellow of "his hand," between the body proper and the instrument of the artist. By simple contiguity: "canvases, brushes, his red hair, tubes, his yellow hand, his easel." As for the two things to represent, their choice reproduces the scene we have already recognized: the top and the bottom, the top from which the ground is bombarded and the substratum, the support, the subjectile at once flat and massive, in this case the plain ("A stormy sky,/ a chalk-white field, / canvases . . ."). A contiguity again effacing the limit between the "plain," as object or subject of the representation, and the "canvases," the subjectile. The motif, we were saying, the excessive exceeded. (97)

Although Derrida does not mention it here, Van Gogh himself exemplifies haunting, in that his move to the south of France was inspired by his love of Japanese Ukiyo-e woodblock prints, encountered through the *japonaiserie* sweeping Paris at the time. The light in the south of France was as close as he could get to how he imagined Japan. The mystorical layers include also the intense yellow of the sunflowers, and the leitmotif of yellow thoughout Van Gogh's oeuvre (the yellow house he prepared in Arles for his imagined collective of artists, the yellow sun setting over farm fields in his copies of Millet). Biographers trace this stylistic intensity to what Van Gogh cited as his worst memory, standing as a child on the steps of his new boarding school, watching his parents departing in their *yellow carriage* (Naifeh and Smith).

The relevant application for the convergence of Fauvism and Trace is the emerging autonomy of *spectacle* in contemporary digital media. Andrew Darley supplies some context, explaining his plan for *Visual Digital Culture*. "I locate and begin to describe a shift away from prior modes of spectator experience based on symbolic concerns (and 'interpretative models') towards recipients who are seeking intensities of direct sensual stimulation. As a possible avenue for further understanding what is occurring within this new aesthetic space of neo-spectacle, concepts of play are introduced and discussed." (Darley 3). In the context of Trace as metaphysics of visceral theopraxesis it becomes possible to recognize the function of spectacle: that FX intensities catalyze mobile Chora of part objects capable of articulating the libidinal economy.

The instructions always return to My, to your intensity: *where is your south of France as Japan, your Venice as St Petersburg?* Such is the orientation of EPS in becoming heuretes, occupying the dimension opened to metaphysics in electracy. It is no surprise to learn that subjectile is another version of Chora, and is understood as instantiated in a singular location. "Acceptance, reception on the subject of a subject, and of something that figures precisely the receptacle, of something that is almost nothing and that must be replaced in its place by place—for the subjectile is nothing other than the empty placing of the place, a figure of the khora, if not the khora itself" (123). Your own place (region, neighborhood) is Chora, the imaginal world of momentous site put into scenario in konsult as genre of education: the Real of desire passes necessarily though My place, mapped in konsult (choragrapy), which is how one becomes electrate.

Border

Chora is the site between, the interface interval mediating egent relations with problem, discipline, culture, and memory (popcycle in short); the play of every hinge, passage, junction and disjunction, subjectile, scene for gathering and arranging realtiy (cosmos)—the operating play that Derrida calls differance. It may be worked (played in every sense). To function as (collective) Subject, actant User of Stack, requires implementation in technology as well as in the other registers of the apparatus. What is this littoral zone of edge, or border, such that it functions as Avatar, Daimon, Genius, Limit? This functionality of edge that opens reality to ordering is explored and expressed through "littoral" geography understood as trope, or concrete logic (Lévi-Strauss). Here is a fundamental responsibility of konsult, as designed imaginal world, to manage relationships and movements (vectors) between concrete and abstract signifiers, particular and general, singular and universal, inside and outside (and all other dynamic dialectics). This dynamic circulates of itself (hence it manifests Being). Derrida confirms the import of the Allegory of the Wave by using the seashore tidal rise and fall as emblem of the ex-pulsional passage, the movement or trace of sense. "Trace" appropriates "sign" in Derrida's program, to name this capacity of *signifiance* to move and transform through time and space the operators of thymos and eros.

In the same way that he differed with Heidegger over the latter's commitment to one unique word of Being, Derrida disagreed with Lacan's fixed point of the Name of the Father as a unary trait without sense. Both are important as far as they go, but indicate the operation of a larger choral field. Developing the fullest implications of surplus value as excess, Derrida demonstrated Trace as the gift of meaning without communication in any number of cases related to signature: that a proper name may return to common noun and vice versa (antonomasia), most famously in *Glas*, unpacking "Hegel" and "Genet" as guidewords thematized in the writings of the respective authors. Hearing in (Maurice) Blanchot the French nouns "white water," Derrida meditated on the whole question of neighboring (from Heidegger), of what is near and far. The functionality concerns how meaning emerges and may be articulated in the egent's mental model. He uses the littoral shore as figure of border in general in *Parages* (Vicinity). Media in the mental model of imaginal world enable a topological reconfiguration of relationships, of how things fit together across time and space. Hence "event" (Ereignis) is as open to collage as is place, and this is a primary advance of Chora on topos in the shift of rhetoric from literacy to electracy, with obvious implications for authoring ubiquitous computing in support of a Just city. The relevance for konsult is the principle that Venice as Allegory supports the effects described in the theory directly through media annotation.

> Parages/Waters/Parts: to this single word [mot] let us entrust what situates, very near or far, the double motion of approach and distance, often the same pace/not (pas), singularly divided, older and younger than itself, always other, on the brink of the event, when it arrives and does not arrive, when it happens and does not happen, infinitely distant as the other shore [rive] approaches. For the shore—let us hear the other—appears in disappearing from view. One part only of this book, its lowest note, is called "Journal de bord," as if to keep the register of a sailing, but all the borders, edges, brinks, from one text to the other, are also shores [rivages], inaccessible shores or inhabitable shores. Not that it—landless landscape, opened onto the absence of the fatherland, seascape, space without territory, without reserved path, without locality—lacks these, but if it takes place, and it must, it will first have to open itself to thought of the earth [terre] as to blazing a path. (Derrida, *Parages* 6–7)

Derrida plays frequently on the French homonym joining negation (*ne pas*) with step (*pas*), that he acquired from Blanchot (*pas au-dela*, the step not beyond). The tonal soundings produce puns, even macaronically across languages, which is the linguistics of *Finnegans Wake*, and these puns function for Derrida the way translation (and etymology) functioned for Heidegger, as the movement (vector) of *signifiance* of how Being is given historically (Rapaport 230). This step/not (*pas*) resonates with the motif of "knowledgeable feet," the signature gait linking Gradiva with the dance floor (choros) of Daedalus. We could pose a situation, to remind ourselves of the practical purpose of konsult, and that the theoretical dimension of metaphysics resonates with the other dimensions, including the historical everyday life world. Justice in Derrida's account differs from Law, Duty, and Utility, adding to the concerns of Amartya Sen, Stanley Cavell, and our other relays. There is no rule or calculation capable of measuring Justice. It comes, it is gifted when an egent receives a call. Orientation to the call of care is through EPS. Recent movements show how social media amplifies a call: #Blacklivesmatter, #Metoo, #Neveragain. May we venture: #Problemsbus

How do you know time is out of joint? Something is amiss. One has the feeling of dissatisfaction (Cavell). It is a response-ability. How did conditions bring us to this point? Movement in space interweaves with temporal movement, in a way that requires bachelor machine systems as the ratio of electracy reoccuping the analogy of the line in Plato. Take the case playing out on the border of the United States with Mexico. This political border is emblematic of every border edge limit troped in metaphysical cosmology. It happened in Macedonia, as migrants passing through Greece from the Middle East attempted to follow the path into the European Union. It is littoral, zone of Unconscious, hence unreasonable, thymotic. What is happening? What is the direction of these events? "Event" is appropriated for electracy as metaphysics (Ereignis, Trace) in a way that interweaves temporality-spatiality within the correspondences of the new macrocosm-microcosm relation of egency. The physical processes of the littoral zone articulate the metaphysical realities measuring Justice. Of course, it is newsworthy, a matter still for the first four estates. Conditions have become so bad in Central America, or the Middle East, anarchy, chaos, failed states, drug cartels, ethnic cleansing, all the forces of disorder, violence, and injustice at work, that families, based on rumor, mythology, hearsay, news, began to send their children, unaccompanied, on the trek to the United States border, in the first case, believing (more or less correctly) that they would be admitted and (unofficially) allowed to remain, even as the United States itself becomes incoherent, psychotic, abject. These routes are vectors and flows of life-death, that is, of Being.

Derrida proposed an ethics of hospitality, which he considered to be "impossible" in practical terms: a relation of not belonging, of guest and host, welcoming to whatever or whoever arrives. It is a risk, he acknowledges, daring a politics beyond Ereignis, not based on belonging (Heidegger's My captured by the nationalist state), retrieving Heidegger's own manipulations of proximity, of what is far or near in space or time. Here is the function of the fifth estate as a global institution, without which hospitality remains utopian. What is inside and what outside of any zone? No more friends and enemies, Derrida recommends, no more "fraternity," since these modes of alliance exclude so many. He acknowledges that total hospitality is impossible within the terms of calculation, expectation, prediction, planning, instrumental advantage, law, duty, ethos. Against those demanding walls and expulsion, Derrida proposes another dimension, emerging through the gift that gives Being unasked, unsolicited, surprising. It materializes or emerges and knocks on your door, like sixty thousand children. Justice is an event of Face, Person, Angel. Is that not an honor, the greatest compliment life can pay, to instantiate for the world a fantasy of happiness? It is a disclosure of Being, for better or worse: an opportunity; a test (subject in process).

EINSTELLUNG

Electrate education proposes to invent an operating function across the divided Subject, the split in reality that is the littoral oscillation or hysteresis or rhythm of systole and diastole, contraction and expansion, falling and rising tides that allegorize the labile condition of metaphysical limit (measure). This rhythm of the tides or cycle of diurnal-nocturnal emblematizes the music of life, the opening and closing of Being, the giving and receiving of possibility, the oscillation of Becoming within which beings strive to linger. Our allegory calls attention to rising waters, appropriate in the epoch of climate change and its denial, evoking all gaps, the zone spreading ever wider, disjoining members of every classification or set—class, race, religion, ethnicity, nation. In apparatus terms, the Internet instantiates in technology and institution the contour and rim of limit, diagrammed through rubber sheet geometry and the epigenetic landscapes of catastrophe theory. In the technological register of the apparatus, what makes Jouissance available to metaphysics is the speed of imaging (of the camera, but also the light speed of electricity).

Psychoanalysis theorizes a logic of imaging, the fourth mode of inference known as conduction, anchored in dreams (tropology), which demonstrate a human capability to work both sides of Un/Conscious, the contemporary reoccupation of *daio*, the division producing the Daimon effect of self-relation with Outside. In *Seminar XI* Lacan uses the dream of the burning child to emblematize the structure: a noise in the real (the accident of the candle being overturned) registers in the dream (the scene of the dead child reproaching his father: *don't you see I am burning?* [siehst du nicht das ich brenne?]). Surrealism was inspired by psychoanalysis to seek this point of intersection between everyday rational utilitarian life and the experience of dream and fantasy, to produce surreality (absolute real). Egents learn to negotiate this division threshold, to find the ratio of incommensurability (the disjoint equivalent of the golden section) organizing surreality. The function of this new dimension and capacity in its institutional emergence is, like that of Kant's Aesthetics, to mediate between the established institutionalized apparati (Science and Religion). Egents are not referees or judges, but creators of an alternative, a third order and lifestyle (a cosmology) demanding the right of capability promoting well-being.

How do egents testify to the littoral zone of Unconscious in one's own neighborhood? We could do worse than to adopt an exercise, borrowed from the filmmaker Wim Wenders, who, in addition to being an important international cinema auteur, is also an accomplished photographer. The opening pages of his collection, *Once: Pictures and Stories*, explain his poetics in a way that shows the affinity of photography with Usufruct, Jouissance, and Trace.

> To shoot pictures. Taking pictures is an act in time, in which something is snapped out of its own time and transferred into a different kind of duration. It is commonly assumed that whatever is captured in this act lies IN FRONT OF the camera. But that is not true. Taking pictures is an act in two directions: forwards and backwards. Yes, taking pictures also "backfires." This isn't even too lame a comparison. Just as the hunter lifts his rifle, aims at the deer in front of him, pulls the trigger, and, when the bullet departs from the muzzle, is

thrown backwards by the recoil. The photographer, likewise, is thrown backwards, onto himself, when releasing the shutter. A photograph is always a double image, showing, at first glance, its subject, but at a second glance—more or less visible, "hidden behind it," so to speak, the "reverse angle": the picture of the photographer in action.... What then is the recoil of the photographer? How do you feel its impact? How does it affect the subject, and which trace of it appears on the photograph? In German, there is a most revealing word for this phenomenon, a word known from a variety of contexts: "EINSTELLUNG." It means the attitude in which someone approaches something, psychologically or ethically, i.e., the way of attuning yourself and then "taking it in." But "Einstellung" is also a term from photography and film signifying both the "take" (a particular shot and its framing), as well as how the camera is adjusted in terms of the aperture and exposure by which the cameraman "takes" the picture. It is no coincidence that (at least in German) the same word defines both the attitude and the picture thus produced. Every picture indeed reflects the attitude of whoever took it (7–8).

Here is a poetics for the electrate selfie, gaining access to "attitude" as the dimension of value formation. "Belief" institutionalized in Religion is nearly impervious to Reason, or demonstrates the power of reason as rationalization. But value grounds belief and may be addressed through transformation of attitude (with these general terms serving as shorthand). Learning in any case involves undergoing change, and the target of konsult is change of value itself. The snapshot is extimate, shot/reverse shot at once. "Once" refers to this uncanny temporality of the photograph, an image captured at a moment, becoming "scarab" or "imsegno," remotivated as My. It is the medium relevant to the fragmented temporality dis/appearing in the flux of events to which Benjamin and Arendt called attention as the matter of the public sphere in an age of mechanical reproducibility. Konsult imaging, in the service of Existential Positioning (EPS), accommodates the complex dynamics of the gaze (of all the circulating @s), by extending recording to include all the -stellungs inventoried in the rich vocabulary of German: not only *Vorstellung* and *Darstellung*, (representation and presentation), but also *Entstellung*—distortion of the sort produced by dream work necessary for latent content to manifest itself. Against the tradition of religious revelation, epiphany or the poetics of correspondences in modernism beginning with Baudelaire in Paris must assume that what is intimated is a lure, deception, trap. *Einstellung* supports authenticity, for when the outside scene touches My unary trait, recording the cosmos of my Being, I get it, I feel it (Roland Barthes called this *punctum*, which was his understanding of how the @ appeared in an image). Digital imaging alters the literal index of photography (the original index of a pro-filmic reality), but not the index of Jouissance. Here is the assignment, an exercise introducing electrate learning: document your neighborhood Chora.

Figure 6. "Rich Family." Stephen Foster Neighborhood, Gainesville, FL. Photo by Barbara Jo Revelle.

Interlude

Murphy's Well-Being (4)

KONSULT DESIGN

Knowledge. Konsult intimates (it neither reveals nor conceals, as Heraclitus said of the Delphic oracle) to the community what is known, what may be learned, in a way that is useful, circumspectly, leading perhaps to understanding and action. The theoretical and historical insight (disciplinary knowledge) is that human desire for well-being (the Good), is displaced into a history of "goods and services," culminating in our time in the commodity form and sign. Capitalism as economy and the corporation as institution were created (invented) to meet the desire for the Good with goods, with unforeseen consequences (gift). How is potential desire realized in actual appetite? It is the same story with every desire: shamans fly of themselves, but we need an airplane, and it is not the same. Apparatus is a Desiring Machine (it begins in Fantasy). *Murphy* evokes this historical event within which our disaster is commonplace. Undergoing prepares the community for action. Expect the Gift Cause.

Interface Metaphor. Installation design calls for a metaphor to guide the interaction or participation of users with the Well. This metaphor is suggestive only, a figure, whose familiarity lends depth of meaning while allowing intuitive participation with the medium. A provocative metaphor supported by knowledge, including electrate conductive inference, is the *Murphy game*. This well-known con game is defined as "any of several confidence tricks in which something worthless is substituted for something of value, often in a sealed envelope." A related definition specifies a certain scenario: Any of various confidence games often having the services of a prostitute as a lure and brought off by switching an envelope containing the victim's cash with one containing scrap paper. In our context this bait and switch trick is a supplement more than a substitute, of something not worthless but dangerous or destructive. "Game" is associated with the theoretical meaning of "gift" (in German, both present and poison): *pharmakon* in Derrida's terms. The lure (prostitute) is the commodity sign, the promotional representation of the use value of the product (everything is for sale).

Assessment. Circumstances conspired to add relevance to MWB, in that Donald Trump is recognized as an embodiment of the classic con man figure, as familiar in American folklore as heroes such as Davy Crockett, lending surplus value to our fables. The value of the *con game* figure is that it calls attention to the active participation of the "victim" in the trick. The confidence agent commits fraud by appealing to the "vicious" (as opposed to virtuous) nature of the mark. It is important to include the historical origins of the pine tar commodity, invented to preserve wood, which is ancillary to the larger history of the spice trade, the primary vector. The fortune of this material, wood, is its association with Hulé, in Ancient Greek, not just "wood" but "forest" (region). The metaphysical dynamic of matter and form is allegorically operative in our condition (dunamis as potential; energeia as actual). Submitted to techne, Wood becomes gift/poison (becoming commodity), generalized through its conceptual appropriation as "matter" (Hulé) into all artefacts. Cabot-Koppers is in the lineage of the first modern corporation (the East India Company), itself produced within the history of the spice trade. The corporations are prostheses of the demand of human bodies for goods, and these goods (through advertising exchange value) promise to accomplish the Good (well-being). Our bodies are the mark, wanting benefit without cost. The marks are not innocent, even if victimized by a murphy game. Technics works for the operant subject (human embodiment).

Wisdom. The fundamental wisdom of konsult, relevant to every one of the Superfund Regions, is that we are complicit as marks in a confidence trick. It is a confidence game in that there is no honest enowning of responsibility. It isn't only corporations that often shirk responsibility, but also citizens, who refuse payment for the sins of the Fathers. The proposal, then, is to design *Murphy* as a fable, with an open moral, whose wisdom implies the lesson of being victimized by one's own desire for good(s). The point is not to blame victims, but to shift the scenario from victim/villain to community well-being in which corporations are macro-persons. The interactive design of the installation tests the claim that the event of living happens through telling. The only moral we receive is one we compose ourselves.

IXOTROPICS

Konsult brings into experience through simulacrum the event disaster. *Murphy* expresses *differend*. "Differend" (Lyotard) locates a suffering that lacks an idiom. The grammatological analogy is with the invention of tragedy as a transitional form during the emergence of literacy in Classical Greece. As part of the invention of new identity formations (individual and collective), tragedy dramatized the relationship between individual and collective experience, focusing on the event of *Até* (individual *folly* that results in collective *catastrophe*). Tragedy contributed to the creation of "Self" as individual conduct, and "State" as political organization, in making intelligible the nature of individual responsibility for collective action. The legend of Thespis, stepping out from the tribal Chorus to speak as an individual, expressed the new experience of selfhood. Generated from this analogy, *Murphy* experiments with consulting that articulates through contemporary disaster an electrate version of *Até*, including an outline of an identity formation and experience native to electracy (the digital apparatus). Psychoanalysis continues to use Greek tragedy and related mythology, especially Oedipus, as a relay for understanding the institution of Family as the most accessible dimension with which to model contemporary experience as system. Deleuze and Guattari wrote *Anti-Oedipus* to expand the network transversally, but their "schizoanalysis" retained the configuration of "hero." Konsult through fable opens the "schizo" protagonist position to further revision. Konsult is not schizoanalytic, but *ixotropic* (not separant but participant, not shattered but *glued*).

Le Quattro Volte. This award-winning film by Michelangelo Frammartino is relevant to the Koppers disaster because one of the "four times" referenced in the title involves the production of charcoal. The four times allude to the four seasons, but also to four modes of Being mentioned by Pythagoras, an ancient native of the region that is the setting for this film. The film (a film poem) documents a passage (vector) from life to smoke. One commentator suggests the passage visualizes a movement of "soul" through the world, which makes it a relay for learning how to annotate vectoral rhythm. The carriers of this force begin with an old goat herder, passing from his death to the birth of a goat in his flock. This kid becomes lost and rests finally at night at the foot of a giant aged pine tree. The slow fade to black, and the ensuing cut to the next season (winter), indicate that the kid died. The old pine is cut down in spring as part of a ritual, trimmed and shaped during festival, and then, in the final volte, "cooked" into charcoal.

This cooking of pine to produce charcoal is the process that also produces pine tar as a by-product (and creosote). It is important that the archive take into account different possible framings, to include a version in which cooking the tree is sacred, associated even with the origins of Philosophy and Western thought, related to the region of Calabria. At this point the charcoal-burners re-enter the scene to cut up the tree (Hulé) and transport it to their corner of the mountains. They conduct their task using ancient skills, their work resembling the pyre for a god or a hero, and we observe it with reverence. Later we see the charcoal brought back to be used by the townspeople who cut down the tree. What we do not see is the byproduct, creosote.

The protagonists of this film are place and mood, so that the viewer is prompted to infer Frammartino's intent. The title, *Le Quattro Volte*, comes from Pythagoras, who lived in Calabria in the 6th century BC and spoke of each person having four lives within—the mineral, the vegetable, the animal and the human—"thus we must know ourselves four times." In bringing the goats, the tree and the charcoal-burning process to the foreground and relegating the humans to a less dominant position, Frammartino intended to create "a pleasant surprise: the animal, vegetable and mineral realms are granted as much dignity as the human one." (Philip French, "*Le Quatro Volte*"). The four turns or times, confirming the four color map principle, correlate with the rhythm of the wide image, the popcycle mystory.

Aristotle proposed four causes operating in physical reality—four dimensions of explanation. Applied to Koppers production of Pine Tar, the causes are: 1) *Material*: that out of which a thing comes to be, as a constituent in the product. The raw material is wood (pine trees). 2)

Formal: the formula of what it is to be the thing in question. How Pine Tar is produced, the chemistry of distillation, the cooking of pine wood that produces the tar. 3) *Efficient*: the origin of the movement or rest. The makers, Cabot-Koppers corporations, are responsible and get credit and profit for the production. 4) *Final*: the end or aim, the purpose of the thing in question. Pine Tar was produced in order to (*that for the sake of which*) treat wood, to preserve it from deterioration in the environment. The Final Cause persists in metaphysics, as the object @, even as teleology is rejected in principle, replaced with autopoiesis in electracy.

These four causes must be supplemented with a fifth force, active in events of purposeful transformation of nature: 5) *Gift*: the by-product, unintended consequences of the process. It is "gift" in the macaronic sense appropriated from the German word: gift/poison. Aristotle anticipated Gift cause with his identification of accident or chance (*tuche* and *automaton*, fate and case). Pine distillation that produces Pine Tar also produces charcoal. Charcoal is a welcome present. The other by-product is creosote, an unwelcome poison. The production of pine tar at the Cabot-Koppers site, beginning as early as 1911, and continuing until 2010, produced environmental disaster. Instruction: count five causes—Material, Formal, Efficient, Final, Gift. Let the emblem of technical intervention in an existing order of reality (nature or culture) be the Happy Meal (every box includes a gift: *look for it*). The final cause of human activity, Aristotle proposed, was happiness, well-being, whose nature he could only describe using transcendental categories: the Good. The Good has no properties in itself, and requires a Polis (political community) to be accomplished. We must ask the fatal question: what is the Gift Cause of Happiness?

Axes of Fable

Literary texts may be analyzed as layered systems, combining two layers of semantics. Natural language is the first order, modeling the lifeworld (real life). Greimas used lexicography to describe literary functioning, beginning with dictionary definitions. The definition of an emotion ("anger" for example) amounts to a story schema, in that the synonyms and antonyms inventory a field of possible behavior, registering the expectations of a particular culture. Consider this entry in a dictionary of synonyms by James Fernald.

> Anger is violent and vindictive emotion, which is sharp and sudden. Resentment (a feeling back or feeling over again) is persistent, the bitter brooding over injuries. Exasperation, a roughening, is a hot, superficial intensity of anger, demanding instant expression. Rage drives one beyond the bounds of prudence or discretion; fury is stronger yet, and sweeps one away into uncontrollable violence. Anger is personal and usually selfish, aroused by real or supposed wrong to oneself, and directed specifically and intensely against the person who is viewed as blameworthy. Indignation is impersonal and unselfish displeasure at unworthy acts, i.e., at wrong as wrong. Pure indignation is not followed by regret and needs no repentance; it is also more self-controlled than anger. (49)

We are engaging with thymos, the passions, in a visceral ontology. These lexical fields are taken up in narratives (secondary modeling systems of literary texts) to set the agenda for actors. The creators of the film *Inside Out* (2015) seem to have taken this lexical schema literally and used it to generate the emotions of a child as actant (masks)—Joy, Fear, Anger, Disgust, Sadness are the five turns included in the mental model. Of course this device is a commonplace of allegory. Our interest is in annotating the vectors of desire, assumed to saturate the entire passional network. Greimas condensed functional structures of stories into six actantial positions (actor-action functions) distributed along three axes: communication (sender-object-receiver = cognition); narrative (helper-subject-opponent = performance); thymic (subject-object = desire, linking the other two axes). Here are the axes of theopraxesis as narrative, informing the actant structure Bratton proposed as relay for User of Stack. Entertainment models modalities of thymos (and eros). Seth Bullock, the sheriff in the HBO series, *Deadwood*, for example, is typed as "angry," and his behaviors through a series of different situations manifest the range of the semantic field "Anger." The Marvel character Jessica Jones, similarly, animates "Female Rage" across a range of situations. The thymic or passional register of feeling individualizes the positional stereotype into a particular character (actor) in the discourse (surface text). With respect to our interactive fable, the point is that a subject-object relationship is modalized within this narrative system, and could be identified through these relationships. In fact it may be possible to generate at least some of the pathemes through permutations and combinations of the modalities of story logic (subject status articulated into wanting-to, being-able-to, doing, knowing). Thus "obstinacy," for example, is a combination of wanting-to and not-being-able-to.

How many variations on one fable are possible (for example, the tar baby story)? *Murphy* may function as a kind of story version of Photosynth, a program that synthesized composite scenes to build 3-D models of tourist sites (originally) based on multiple individual images. One lesson of the prototype was that there is considerable redundancy in tourist photographs, for example, since people tend to frame pictures in similar ways from the same position. Egency may be formed out of redundancy. Here is a version, for example, of a tale from Tibet found in many folk traditions, concerning a well, whose wisdom resonates with *Murphy*.

> In long-past times there lived a band of monkeys in a forest. As they rambled about they saw the reflection of the moon in a well, and the leader of the band said, "O friends, the moon has fallen into the well. The world is now without a moon. Ought not we to draw it out?"
>
> The monkeys said, "Good; we will draw it out."
>
> So they began to hold counsel as to how they were to draw it out. Some of them said, "Do not you know? The monkeys must form a chain, and so draw the moon out."
>
> So they formed a chain, the first monkey hanging on to the branch of a tree, and the second to the first monkey's tail, and a third one in its turn to the tail of the second one. When in this way they were all hanging on to one another, the branch began to bend a good deal. The water became troubled, the reflection of the moon disappeared, the branch broke, and all the monkeys fell into the well and were disagreeably damaged.
>
> A deity uttered this verse, "When the foolish have a foolish leader, they all go to ruin, like the monkeys which wanted to draw the moon up from the well."(http://www.pitt.edu/~dash/type1335a.html)

5 Choragraphy

CAPABILITY

The care of global well-being in the digital apparatus depends upon a metaphysical annotation of appetite as force in reality. We need to design and test this annotation, exploiting affordances of digital media. Konsult addresses this challenge within the framing of Amartya Sen's vision of Justice as capability. Sen's vocabulary evokes the tradition not only of Justice, but of the primary Greek virtue of *phronesis* (Prudence) initiated in Aristotle's ethics, a tradition of metaphysics to be reoccupied for electracy (what are judgment and decision today?) (Ulmer, *Avatar Emergency*). Aristotle's *Ethics* and *Metaphysics* are a relay for invention, expanding the context of Plato's *Republic* in previous chapters, to identify opportunities for invention. Considering the purpose of this discussion to orient the design of konsult, it might be worth unpacking more fully the philosophical register of our heuretic CATTt. Our invention project continues building on the remotivation of allegory and dialogue, as devices of pedagogy. Metaphysics is poetry (art), in the way that it abstracts the ontological from the ontic, as John Protevi put it. In our Allegory of the Wave, the ontic factical scene of Venice and the wanderings through its laybyrinthine streets and canals of the poet Joseph Brodsky as conceptual persona, figure the learning conduct of theopraxesis. What are the operating principles of the correspondences governing the vectoral movements of *signifiance* in this scene (addressed to you as instructions)?

1. The egent encounters a situation, a disaster (some condition of aporia)—for example, the scene of the Superfund site in Gainesville, Florida (this is our prototype). The disciplinary baggage associated with "metaphysics" should not distract from using that framing to focus on what is at stake in this encounter: what is real? (ontology); how do we know (epistemology); what action should we take (ethics, politics); How do we annotate (aesthetics). Sen's emphasis on choice, preference, values, goals, capacity, places his vision of Justice within metaphysics. Aristotle's *phronimos* exercises *phronetic* perception, meaning that s/he must recognize (spontaneously) the nature of the situation, draw upon past experience and disposition, to decide what action will bring about the best outcome for community. In American mythology the *phronimos* too often is imagined to be "the right man with a gun," the Frontier ethos mythologized in Westerns and appropriated as ideology by the National Rifle Association in America (Ulmer, *Miami Virtue*). Alternatively, "everyone a *phronimos*" is the goal of konsult.

The initial encounter is in part aesthetic (even if judgment ultimately draws upon all faculties in concert). Political and ethical decisions concern contingent circumstances, not necessities, since human choice (*prohairesis*) is involved, such that things may be otherwise than we find them. Capacity is synonymous with virtue, power, terms that bring us to one of the points of invention in the tradition. The sensorium is our embodied interface with the environment. Each sense is a capacity, a potential for experience according to *the appetite of the organ*—the eye to see, the ear to hear, the brain to think, sex to mate. There must be both hearkening and sounding, the commentators note. The organ possesses the potential (*dunamis*) for experience, but it must be exercised or actualized (energeia), in an interaction between inner and outer worlds. The importance of choice is noted here, relative to the presence or absence of capacity—its actualization or its privation (*steresis*). (Protevi 56). Here is the rationale for theopraxesis: one has a capability to learn; it is necessary to act upon this capability in order for learning to occur; this acting happens through making. One understands what is necessary (*theoria*), and wills an action (*praxis*), but these two virtues do not suffice: there remains one further power or modality—the feeling of capability, associated with imagination. Here is the hinge or threshold of electrate education.

2. The fundamental action of ontology is the encounter in which the egent recognizes an entity in the world. *There is a tree* (to use the clas-

sical example). The intuitive power of intellect (*nous*) recognizes this being, and performs the gesture of indication, pointing, saying "this such" (*tode ti*). All of metaphysics, we are told, is condensed in this event of encounter and statement: "there is this tree" ("this is a tree"). How to retrieve this event for Second Nature? Poets begin in metaphysics also, but are less concerned with substance, to linger over the accidents, the qualities of the tree, its individuality as such. The singularity of an entity remains outside this event, other, unknowable, but appropriated into knowledge, however distorted within conceptual categories, as both individual (one) and particular (many). *There is this catastrophe.*

What is named (substance) is life, energy, with substance constituting a compound intellectually apprehended as matter (potential, dunamis) and form (actual, energeia). Aristotle's prototype for *ousia* (substance) was the living organism, with substance being not a present thing (as proposed in the Categories), but a process of passage or temporal movement. "Entelechy" is Aristotle's neologism to name this being-at-work-remaining-the-same, his solution to Plato's aporia regarding how the eternal universal real (form) interacted with perishable changing matter. Our equivalent for Second Nature is the artefactual revelation of disaster.

Plato introduced Chora (space of generation) that Aristotle made immanent as force of generation within the individual entity. Beings become what they already are (in the manner of a seed becoming a tree). The insight from the example of human generation (also one of Plato's metaphors for Chora) was that matter (woman, womb, mother) is an active partner with man (semen). This figure is an opportunity for invention. We have proposed to annotate life beyond biology as the operation of desire in terms of vectoral rhythm. The other beginning is this trace of generation, genesis, appearing as emergence rather than telos, in every dimension of reality. John Protevi calls attention to "generation and destruction" as one of the fundamental kinds of movement used in the tradition of metaphysics to guide the account of reality. Here is the movement tracked as vector of desire featured in electracy. The General Accident (Virilio) manifests the actor network of desiring machine (apparatus).

Protevi argues that Derrida distinguishes his deconstruction from Heidegger's project to determine the sense of Being by returning to the aspect of Plato's Allegory of the Cave that Heidegger neglected. Heidegger reoccupied the movement from cave to sunlight exclusively with reference to the metaphorical transfer (vector) between "light" and "knowledge." Indeed, this etymological and paronomasic movement of signification structures all of literate theory and the vocabulary of "seeing" as "knowing." Derrida following a principle of deconstruction takes up the neglected affordance of the metaphor to develop the ontology of Trace through the ontic qualities of the sun as heat and warmth associated with the function of light in the life cycles of growth and decay. The quality of what is meant by Existential Positioning System (EPS) enabled by the vectoral or directional sense of Trace is explicated in Protevi's working through this Derridean turn of the allegory.

> Now of course the analogy between the constitution of geometrical objects, the Husserlian context for the development of Derrida's notion of différance, and the generation of human species-being doesn't match completely, but it does enable us to think. Geometrical objects are free idealities; human species is a bound ideality. But we certainly can see a generated structure: the species does not live in some Platonistic caricature—as Aristotle says, no universal is a substance—and a structured genesis: most of us do function pretty much the same, the condition of possibility of scientific medicine. Now this time/space of generation must be understood on the basis of an economy of exteriority, for looking at the mother and child graphically displays for us the becoming space of time, a phrase applies that holds at least two levels. First of all, at that level of the soul's counting off of the two "nows," time is spaced as the differance of the soul's counting, the auto-affection that generates another now with an identical structure, separated by a "between." And, on the second level, this spacing is displayed, it stands before us in the flesh, we might say, graphically displayed in the element that would correspond to the writing down of geometrical objects. Time's spacing is displayed in the spatially dispersed bodies of the mother and child: the (m)other whose alterity is constitutive of the child's self, and "as such," is a past that can never be made present to the child, an "as such" that can never appear. (190–91).

Deconstruction works by developing the neglected potential of tropes, of the (dead) metaphors sedimented in concepts. Literacy imagined knowledge as light and sight, as figured in the vision of the Sun outside the Cave. Derrida takes up the other associations available through the warmth and heat of the Sun. He used the German term *Geschlecht* to gather the terms naming how genesis or generation functions in time. Opening his first essay devoted to this theme, Derrida notes that Heidegger said little if anything about sex. "Perhaps he has never said anything, by that name or the names under which we recognize it, of the 'sexual-relation,' 'sexual-difference,' or indeed of 'man-and-woman'" ("Geschlecht" 65). He adds in a note, referring to his title, "That word, I leave it here in its language for reasons that should become binding in the course of this very reading. And it is indeed a matter of 'Geschlecht' (sex, race, family, generation, lineage, species, genre/genus)." The primary model of emergence (life force) named by Trace is that of Geschlecht in all its senses (*Avatar Emergency* explored Trace as Geschlecht in my own case).

3. The epistemological dimension of Aristotle's account concerns the natural capacity of humans for reason, with reasoning being itself a kind of movement in conceptual space-time. Our invention process indicates that there are movements of intelligence similarly native to electracy. Aristotle observed a correspondence aligning the organization of nature as substance and accidents (things with properties), language with its grammatical structure of subject and predicate, nouns and adjectives, paronymy, declarative propositions, and mind or thought with its rational powers of logic. Form is a nonsensuous reality, whose operations Aristotle codified in his logical square, tracking the interactions of presence and deprivation through the relations of contraries, contradictions, and complements (the series of oppositions). It is important to note that the purpose of the logical square is to account for the possibilities of change supported within conceptual space (literacy). Form realized in matter produces substance. This nature is accessed and manipulated in writing (Philosophy) through a deep unity, the idea (eidos, shape). The system of correspondences is also an opportunity for invention. Electracy reoccupies this template of signification in terms of digital media, to identify and put into operators the equivalent of logos—bachelor machine dada conduction, managing change in imaginal space-time.

The world is intelligible, shows itself or shines forth, in this Classical model, such that humans feel themselves addressed (disaster becoming Person). This intelligibility is the clue to happiness, in that what is most proper to humans (for Aristotle) is this power of reason. A crucial point in understanding well-being against disaster is that what motivates actualization of virtues is an object-cause-of-desire, that Aristotle identifies as an unmoved mover, a universal final cause that was addressed through theology (God as prime mover). The experience of contemplating by means of reason the work (ergon) of nature (reality) Aristotle called "eudaimonia," translated as "happiness," which is confusing, since what he means is closer to what the psychologist of creativity, Mihaly Csikszentmihalyi, called "flow"—the pleasure associated with working in a state of complete absorption. Life works (ergon). Aristotle thus declares that the good life, the best activity, is a life of study, especially study for its own sake (contemplation). The electrate template proposes as supplement to this literate tradition the principle that the world is felt, undergone as passion, organized as sense (direction) without rational utility (Man is a useless passion, Sartre said). The crucial point is that the function of konsult as metaphysics is to access, annotate, and ultimately manipulate the movements of reality, rendered available in electracy, including Second Nature (Phusis) of artefacts opening a virtual demansion. The argument is that this movement is what Theory named Enjoyment, in the historical passage of generation (genesis) through time. The challenge is to bring into education this object-cause-of-desire, which Lacan identified as the object @, a bit of litter.

The prime mover in electrate metaphysics, then, is what Derrida addressed in the term Geschlecht. Hans Blumenberg, in his critique of secularization, makes the point that Christian Theology appropriated for its own vision of perfect happiness the eudaimonia from Greek philosophy, modifying it as contemplation of God. Part of Blumenberg's point is that new paradigms do not so much replace a previous paradigm as *reoccupy* the old questions, in order to supply new answers. Modernity does not eliminate medieval theology by secularization, but reoccupies its questions. In what follows we will *retrieve* (McLuhan's version of reoccupy) the metaphysical question of the relation between potentiality and actuality, and the new priority assigned to potentiality through capability, as an emergent manifestation in electracy.

POTENTIALITY

The problematic of Trace concerns annotation of desire in time, to bring it into education relative to well-being against disaster. Sen's approach to Justice and well-being through capabilities and capacities positions his policy initiative in a way relevant to Trace. It is not only a matter of recognizing the metaphysical nature of potentiality, but of participating in the invention of metaphysics that deconstructs the literate commitment to actuality over potentiality. Giorgio Agamben explicitly embraces the program of capability, in terms that echo Derrida and resonate with the project of apparatus invention.

> Contingency is contained in a barrier that always necessarily inscribes its expression in the form of a past: something could have been otherwise than it is. This temporal articulation in fact conditions Western science's entire representation of possibility (and this is as true of linguistics as of all other disciplines). That said, is it possible to grasp contingency otherwise than as "something that could have been"? Is it possible, in other words, to call into question the principle of conditioned necessity, to attest to the very existence of potentiality, the actuality of contingency? Is it possible, in short, to attempt to say what seems impossible to say, that is: that something is otherwise than it is? This appears to be precisely the task of coming philosophy: to redefine the entire domain of categories and modality so as to consider no longer the presupposition of Being and potentiality, but their exposition. (*Potentialities* 75–76)

In this context we may specify further the scenario of electrate education. In *Heuretics* (1994) I proposed that "chora" is to electracy (digital apparatus) what "topic" is to literacy (alphabetic apparatus): a rhetorical system of storage and retrieval of materials, organized to assist the transformation of information into knowledge. Electracy adds: the transformation of knowledge into experience. The topical method of invention that organized education in the West throughout the manuscript era and beyond developed Aristotle's metaphysics into a pedagogy (his isotopy correlating thought and language with the operations of nature). The genre of electrate pedagogy is konsult, whose counterpart for literacy is dialogue. To promote chorography as the practice organizing konsult, then, shows the holistic approach the EmerAgency (as relay for Internet learning) takes to consulting as collective pedagogy. The goal is not just to express some opinion from the literate disciplines about policy debates, but to design and test an electrate metaphysics (account of reality), structuring the future of the public sphere as a fifth estate in a digital apparatus (just as Aristotle's metaphysics was the frame within which science became possible, and ultimately journalism as well). This framing ambition may not be accomplished all at once, and need not be, but is the guiding idea directing many steps (experiments) along the way. Conventional consultants enter temporality in the mode of futuristic scenarios, trusting narrative structure as adequate to the movements of change operating in reality. Konsult submits conventional scenarios to the innovations that transformed narrative and discourse in the modernist avant-garde, as vehicles (metaphors) of vectoral sense.

Our point of entry into the function of Chora as rhetoric is with the invention of Philosophy in the Academy and Lyceum, the first schools in the Western tradition, founded by Plato and his pupil, Aristotle. Giorgio Agamben retraces the genesis of Philosophy, including Heidegger's reading of the Greeks (his other beginning), and his influence in turn on French theory (Derrida). The method of invention is heuretics, with the first point to register being that literacy in every feature of its history is an invention, an intentional creation, design, and implementation including identity behavior, institution formation, and technology and its practices. The particular moment within this holistic matrix that Agamben foregrounds (after Heidegger) is the conceptual invention of "truth," noted in the Greek term *aletheia*. Heidegger used his etymological procedure to translate the abstract principle of truth into an experience and event of un/concealment (disclosive withdrawal). The other beginning shifts away from "proof" to "revelation."

The importance of "event" for chorography is that it includes time as the sense of Being. The relevant insight is that truth as event (as experience and phenomenon) happens only within the prosthesis of written language (the apparatus frame). Within that frame a double movement occurs, indicated in the phrase *It gives* (a gift). The gift given is the *thing*. There are two dimensions of this event: That the gift appeared; what the gift is. The What-is that appears, emerges through an opening of withdrawal, a clearing and lighting up, the shining of This (That)—beauty. The opening is Chora. Aristotle's (fatal) Decision (fatal in that it determined the direction or Way of the West up to our own epoch) was to codify out of the Greek beginning a metaphysics of What (substance). There are potentially two beginnings of Western philosophy, then, each with its own end (completion or goal, telos), only one of which was made actual or realized (the one we are living now). The other invention foregrounds and develops the operating features of this movement of disclosive withdrawal—the shell-game of Trace.

Theory proposes that the "other beginning" (Heidegger) has become practical in the conditions of electracy: to develop an emerging or coming metaphysics (electrate civilization), an ontological rhythm of opening/closing, which is implicit in Aristotle's distinction between dunamis/energeia (potentiality /actuality). The way of potentiality is to notice that what we talk about when we talk about Being is precisely language as such, language itself (its capacity for meaning). The experience of truth is an event made available within, a capacity specific to, written language (the oral apparatus has its own metaphysics of right/wrong). Agamben declares in *Infancy and History* that the question motivating all his books is what it means to say "that there is language" (5). The implications for a konsult on well-being are evident: Justice requires that the human capacity for language (in the extended sense of apparatus) be actualized for each individual. The heuretic principle of cause is to use the invention of literate metaphysics as a template for our own invention. Metaphysics as worldview continues in electracy, just as do narrative, politics, education. The other beginning leads not to "truth" and "science" (which continue in any case) but to experiences and practices native to a digital apparatus. As will be developed in this discussion, the movement of *significance* in Trace is that of system feedback loops, circumspective slippages of sequence and series that treat the conventional circles of hermeneutics the way modern geometries treated the lines of Euclid.

The Coming Philosophy

In his book on Benjamin's conceptual innovation—reframing concepts not as essences but as procedural possibilities, articulated as -ability (*-barkeit* in German)—Sam Weber cites a passage from Derrida's *Echographies* that shows Derrida's affinity with Benjamin's program of a coming philosophy.

> If I had time, I would insist on another trait of "actuality," of what is happening today and of what is happening today to actuality. I would insist not only on the artificial synthesis (synthetic images, synthetic voices, all the prosthetic supplements that can take the place of real actuality) but first of all on a concept of virtuality (virtual image, virtual space and thus virtual

event) that can no longer simply be opposed, in total philosophical serenity, to actual reality, as one formerly distinguished between potentiality and act, between dynamis and energeia, between the potentiality of matter and the defining form of a telos, and hence also of a progress, etc. This virtuality impresses itself even upon the structure of the produced event, it affects the time as well as the space of the image, of discourse, of "information." In short, everything that relates us to the said actuality, to the implacable reality of its supposed presence. A philosopher who "thinks his time" should today, among other things, be attentive to the implications and the consequences of such virtual time. To the novelties of its technical implementation but also to what in radical innovation recalls of possibilities that are far more ancient. (Derrida, "Artefactualités," qtd. in Weber, *Benjamin's -abilities* 51)

Our approach to Justice through capability commits us to a heuretics of potentiality, relative to an electrate metaphysics (substance : actuality :: element : potentiality). The other beginning already shows this attitude, that treats the history of Being as open to further invention. Such is the significance of the "history of the present" found in Foucault, suggesting that the world as we find it is contingent, and could be otherwise; that the future is open to revision. Walter Benjamin developed a practice that offers some tools and devices for operating with reality as potential rather than actual. As Samuel Weber demonstrated, Benjamin formulated his concepts as passages between potential/actual, signaled by his usage, naming his terms with the suffix "-ability." Key terms covered in the first part of Weber's study include criticizability, impartability, translatability, citability, with the second part developing legibility, the principle as it informed all of Benjamin's work through the dialectical image and the Arcades project.

The text central to this reoccupation of the ratio potential/actual is Walter Benjamin's "On the program of the coming philosophy," an essay published early in his career. Benjamin articulates a task for the approaching or future philosophy, a philosophy to come (*Zu-kunft, a-venir*) that Giorgio Agamben takes up in turn, and that motivates important strands of French poststructuralism. What makes this task relevant to electracy is its ambition to reintegrate into a unified mode the kinds of thought, knowledge, and experience specific to each of the three apparati: religion (orality), science (literacy), and entertainment emerging in electracy. Relevant to theopraxesis, the task of the coming metaphysics is to support a cooperation and correlation among the three institutional and epochal modalities. To put it briefly, electracy does for emergence what literacy did for telology (the shift from substance to system) as the vector of life.

Benjamin's point of departure is Kant's three Critiques, acknowledging Kant's prescience in introducing a third faculty, granting equal status to imagination (taste, aesthetic judgment) with pure and practical reason (understanding and will—moral freedom). Knowledge is said to have two sides. The first side concerns certitude of what is lasting, permanent, present. We recognize this first knowledge as the kind featured in Aristotle and the Greek decision to focus reality in terms of actuality—that which is present is necessary. This focus promoted empirical science, reaching completion (its telos) in our present techno-utilitarian epoch. The other side of knowledge (admitted but neglected in the tradition as illusory) is experience of the ephemeral. This latter kind designates the everyday modality that Heidegger foregrounded as relevant to the other beginning for a new metaphysics, concerned with appearing and destruction. It is worth citing Baudelaire (protagonist of Benjamin's Arcades project) to clarify ephemerality as the primary feature differentiating modernity from previous epochs, with Fashion as its institutional vehicle. Baudelaire's new philosopher, the figure attuned to the contemporary, is the dandy/flaneur, wandering or drifting in the industrialized city, and this scene instantiates the poetics of correspondences central to electrate logic.

> He is looking for that indefinable something we may be allowed to call "modernity," for want of a better term to express the idea in question. The aim for him is to extract from fashion the poetry that resides in its historical envelope, to distil the eternal from the transitory. If we cast our eye over our exhibitions of modern pictures, we shall be struck by the tendency of our artists to clothe all manner of subjects in the dress of the past.... This is evidently sheer laziness; for it is much more convenient to state roundly that everything is hopelessly ugly in the dress of a period than to apply oneself to the task of extracting the mysterious beauty that may be hidden there, however small or light it may be. Modernity is the transient, the fleeting, the contingent; it is one half of art, the other being the eternal and the immovable. (Baudelaire,"The Painter of Modern Life," 403)

The insight guiding Benjamin's formulation has its contemporary version in Derrida's generalization of iterability or citability of any mark in any medium. This capability of the re-mark, to support different signification through repetition, constitutes precisely the dimension of language itself, language as such, however mounted. This potentiality of the mark itself to generate meaning has metaphysical power, and is the dimension that our theory foregrounds for konsulting. Benjamin's concepts are designed to move thinking away from literate teleology, substance, actuality, completion, toward difference, becoming, transformation, invention. For this purpose his terms gather and categorize not according to the average of a family resemblance (essence), but seek a limit, an extreme edge or threshold beyond which an identity transforms and alters into difference (the moment of catastrophe, the fold). The historical process included in this thinking resonates with Heidegger's Ereignis (event, appropriation, enownment), bringing into practice the temporality of becoming by which a concept splits, separates and departs from itself over time. This potentiality of *significance* to mutate lends thought a peculiar movement (vector) that Benjamin correlated with a new mode of "idea" adequate to modern media of mechanical reproducibility whose prototype is cinematic montage. The imaged idea does not describe but circumscribes: egents are not "inspectors" but "circumspectors." The dialectical image is a version of the *sensible idea* (Merleau-Ponty).

Benjamin's point of departure is Kant's *Critique of Judgment*, in which Kant promoted "taste" to the status of a faculty, a capacity of aesthetic discernment with power or potentiality equivalent to understanding and reason. We are addressing now the reoccupation and retrieval of the imaginal world. Taste is grounded in an individual orientation on an axis of dis/pleasure, a capacity to be affected on a range of attraction/repulsion, which is communicable through this common sensibility of the human embodied sensorium. Taste, in other words, is the ground of electrate metaphysics, accessing the prime mover. The task of the coming philosophy, first declared by Benjamin after Kant, and taken up by subsequent thinkers guiding our invention, is to create this modality of intelligence that is neither reason nor will, but feeling (vector) of attraction-repulsion. Benjamin proposed to shift Kant's innovation from knowledge to language itself. As Weber explained, Gilles Deleuze follows Benjamin's shift, remaining within metaphysics (it should go without saying) but shifting attention from actuality (energeia) to potentiality (dunamis), specified as "virtuality." We may jump outside this argument for a moment to note that the philosophers are adapting metaphysics to the terms of contemporary mathematics, in which Aristotle's causality, the direction of becoming towards completion in a predetermined end, is replaced by emergent and unforeseeable becoming within a frame of complexity, chaos, catastrophe, autopoiesis, and related mathematical principles.

The task for a coming (electrate) philosophy is to adapt conceptual (literate) language and thought to the oxymoronic conditions of a figure without telos. The value of Benjamin is that he pushes potentialization or virtualization of thought beyond literacy into image media, in his design and testing of the dialectical image as a hybrid of philosophical dialectic, cinematic montage, and modernist poetics (Baudelaire). His archival treatment of Paris is a monument of electracy, in that it returns to the Paris of the nineteenth century, as scene of the invention of "pure art" (pure language) in the bohemian opening of a new dimension within the industrial city, composed through iterability. Benjamin's experiment is made almost entirely of citations, to demonstrate the potentiality of language, and specifically of the dialectical image—a scene of the past whose possibility for meaning becomes recognizable, legible, at a certain moment in the present, as a flash of epiphany. He is troping "Paris." This flash (flash reason) of epiphany may be designed, composed, and this is the task for konsult: to compose and augment dialectial images (sensible ideas) to probe for Justice through disaster. The importance of the dialectical image is that it submits events, moments of time, to the manipulations of montage. Iteration: there is a certain pattern or rhythm to the movement of time, in the manner of retrospection at light speed. The argument is that the movements of time native to the previous apparati (season cycle in orality; linear progress in literacy) give way to the timing of moment in electracy (momentous site), whose annotation we are learning.

Aletheia

Heidegger is a resource for inventing electracy, since his originality in the tradition of metaphysics is to have transposed Aristotle's Ethics into ontology. His insight was that the greatest danger (the completion of literate metaphysics in our techno-scientific civilization) is also the opportunity for rescue. The autarchy of technics (Second Phusis) now transforms the decision of a *phronimos* into an ontological opportunity: not just that a given political or ethical behavior might be otherwise, but that reality itself may become other than we find it. Human choice is ontological. Heidegger retains the terms of the tradition from Aristotle, to convey a shift of emphasis from telos, cause, being as permanent present product (from a preference for *energeia, actualitas,* the what-is of substance), to becoming possible, potentiality, *dunamis.* "Translated literally," Heidegger writes, referring to Parmenides,

> the *esti* thus emphasized does mean 'it is.' But the emphasis discerns in the *esti* what the Greeks thought even then in the *esti* thus emphasized and which we can paraphrase by: 'It is capable.' However, the meaning of this capability remained just as unthought, then and afterward, as the 'It' which is capable of Being. To be capable of Being means: to yield and give Being. In the *esti* there is concealed the It gives" (*Time and Being* 8).

Here is the fundamental issue for konsult inventing *capability* as the measure of Justice. There is much to unpack in this passage, but for now a point of relevance is the consequence of Heidegger's shift of emphasis, from presence to absence, from life to death. What most belongs to humans is our capacity for death, our finitude (ephemerality). EPS has its point of departure in the history of metaphysics, which rendered manifest the movement of Being through the movement of the heavens. Heidegger embraces Aristotle's association of Being with movement, understanding movement as temporal as well as spatial, mental and logical and cosmological as well as physical. As John Protevi noted, Derrida goes beyond Heidegger in shifting emphasis to natality, or to include the birth pole of the life-death pairing, hence archi-trace as Geschelcht (gender, lineage, race, sex). The technology of EPS involves ubiquitous computing: to track all dimensions and vectors of movement. Well-being must be undertaken through the mobility not only of wellness but of Being itself. Thinking opens a path, Heidegger proposes, and konsult constructs the EPS (Existential Positioning System) for this passage as theopraxesis (thinking-acting-making). Mortals experience time as care (*Sorge*), through moods such as Anxiety, and the most relevant trajectory is not only biological (entelechy), but historical (Ereignis, event), in an environment not only natural but artefactual. Any individual choice, and even any policy decision deliberated in a community, is belated, enframed by an epochal decision, a fatal commitment of the civilization, such as the one made by the Classical Greeks that determined the destiny of Western civilization through the epochs of the literate apparatus.

Part of the purpose of konsult is to bring theopraxesis into education. Heidegger found the clue in the Greek word for "truth"—aletheia—whose etymology Heidegger exploited to translate as "unconcealment." Being is experienced as a disclosive withdrawal: the withdrawal of the opening that gives the gift of beings (That things are) is ignored and forgotten in favor of the product (What things are). We are at the end (telos) or completion of one possible relation with Being (beings as useful), and Heidegger suggests that there are other possibilities (potentiality of Being). Heidegger's thought opened a path to electrate metaphysics by offering poetry in particular, and the arts in general, as the mode of signification appropriate to the task of thinking the coming community. Part of the project of konsult is to design and test this alternative operating rhetoric, following this invention thread of potentiality and capacity. The hypothesis is that theopraxesis as heuretics grounds education across all media, disciplines, and everyday life citizenship in electracy. The Justice we seek is coming, not actual.

Aristotle's metaphysics includes a template to reoccupy for the invention of categorial elements, in his strategy of form and matter, which in practice meant applying his logical square (the inferential movement of opposition—contraries, contradictions, complements) to the elements of matter (Earth Air Fire Water). That is a choral template for articulating the Trace of attraction-repulsion in history. Heidegger adopts a similar strategy, replacing the logical square of conceptual thinking with the Fourfold (*das Geviert*) chiasmatic belonging together of Earth Sky Divinities Mortals borrowed from Hölderlin. For our purposes, these programs make explicit the template of relationships also organizing the popcycle of Mystory.

STERESIS

What is at stake in Capability as element of electrate Justice may be observed in this reminder of its place in Aristotle's account of "virtue," referring to the differences among *theoria*, *praxis*, and *poiesis*. "Aristotle calls the first *entelecheia* a fully developed, mature ability so far as it remains ability. In some particular cases the formula: 'I can..., I am able

. . . I perfetly understand how to . . . , but I do not act at this moment,' may serve as an illustration of the meaning of the term. In *De anima* II, 5 Aristotle explains the difference between the first and the second *entelecheia* as follows: A newborn child is able, as a human being, to read and write, because he can be instructed in grammar. That is to say: he possesses the potency to know grammar = he knows grammar in potentiality. . . . Mastery of grammar is the first *entelecheia* with regard to the capacity to learn which the child possesses. The reading and writng activity is the second *entelecheia* with respect to the 'I can' of a person actually knowing grammar" (Chernyakov 103). Aristotle's point concerns the relation between knowledge and action, soul and body. "[The soul] is a coherent system of such interconnected abilities (capacities, faculties, functions), which can immediately manifest themselves in an appropriate action—in the body possessing organs, by means of it or in relation to it" (104). The issue for konsult is this feeling "I can," and the path from the first to the second entelechy.

It is worth emphasizing that Agamben's *Potentialities* is an implicit commentary on choragraphy and grammatology in the tradition from Aristotle to Derrida. The immediate relevance may be inferred from the title: *Potentialities* is a book about human capacity, capability, grounded explicitly in a critical history of Aristotle's Metaphysics, specifically the distinction between *dunamis/energeia* (potentiaity/actuality). Agamben frames this history in his own project, itemizing the tasks of "the coming philosophy" (adapted from Walter Benjamin and Kant), alluding to a "potential" modality of thought. Agamben's contribution is to approach metaphysics from the side of experience—"capacity" as experience, as a feeling of "non/power": *what does it mean to say and mean "I can"*? Such is the modality of electracy.

Agamben focuses on a feature of Aristotle's account of Being as substance (form/matter composite) that is often overlooked, and we are reminded that the review of the invention of literacy is a relay for a heuretics of electracy. The relay in this case is Aristotle's solution to the aporia of how something not actual may yet exist. His solution was derived from his operant logic (movement) of contradiction, organizing qualities by presence/absence. Thus a potential to be or do is also to not be or not do. Indeed, what distinguishes human being is just this capability of incapacity, an im/potence that is a basis of human freedom. This power of choice turns out in modernity not only to be important for ethics, but also ontology: the world as we find it may be otherwise. The context is Heidegger's "destruction" of the history of Being, showing that our actual utilitarian techno-scientific civilization (the age of the world picture), saturated with commodified "goods," is the completion (telos) or realization of the Greek decision that reality is a product. It was a long time in coming, we might say. Agamben uses the capacity for incapacity as the position from which to step back out of the propositional system of literacy, to follow Heidegger in the project to develop another possible metaphysics available in the apparatus, now made practical in electracy. This movement is that of the *pas* (step/not).

The emblem guiding this move is the Melville story, "Bartleby, the Scrivener: A Story of Wall Street." In Deleuze's term, Bartleby is a "conceptual persona," whose story is a "vital anecdote" showing the implications in a problem field of living a certain idea, similar to Socrates in Athens or Brodsky in Venice. The idea in this case is to invoke incapacity as freedom. Confronted with a routine request from his employer, Bartleby articulates his paradigmatic formula: "I would prefer not to." This preference turns out to be metaphysical, relating not just to a task at work, but to *ergon* as such (to actuality realized through production). Bartleby, in other words, is to "capacity" what Socrates is to "dialectic." He circumscribes a mystic position in narrative. Agamben traces Bartleby's formula back to Hellenistic skepticism, a stance of doubt, suspension of judgment with respect to reality, interruption of process, associated with the method of *epoché*, the phenomeological reduction revived by Husserl. He performs the step/not (*pas*). Bartleby thus may be associated with the modernist break with tradition, a procedure for overcoming the condition of alienation through devices of estrangement (defamiliarization) that modernist philosophy shared with vanguard arts, codified in the theory and practices of Russian Formalism and Bertolt Brecht.

TRACE

Derrida introduced Chora as an opportunity for shifting the relation with Being from actuality to potentiality, and Agamben maps the various incarnations of Chora from its beginnings to the present. The task of the coming philosophy is to invent choragraphy as a practice of electracy. Within that general task is the more immediate goal of the EmerAgency to design and test konsult, a genre applying choragraphy to policy dilemmas as an interface for digital education. The challenge of the genre is to introduce egents to the dimension of capacity (the virtues) in their own embodiment (My), augmented within digital metaphysics (this experience is what is revealed through epiphany as practice). In the spirit of building an archive in support of this project, here is a passage from Agamben, describing the dimension of capacity in question, and its relation with Chora.

> In the dark, the eye does not see anything but is, as it were, affected by its own incapacity to see; in the same way, perception here is not the experience of something—a formless being—but rather perception of its own formlessness, the self-affection of potentiality. Between the experience of something and the experience of nothing there lies the experience of one's own passivity. The trace (typos, ikhnos) is from the beginning the name of this self-affection, and what is experienced in this self-affection is the event of matter. The aporias of self-reference thus do not find their solution here; rather, they are dislocated and transformed into euporias. The name can be named and language can be brought to speech, because self-reference is displaced onto the level of potentiality; what is intended is neither the word as object nor the word insofar as it actually denotes a thing but, rather, a pure potential to signify (and not to signify), the writing tablet on which nothing is written. But this is no longer meaning's self-reference, a sign's signification of itself; instead, it is the materialization of a potentiality, the materialization of its own possibility. Matter is not formless quid aliud whose potentiality suffers an impression; rather, it can exist as such because it is the materialization of a potentiality through the passion of its own impotentiality.
>
> In the *Timaeus*, Plato gives us the model of such an experience of matter. Khora, place (or rather nonplace), which is the name he gives to matter, is situated between what cannot be perceived (the Idea, the *anaistheton*) and what can be perceived (the sensible, perceptible as *aisthesis*). Neither perceptible nor imperceptible, matter is perceptible *met'anaisthesias* (a paradoxical formulation that must be translated as "with the absence of perception"). Khora is thus the perception of an imperception, the sensation of an anaisthesis, a pure taking-place (in which truly nothing takes place other than place).

> Derrida's trace, "neither perceptible not imperceptible," the "re-marked place of a mark," pure taking-place, is therefore truly something like the experience of an intelligible matter. The experimentum linguae that is at issue in grammatological terminology . . . marks the decisive event of matter, and in doing so it opens onto an ethics. Whoever experiences this ethics and, in the end, finds his matter can then dwell—without being imprisoned—in the paradoxes of self-reference, being capable of not not-writing. (*Potentialities* 217–18)

This choral experience of one's own potentiality is also fundamental to Dasein in Heidegger's terms, as the source of EPS, meaning as direction, orientation of purpose or project in the world, and in this account we discern the articulation of theopraxesis for Heidegger. "The soteriology of 'temperance' spoken of by Aristotle consists, according to this interpretion, in acquiring this tranparency, sonority of the 'whole life.' The end of the action, its ultimate for-the-sake-of-which, is Dasein itself insofar as it is disclosed for itself in its resoluteness to be itself. And on this primordial disclosure Heidegger hinges all the other kinds of truth, including 'scientific' truth traditionally understood. Actually, this is what the project of fundamental ontology consists in. Fundamental ontology, building on the basis of the Aristotelian ontology of human action, has as its object 'the how' (*das Wie*) of the disclosure of Dasein's being for Dasein itself; the structures of this disclosure are called *existentialia* in *Being and Time* (Chernyakov 114). Mystory is the genre through which this disposition of Dasein may be disclosed, for the egent first of all. Such is the premise of electrate education: a feedback network of reciprocal invention among all the virtues, such that creativity in science (for example) depends upon the egents' ability-to-be, augmented in the feedback loops of digital technology. Konsult designs the scene (mise-en-scene) of this event.

It is useful to remember in this context that "electracy" is a portmanteau of "electricity" and "trace," and that Trace is in the family of electrate guidewords for apparatus invention: Enjoyment, Jouissance, Trace. The justification for the citation is its rehearsal of the concept and its field guiding our project. Our role is to bring this history into heuretics, to outline a practice of chorography as education. Each apparatus reconfigures the hierarchy of the human sensorium. Walter Ong famously documented the shift from orality to literacy that occured in part through the promotion of sight over hearing. The equivalent in electracy is to include the erogenous zones among sense organs (as recommended by Brillat-Savarin in *The Physiology of Taste*), positioned at the top of the hierarchy. The senses are no less than six, Brillat-Savarin observed. Lacan explicitly updated Aristotle's *steresis* to include sexual im/potence as a manifestation of Unconscious, orienting electracy beyond thought and will in the dimension of desire. The phallus (phallus/vulva as the original 1/0 or Yang-Yin, *Taijitu*) emblematizes this metaphysical complex of actuality/potentiality as the sensorium measure of emergence and generation (Geschlecht). Konsult works with genital sensorium the way dialogue did with vision sensorium, or ritual with acoustic. The vocabulary of "theory" created in literacy is sight-based. Our philosophers are inventing an equivalent for libidinal theopraxesis, which consitutes a threshold of resistance separating electracy from literacy.

Coming into focus is the understanding of Chora as interface aligning experience, history, nature, technology, within an apparatus. Konsult testifies to this relationship as an appropriation of Being (Ereignis), specifically as well-being relative to bare life (Agamben). The existential insight into Western metaphysics and its commitment to the ends of "life" as reality, noted that human entelechy ends in death (humans are the animals *capable* of death). EPS orients us to this movement of living, such that egency supports thriving, against disaster, as the edge of Justice. Potentiality is the opposite of entelechy as a relation with Being. The experience most instructive of human capacity as potentiality is love (passion), keeping in mind the psyche means "soul" (marking a genesis from Plato to Freud). The relevant point is that electrate metaphysics emerges out of love/hate (passion) and its expression in the arts, in the way that literate metaphysics emerged out of reason (logic) and its expression in mathematics (measuring). It is worth being reminded that when we say "metaphysics" we mean an orientation to reality put into practice in an apparatus, from the beginnings in philosophy to institutionalized science today. "Chora" names the opening making room for human freedom to come into its own, to manage mind, language, society and nature to produce an institution of Justice. The priority for electrate education, then, is egent capacity for Enjoyment, supplementing literate disciplinary specialization.

Trobar

In electracy pedagogy orients discipline, just as creativity subordinates proof. Agamben describes the qualities and functionality of Chora relevant to a practice of choragraphy as electrate pedagogy.

> The topology that is here expressed tentatively in the language of psychology has always been known to children, fetishists, "savages," and poets. It is in this "third area" that a science of man truly freed of every eighteenth-century prejudice should focus its study. Things are not outside of us, in measurable external space, like neutral objects of use and exchange; rather, they open to us the original place solely from which the experience of measurable external space becomes possible. They are therefore held and comprehended from the outset in the topos outopos (placeless place, no-place place) in which our experience of being-in-the-world is situated. The question "where is the thing?" is inseparable from the question "where is the human?" Like the fetish, like the toy, things are not properly anywhere, because their place is found on this side of objects and beyond the human in a zone that is no longer objective or subjective, neither personal nor impersonal, neither material nor immaterial, but where we find ourselves suddenly facing these apparently so simple unknowns: the human, the thing. (*Stanzas* 59)

Such is a rationale for prioritizing arts and letters disciplines adapted for electracy. Konsult educates within the *littoral demansion* of the location and movements, the topology, of this zone of the third area. Theory in a generative CATTt makes it possible to state in phrases such as "*littoral demansion*" exactly what is meant, naming a practice irreducible to conventional conditions. This context demystifies to some extent the positive value placed on the productions of "children, fetishists, savages, and poets," being to Modernism what Classical Antiquity was to Renaissance artists and philosophers. The expression of *signifiance* (intensity, vitality) found in such works is a relay for electrate intelligence, to supplement the propositional logics of conceptual thinking that are the foundation of literacy. Aristotle excluded these practices (Plato expelled poets from the *Republic*), to preserve the neutral modality of declarative propositions capable of determining true/false. Electracy takes up the remaining modalities, in designing thymotic metaphysics of attraction/

repulsion. As a resource for aesthetic metaphysics Agamben gives special place to the troubadour poets, to clarify this choral dimension as the "pure experience of the existence of language," with an emphasis on "experience." In a practice as much philosophical as literary, the poets (including Dante) "grasped the pure existence of language by means of the figure of a woman who was held to be the supreme love object and through whom the mother tongue was explicitly opposed to grammar" (*Potentialities* 71). This case extends and clarifies the scene of natality figured in the sea foam of Aphrodite rising from the waves: the quality of the experience as potentiality. We recognize that we are in the poetics of correspondences, the Symbol of imaginal world, ontics intertwined with ontology.

> Here man is not always already in the place of language, but he must come into it; he can only do this through appetitus, some amorous desire, from which the word can be born if it is united with knowledge. The experience of the event of language is, thus, above all an amorous experience. The birth of the mind from which the word is born, is thus preceded by desire, which remains in a state of agitation until the object of desire is found. According to this conception, the amorous desire from which the word is born is more originary than inventio as a rememorization of the being-given of the word. With the Provençal poets, the classical topic is already definitively surpassed. What they experience as *trobar* goes definitively beyond inventio. The troubadours do not wish to recall arguments already in use by a topos, but rather they wish to experience the topos of all topoi, that is, the very taking place of language as originary argument, from which only arguments in the sense of classical rhetoric may derive. Thus the topics can no longer be a place of memory in the mnemonic sense. Now it is presented in the traces of the Augustinian appetitus as a place of love. *Amors* is the name the troubadours gave to the experience of the advent of the poetic word and thus, for them, love is the *razo de trobar* par excellence. (Agamben, *Language and Death* 68).

Agamben helps understand the experience of this register of capability, of human freedom grounded in the privative capacity to withhold, to choose not to (be or do). This privation is experienced through the facticity of existence, the site where the withdrawal of disclosure may be apprehended. He suggests that the experience that most fully represents the complexity of radical incapacity (the capacity for death, finitude), the freedom that follows paradoxically from absolute powerlessness, is love (passion), which is the scene of electrate metaphysics. In previous apparati this condition was put in service to some other reality (God; Nature). In electracy passion itself is the real in question. On one hand passion motivates action, the mood of wanting and being able, and on the other the loss of control or mastery. In love (passion) one undergoes an event of pure receptivity that distinguishes capacity from its peer faculties of reason (knowledge) and will (intention), which clarifies and articulates the relations of theopraxesis. The choral principle is to expand from any one foregrounded concept to the family of related terms, hence to consider the passions as a network, a system, of which love is one among others (Lacan's set was love, hate, ignorance): the passional system. From science emerges nuclear energy (for example). Electracy takes up the decision of usage: Enjoy nuclear power!

The lesson for apparatus invention in Agamben's account is that the issue is not *Erlebnis* (immediate lived experience) but *Erfahrung* (living reiterated in the fold of language to be undergone retrospectively). The challenge for choral interface is to introduce between living and telling this order of simulacrum (existing images) correlating visceral libidinal embodied triggers of catalysis with Absolute (archive of civilization), such that konsult supports Jouissance the way dialogue supported reason. At stake is the potentiality of thymotic Justice. We learn from Trace that the feedback is topological, not circular. EPS maps this moebius loop. The lesson is not in corporeal sexuality (act of reproduction) but in the emergent Troubadour invention of a paradigmatic relationship, a scenario of courtly convention, the Dark Lady and the poet desiring what is not attainable, all of which is a metaphysical scenario (allegory). Our Presocractics work in Hollywood and Bollywood. Based on a detailed review of medieval medical theories (sensation becoming phantasm in imagination), Agamben uses this invention to explain how the imagination (the faculty augmented in electracy) functions, because the imaginal is the dimension reoccupied. The insight of the invention is that poetry creates an opening in facticity, a further dimension, mapping precisely the event of contact between inner experience and external environment. This contact triggers epiphany (revelation, flash reason), and this is the modality of learning and configuration that must be syncretized with literate schooling. The structure is that of Chora, mediating between Being and Becoming, with poetry holding open the choral dimension for arts aesthetics, generalized as function of logos. Part of the lesson has to do with happiness, figured in the complexity of the Troubadour *joi d'amour* (that Nietzsche also endorsed as the *Gay Science*), fixing desire on the unattainable. Here is the aporia of theopraxesis: no reappropriation of self, no self-coincidence, but actantial egency (that is, if you want to fly, take a plane). This is how the dream of becoming god is realized in a machine. The argument is that desire is satisfiable by means of imagination, realized through language: Fantasy against Anxiety (the theme of Lacan's seminar on Anxiety). Electracy is the apparatus of imagination, as literacy was of reason. Here is the fundamental orientation for the coming education in a digital apparatus, seemingly not yet acknowledged.

Agamben generalizes the Troubadour historical invention of courtly love to a new model of invention or creativity that is to electrate logic what Aristotle's topics is to literacy. Language as practice has two fundamental capabilities (two modes of exhibition): saying, and showing. Literacy is the hegemony of saying, which is why Plato's copy subordinated Lucretius's simulacrum. Aristotle's metaphysics developed an isotopy coordinating Euclidean space, logical dialectics (opposition) in language, and reasoning (thinking). Electracy shifts to the dimension of showing (indication, gesture, simulacrum, augmented in digital imaging and design)—as supplement, not replacement. Agamben outlines the isotopy articulated for this register: topology (labyrinth) as space, fetish emblematics as logic, and passion (love) as psychology. The register of showing does not replace saying, but develops this faculty to supplement those already institutionalized in the historical apparati. Modernism adopted as the sources or authorities for its innovations in this capacity the productions of children (Piaget), aboriginals (Lévi-Strauss), the insane (Freud), and poets (Benjamin). Agamben clarifies what must be learned from these sources that explore the capacity of language to support modalities of the un/real—the un/attainable, imaginal. Heuretics as the methodology used to compose a poetics of electrate metaphysics, thus, to pass from topos to chora, must extend the logic of invention to include *trobar* as instatiation of heuretes (one who finds), both for its own practice, and as pedagogy. Trobar devices address, activate, and circulate signifiers of desire in the dimension of form, medium, and object, bearing some discontinuous correlation with semantic effects. It is the matter of sense, at once meaning and direction (vectoral part-objects). It is worth noting in this context that Jacques Lacan adopted as motto Picasso's saying, "I do not seek, I find." (Miller 214). Trobar contributes to the passage from literacy to electracy by providing devices of creative invention.

THE LITTLE PHRASE

Agamben represents a philosophical relay locating Chora in the invention of Troubadour poetry, along with an analysis useful for tracking the mechanism from Plato's *Timaeus* to Derrida's Trace. Algirdas Greimas, in *The Semiotics of Passions*, adds formal value, suggesting how narrative scenarios might become electrate, a lesson confirmed in Bratton's suggestion the User position of Stack is not Subject but actant, that is, not an individual person, but a position in a scenario. The functionality of learning as feedback loop relating Erlebnis and Erfahrung at light speed becomes clear in Bratton's speculations about person innervation as Stack User (with relevance for why electracy needs to trope Justice).

> I believe that instead of pleading the Jeffersonian wounds over and over, the more radical and prudent line of sight is toward carving defensible space around the nonhuman *User* in order to explore the literatures by which human beings can become part of this set. This plays with role reversal and drag, as in Jean Genet's *The Balcony*, or the old Google Glass App that let the *User* control the pitch and yaw of a quadrotor drone by tilting his head, even though we all know the drone is really controlling his neck muscles (sic). Recording becomes playback and playback a variation on recording, swapping tempos: the ultimate promiscuity of the roles—apparatus, interface, and subject—all can be recast by one another in the arc of watching someone else watch you, and to watch yourself watching it over again while pretending to be the camera. (Bratton 288)

Bratton's Stack of User Real-Time metalepsis supports the bachelor machine of electrate simulacrum: a meeting of Diana's Bath and Liquid Architecture in Konsult. We learn from Greimas how to shift focus in consulting away from conventional projection of mimetic representation into the figural (simulacra) as a different way of addressing possibilities for transformation or change out of present circumstances. Konsult coordinates the empirical body with egents's transcendental subject through the interface of "conceptual persona" (modeled by Sterbak and Brodsky in Venice). It is the problematic of Trace: the contamination between actual empirical and potential transcendent—the interweaving of these dimensions (Protevi 188), with digital media. The point of poetic correspondences is this position of contact between the sensible and intelligible dimensions of event, with the sensory body articulated through *signifiance* as mediating between the inner individual and the exterior state of affairs in the world in a topological feedback loop managed as interface. The function of egency interface is that individuals receive the effects of collective actions. This relationship is figural (*signifiance* is emergent), augmented in the apparatus as spectacle FX. The relevant point is that electracy, responsible for institutionalizing the digital apparatus, must develop for pathos what literacy developed for logos, or orality for ethos, augmenting the undergoing of attraction/repulsion—the capacity to be affected that is to electracy what true/false propositional logic was for literacy or right/wrong conduct for orality. The source domain for the relevant practice is the arts, and the capacity of aesthetic form to capture and augment intense personal sensory experience that exceeds abstract categories, and that registers, rather, a singular manner of existing that has everything to do with quality of life and well-being. The fifth estate constitutes the site for a politics of visceral *manner*. Here is the contribution the Humanities makes to digital education.

Greimas's semiotics of the passional (thymic) dimension of discourse, grounded in the instance of Marcel Proust, informs our heuretics of choragraphy. The description is heuretic in that its analysis of how Chora is manifested in Proust may be generalized into a template, not only for further analyses, but as a poetics of simulacrum, imsegno, secondary modeling. The epiphanic experience outlined here has not only critical but also ontological importance in demonstrating the genesis of valency and value (opening Justice to design). Specifically, in the context of a konsult on Justice as capability, Greimas's semiotics pinpoints precisely the "how" that Heidegger sought, the mechanism of potentiality and capability in the affordances of discourse in culture. The figural event involves a transformation that Heidegger described as an appropriation of Being—Ereignis as a particular relationship with Being (with life energy). Humans are not born in the open (as Rilke put it) but must become their being (let it come for them): fate is feedback. Different relationships with Being are possible, such as the utilitarian appropriation currently hegemonic, in which everything is equipment for (commodity) production, and every situation is a problem for solution.

How might a different value (attitude and comportment) emerge? How might individuals collectively separate and step back from the present ethos (habitus)? A relay is dramatized in Proust, "Swann's Way," the first volume of *In Search of Lost Time* (or *Remembrance of Things Past*). A work of art, in this case a sonata for piano and violin, by the (fictitious) composer Vinteuil, the first few bars of which attracted Swann's sophisticated attention one evening at the Verdurin's salon. Swann's capacity for this experience was latent, virtual, part of his competence and that of his culture—a primary potentiality that in principle could have been triggered by any work. Actantial existence breaks out into several primary modalities: wanting-to, knowing-how-to, being-able-to (theopraxesis). In fact, semiotics reveals that Western culture assumes that want or desire include capacity (being-able, can), with the caveat that other cultures and civilizations have different assumptions. Apparatus shows that the assumption is not just cultural but metaphysical. The ambition of theopraxesis as electrate comportment is to correlate these modalities.

At the level of experience in the prototype, Swann's encounter with the sonata erases the concerns of his empirical subject, producing by means of the musical form the opening that is Chora, available for inscription of a new value (and this is a primary purpose of electrate education): in Swann's case, the possibility of falling in love with Odette. The literature models a relay for konsult interface. This initial event (epiphany) is just the beginning of the new capability of experience as *Erfahrung* (aesthetically mediated). The formal features of the art supply a system of relationships—aesthetic, as distinct from the dialectical logic of Aristotle's topics—that project a syntactic route, beginning with a valency (care), around which accumulates a semantics creating a positive object of value. We recognize it as the formation of simulacrum (sentient doll). The operating power of this system is formal, aesthetic, emergent within the scene. Such is the import of "figural" (spectacle)—it is customized, singular, one-off (art). The "little phrase" of the sonata heard in the salon setting (outside) gives form to the matter of Swann's inner feeling, the formal structure constituting a prosthesis facilitating passage between inchoate existence (potentiality) and transcendent being (auto-affection). Greimas describes the association relating Swann's experience of Odette and the musical phrase.

> A syntactic framework, based entirely on aspectual arrangements, is outlined behind the figurative and sensory description of the musical phrase: lateness, delays, expectations, surprises, incidences, and decadences. These aspectual figures are explicitly associated with Odette de Crécy, the object of value. At a moment when each time the phrase is heard Odette's image is called up, Proust writes:
>
>> The violin had risen to high notes where it stayed as if waiting, a wait that would continue without its stopping to hold the notes, in the exaltation he experienced seeing the expected object approaching, and with a desperate effort to last till she arrived, to welcome her before dying, to keep the way open, with all its last strength, so that the object could come through, just as we hold open a door that would close if we were not holding it open.
>
> We have already shown that worry created two distinct roles in Swann: the birth of a new Swann, according to seeming, who commits himself to passion, and by contrast makes the former Swann a subject according to being. A whole world of discourse is set up around the new Swann, a world that includes another kind of space, another perception of time, and other system of reference, thanks to the generalization of simulacrum and the spreading of the sensitized arrangement onto all actors, places, or moments. (Greimas and Fontanille, *The Semiotics of Passions* 19)

The challenge for My konsult is to provide an interface that maps the coordinates of both "Swanns," both subjects of the egent, empirical and transcendental, the one physically existent, and the other a simulacrum, for it is just this pairing that produces electrate capability, the basis of global Justice. This construction is theopraxesis, basis for all learning in electracy. For Justice to materialize, this momentous site of valency (of simulacrum) must be created. Such is konsult design.

Flesh

A consensus among commentators designates Proust's novel—specifically the scene of Swann's experience of Vinteuil's sonata (the "little phrase")—as the exemplary contemporary instance of what Agamben calls *trobar* invention. The scene is paradigmatic for Benjamin, Greimas, Guattari. The focus for the moment is Merleau-Ponty, who declared that Proust (in this scene) had created the definitive example of a *sensible idea* (similar to Heidegger's "hermeneutic concept") grounding a new ontology that we appropriate for electracy. Whatever problems deconstruction had with the phenomenological reduction, in the context of grammatology and apparatus invention Merleau-Ponty is a major figure, learning from the entire mix of innovations in the first half of the twentieth century, in order to develop a relay for electrate ontology. Truth appears in a disclosive withdrawal (aletheia): the exhibition is by seeing and saying, showing and telling, indication and statement (to which must be added: listening, reception). Literacy promoted the saying, subordinating showing within the affordances of alphabetic writing. Electracy (Modernism) shifts priorities to showing, indication, gesture, extending ontology beyond language and discourse into the image and diagram (and the technical prosthesis evolving within the digital apparatus). Merleau-Ponty develops the metaphysical capabilities of perception itself, which is sensation or human sensory experience organized in aesthetics, in each of the arts. What grammar of natural language was for Aristotle, graphic design FX in art is for Merleau-Ponty.

How does sensible idea function as ontology? It is catalytic, not analytic, accessing Aristotle's "second entelechy," the movement from impotence to power through visceral memory. Swann attends the Verdurin salon, where he hears Vinteuil's sonata, even just the first few bars, the violin overture, the hook, and he undergoes an event (Ereignis) of intensity, triggering his potentiality. The apparatus analogy helps us appreciate what is at stake for konsult. The literate equivalent is Socrates forming a concept. He famously would stand lost in thought as he worked out the pattern in his head (without benefit of writing), to the point that people gathered around to observe and wager on how long it would take. The mental model of problem solving in literacy is the field of concepts, organized by the synchronic and diachronic axes, textile grid. The logical square manages the vectors of signification shifted around in this matrix, tracking "love" through the dictionary. Beyond concept, the sensible idea (*signifiance*) introduces the vectors of the imaginal world of electracy supplemental to and exceeding this conceptual grid.

It was not the first time Swann heard that melody. Rather, he recognizes it now, in the context of a situation, relating to a woman he met at the salon (Odette). The first point is that the "idea" is "sensible" rather than conceptual (rational). "Idea" is a catachresis to name this other mode of ordination of reflective judgment. It is felt more than thought. As firstness, it must be experienced, heard, undergone, and this emotion of the music is to the electrate apparatus what entailment in written logic is to literacy. It is an encounter of flesh, with Swann's body as pivot or hinge, the chiasmatic, topological crossing of outside within (Lacan's extimacy). "Flesh" in Merleau-Ponty's ontology replaces "substance." It is ontological in that through the carnal body humans receive (and produce) the reality of the *Umwelt*, the milieu, which is of the same flesh (enveloping subject-object), generated with part-objects circulating as letters through the Outside. The association created in Swann's imagination between the melody and the feeling for Odette constitutes an "initiation"—Merleau-Ponty's translation of Husserl's *Stiftung* (foundation, institution, monument). The formation of the sensible idea marks an entry into the transcendent field of Being, opens a dimension of choral space-time, a "landscape" of alterity within creative practice becomes ontological (Merleau-Ponty, *The Visible and the Invisible*).

How does a personal experience of art become "idea"? Merleau-Ponty's use of "idea" in the phrase "sensible idea" is a placeholder for us, to be replaced by usage of "event" (for example) to name the functionality for digital recording that "idea" acccomplished for writing. The idea (Eidos as shape relating ontic appearance with ontological import) is in art in the way melody is in the notes (compare Walter Benjamin: ideas are to thought as constellations to stars). Deleuze refers to this effect of sense as "expression" (and as "event" and "simulacrum") in *The Logic of Sense*. Perception and language are inherently reversible, one into the other chiasmatically, to begin with. Merleau-Ponty merged Saussure's linguistics with Gestalt theory, to propose that perception is not of raw sensation, and not immediate experience (*Erlebnis*), but an articulation of patterns given organizing world (*Imsegno*). Melody is a Gestalt in time, an emergent pattern produced through formal coherence. Perception guided by art is for electracy what reasoning guided by logic is for literacy. Perception works diacritically in the same way that language does, with signification emerging by means of a system of formal (aesthetic) relationships. The figure-ground switches of attention and intention organizing Gestalts (felt ideas) function diacritically, not as reference or content, in other words, but as difference enabling signification. Fragments of material sensation, organized within art forms, are folded back onto the world to become figures capable of signification. In the context of apparatus, the "pure art" invented by the avant-garde functions as annotation and catalyst of these perceptions, from which emerges a possible practice not of science but of pleasure.

In Swann's case, a systematic analogy (allegory) is instituted between the formal, aesthetic features of the sonata, and the feeling for Odette (Klossowski's simulacrum). Such correspondence is metaphysical, constructive of reality. The event is foundational (as *Stiftung*) because it initiates a field of relationships structuring Swann's lifeworld in general, but uniquely, and here is the key to electracy: cosmology is personal, mediated by the cultural archive. A passage is opened through this idea between the visible and the invisible Swann, catalyzing his ability-to-be. Idea returns to its original sense of *Eidos* in Greek, as "shape," in order to develop the other direction of meaning in electracy. These Gestalts are not simple associations, Merleau-Ponty explains, but function more like a fetish in Freudian theory. Fetish is the "thing" of electracy: object-subject mutually saturated. Winnicott's transitional object is another example, mediating the mother-child relation, constituting "potential space" as resource for all subsequent creative intuition for that person (visceral intelligence). Anything has the potential to become the emblem of reality for Swann, and this potentiality is the invisible dimension of the world, rendered as apprehension within aesthetic annotation (reoccupying the burning bush, so to speak). The presence/absence binary of Aristotle's metaphysics is shifted in Merleau-Ponty to present/latent. The contingent event, once triggered, becomes necessity — and this is the "necessity" that Heidegger translated from Anaximander as "usufruct." Lacan took up "flesh" explicitly for psychoanalysis as "gaze" — the experience of being-in-the-world. Today surveillance instantiates gaze, meaning it is the technology of the coming philosophy (for better or worse). This catalysis of triggering (punctum) is what must be captured for the apparatus, harnessed for capability, just as literacy harnessed (augmented) reasoning, keeping in mind the resource accessed in this way is the visceral orientation of the body acquired in infancy (Kristeva's chora).

Konsult generalizes the sensible idea to learning as such. For now, it suffices to note the description of the shared chiasmatic field of Being as a landscape (quantum field) throughout which are disseminated multitudes of monuments (*Stiftungen*). This landscape is a mental model designed and projected within the apparatus, organizing the correspondences of microcosm-macrocosm, now constructed uniquely for each person and shared within the system of egency. Not one cosmos, but a cosmos of one (cosmological multiplicity). For a collective singularity to be possible a device and practice capable of correlating conflicting simultaneous inaugurations is required. The importance of a shift in ontology from actuality to potentiality is apparent, in that in virtual reality the rules of non-contradiction and incompossibility may not apply, similar to the way in manuscript education each student constructed his/her personal memory palace and commonplace book in order to manage the topical archive. It is rather a quantum ontology, organized by probabilities. Deleuze remotivated Leibniz's monad in this same context. Egents design sensible idea creating a capacity to receive disaster as Avatar.

Element

The lessons of Merleau-Ponty's phenomenology of perception take on their full import for apparatus invention when the sensible idea is considered from the side of painting. A short-hand version is to say that Merleau-Ponty intended to do for imaging what Aristotle did for writing: create a metaphysics, that is, a categorial operating practice for the apparatus. Merleau-Ponty's primary case for painting as ontology is Cézanne (and also Paul Klee), but the point of departure for using Cézanne as a relay for philosophy is the individual embodied human situated in the world, with carnal self-experience (auto-affection) as the hinge (pivot) for the measure of Being: in short, *Phusis*. Electracy makes Second Phusis accessibe to apparatus invention. Cézanne and Cubism after him recorded landscape in motion, which we recognize in our context as the work of metaphysics. Céznne learned to shift his expression of libidinal energy from thematic scenes of murder and lust (in his early period) to the brush-work of formal design, to *signifiance* (late period). Especially relevant is the emphasis on the body in motion, motility and proprioception. As Protevi explains, literate metaphysics was invented by a systematic organization of movement as measure (life is self-moving). Electracy reoccupies this care for movement.

The ontology is not of things or objects, not entities in literate terms, in other words, but what Heidegger theorized as Ereignis (Event), experimenting with various spellings to signal the difference (*Seyn*, Be-ing). Be-ing concerns the *manner* in which an individual appropriates (enters relations with) Being. This manner is singular, named with a vocabulary of *Wesen*, *west*, attending to one's *manner* of dwelling, of inhabiting embodiment. Flesh is the inter-experience of one's own manner (style) as a way of being, in relation with others. Neuroscience recently explained the physiology of what Merleau-Ponty (and Heidegger) were proposing with this ontology: mirror neurons in the brain that give humans a capacity for imitation, accounting for a range of behavior from learning to fashion through a gestural mimicry and caricature. Most significant for ubiquitous computing is not only the routes of motility open to chorography, but the fact that this capacity for movement is experienced as power (virtue). Cézanne's "little sensations" exemplify Merleau-Ponty's "element" in practice, discovering how to annotate the vectors of desire.

> The flesh is for itself the *exemplar sensible*. It is so because its manner of being is elemental: . . ."to designate it we should need the old term 'element' . . . in the sense of a general thing, midway between the spatio-temporal individual and the idea, a sort of incarnate principle that brings a style of being wherever there is a fragment of being" (p. 139). This teaching was prepared in the *Phenomenology of Perception* especially in the analysis of the corporeal schema, or postural model. The body is able to move itself because it has an awareness of itself and of its situation in the world; this awareness is the postural schema. But the postural schema is not a particular image; it rather gives the body to itself as an "I can," as a system of powers organized according to the transposable schemes for movement. The continual autoproduction of schemes in the body's mobilizing of itself "gives our life the form of generality and prolongs our personal acts into stable dispositions." Thus "my body is to the greatest extent what every thing is: a dimensional this . . . a sensible that is dimensional of itself" (Lingis, Translator's Preface 260).

Lingis gathers into a constellation a number of key notions: the style of the proprioceptive body, feeling the "I can" of potentiality, composable as sensible ideas through the elements. "Element" is a major innovation, replacing "substance" to theorize how flesh is ontological, and begs for comparison with Asian martial arts traditions. The historical relay for categorial elements comes from the Classical Greeks (Earth Air Fire Water), the original materialist cosmology proposed by the Presocratics, reoccupied for electracy. Plato described Chora as a violent vortex that sorted original chaos into these elements (the informing of matter). Merleau-Ponty updates this description to characterize flesh as the overlap of two vortices, chiasmatic interior-exterior flesh, the body as tourbillon. It is significant for us that in *Seminar XI*, Lacan refers to Merleau-Ponty's flesh as the point of departure for his own development of gaze. Perhaps it is important to remember the purpose of this emphasis on Phusis as disclosure of emergence, which is egency—the overcoming of alienation and reification that disrupted agency and concealed the experience of being-in-the-world. Electracy reoccupies this event in relation to Second Phusis—world-production through technics.

In practice the elements refer to the formal aesthetic features of Gestalts, transforming points, lines, planes, colors, sound, movement and all the other properties mobilized into signification in the arts that make it possible to categorize the world with reflective judgments. Art is ontological because it has this choral capacity to receive and express the forces of the Real (pivots and vectors, the rays of reality), constituting the equivalent of grammar for electracy. Merleau-Ponty quotes Paul Klee's exemplary saying, slogan for image ontology, that art does not reproduce the visible, it makes visible. Heidegger also references Klee's paintings at the beginning of *Time and Being*, giving an account of Ereignis as the turn away from Dasein, to set aside the hero's project in favor of the mystic's *Gelassenheit*. A related authority for elemental ontology is Rimbaud, the letter of the seer (voyant): the world manifests itself through the artists's visions. This experience of dictation or receiving visions, often noted by artists, takes an ontological turn in modernism, the invention of "pure art" in bohemian Paris (whose first generation is Manet, Baudelaire, and Flaubert): the autonomy of language, generalized in the answer to the metaphysical question: what is there? *Il y a* (there is). Art is conducted in a "middle voice" or feedback loop that is at once active-passive (the stance of potentiality rather than productivity). It is perhaps obvious in our context the extent to which flesh anticipates and is appropriated as text by Tel Quel and French theory in general.

Cézanne is the representative figure of this image ontology beyond concept. Merleau-Ponty differentiates his new ontology of perception not only from the Cartesian cogito, but also from Renaissance perspective as the equivalent of the cogito in the visual arts. The whole mimetic system generated around the fixed viewing position, the single immobile eye, the rationalism of Euclidean space and Cartesian cogito, is contrasted with the non-Euclidean, topological principles of modern mathematics, and the abstract expressionism of modernist art. Aristotle's topical logics assumed homogeneous empty Euclidean space as part of their functionality, while electrate simulacrum assumes topological relationships such as envelopment, neighboring and the like. Similarly, literate concept, idea and contradiction, are replaced by graphic dimension, pivot, hinge, articulation and so forth. Cézanne's style emblematizes the idiosyncratic *Wesen* or becoming of perception itself, specific to egent manner. Gestalts of graphic properties function as logos, supplying elementary coherence without benefit of concepts. The hawthorn flower — its pinkness, its roseness — projects a filigree or armature through potential Being, a "ray" or vector of the Real that Marcel Proust used to navigate the in/visible in his novel. Cézanne painted Mont Sainte-Victoire at least sixty times.

The sensible idea of the mountain is the invariant signification of these variations (Carbonne, *La visibilité*). The crucial point is worth remarking, emblematized in the term flesh: the sensible idea through FX annotates the vectors of desire (attraction-repulsion), just as (in literacy) the concept through definition annotates the sequences of reason. The "little sensations" of how warm and cool colors affect perception ground a modernist reform of space-time, with the prototype of such grounding in embodiment being the phi phenomenon responsible for causing a sequence of still images, projected at a certain rate, produce the illusion of movement. Thierry Kuntzel coined the term l'*Emouvoir* to name this special effect: "A word untranslatable in English, but which condenses very happily in French, the idea of movement, that of the film's (as film-strip into film-projection), and that of the spectator's, moved visually, psychologically and unconsciously; in émouvoir, to move and to be moved are uniquely fused to render that startling effect produced by the perception of images which must be represed in order to be seen."

(Augst, "The *Défilement* Into the Look . . ." 250). A proper electrate ontology requires animation.

Figure 7. "Night Car." Stephen Foster Neighborhood, Gainesville, FL. Photo by Barbara Jo Revelle.

Interlude

Murphy's Well-Being (5)

Vortex

Murphy is a konsult experiment. The four turns of the popcycle organize the database: each track of the archive is organized by one of the four primary tropes of rhetoric (the cardinal tropes): Metaphor, Metonymy, Synecdoche, Irony. The four turns, four vectors. These tropes represent four primary kinds of relationships, and when run in (non-linear) sequence, produce the rhythm of the konsult. *Murphy* as interactive installation, through the generation of fables, offers counsel in the manner of circumspective indication (which may in turn be comprised of narratives and arguments). The goal is an affective retrospective advisory introducing a dimension of telling into neighborly living. The event fosters attitude adjustment (happy hour).

The media structure relevant to the design and effect of *Murphy* is the emblem *ideogram*. Interactivity depends upon user competence (enculturation). Cinematography is now the GCI (general cultural interface) of media civilization. The juxtaposed screens of *Murphy* constitute a basic form of filmic (image) discourse: montage (editing). It is worth recalling that Sergei Eisenstein derived his version of montage in part from the model of Japanese (and Chinese) ideogram or pictogram writing. Eisenstein's point of departure was the use of editing to construct narrative action in D. W. Giffith's films (*Birth of a Nation*, for example), which he promoted into a filmic equivalent of conceptual or abstract reasoning. His ambition (in the context of the new Soviet state) was to help an illiterate mass public understand the philosophy of Karl Marx in *Capital*.

The relay for intellectual montage is how ideograms combine graphic icons of concrete or sensory items to evoke a third signification that is not itself directly perceptible. "Heart" + "Knife" = "Sorrow" is one of his examples. Ezra Pound's vortex image similarly is based on ideograms. The relevance is not only this two-step equation (the result is not a sum but a "product"), but, in the context of interactivity, the fact that the meaning is an event in the mind of the vuser (viewer-user). It is a Gestalt perception, an inference, or what today is more commonly called a simulacrum: a copy for which there is no original. The fable vusers generate is a simulacrum of the *writing of the disaster*. Through the simulacrum the disaster becomes interlocutor. The figure of ideogram is more basic than the moral of fable, although ideogram and fable both assign primary responsibility for "meaning" to the receiver.

Happiness. The Chinese character "Happiness" is a combination of two figures: music + singing. "Music" depicts the ancient drum on its stand, with stretched skin, and a straightened right hand striking it. To this graphic is added "mouth," for "singing" (in the character, "mouth" is the lower rectangle, beneath the hand striking the drum). This montage for "happiness" as relay for our fable/ideogram supports the relevance of developing the historical connection with "Stephen Foster," for whom the polluted neighborhood is named. Stephen Foster composed the song "Old Folks At Home" (1851), the opening lyric of which is, "Way down upon de Swanee Ribber" (in the original dialect). Foster had never been to the South, and got the name of the river from a dictionary, looking for a river name that worked with the song syntax ("Swanee" rather than "Suwanee" was dictated by the form). The song was a hit, and eventually was adopted as the official song of the State of Florida (with lyrics bowdlerized to remove terms now considered racist). The song evokes a nostalgic image of well-being.

HOLE

"Hole" is a puncept, in that "hole" as electrate inference functions to gather or assemble disparate dimensions of the world into holistic frame, to support transversal comprehension. The image in question is received as a kind of rebus, a sign expressed within a discourse that is to the community what a dream is to an individual. Konsult translates what disaster expresses regarding relations among culture, nature, and technics. "Hole" was Lacan's shorthand for the breakdowns within normative practices, discourses, and behaviors productive of alternative expression, producing contamination (networks) across semantic fields. Jouissance emerges "beyond the pleasure principle" (to adopt the title of Freud's famous study), manifesting what Freud finally decided to call the "Death Drive,"—a repetition compulsion of traumatic (dis) satisfaction. Konsult shifts attention to corresponding repetitions at the collective level. What is it about disaster that we enjoy (considering how often it repeats)? Do disasters literalize Death Drive on a collective level? The image we are contemplating is feedback for the community, expressing the return of the repressed, of what we do/not want (to know/feel). Dream images, that is, are part of an Unconscious discourse (by definition collective, intersubjective) that is structured "like a language." The image evokes words and unfolds into sequences and constellations of associations. Konsult renders legible the event as an idiom of corporate actant being.

Murphy interrogates the Superfund hole—what it may express as a collective rebus, as Daimon, Avatar, lending corporation a face: revelation of Second Phusis. Heuretics follows the inventions. egents notice and query the pine tar production (within technics) that is the direct source of the disaster—the gift cause of pollution (contamination). We tracked the historical genesis of the invention, placing it in the series of Final Cause (that for the sake of which), through the damage done to sailing vessels engaged in the spice trade, the competition of trade routes to India, resulting in the Gift Cause of the discovery of America by Columbus. The local gift is creosote (arsenic et al.): the material that threatens the regional well-field (well-being) is a by-product of the production of pine tar (ava-tar) used to seal and protect wood from decay (entropy). Pine tar is *sentient doll*, prosopon of Avatar, explaining to us our ethos (it is Krishna to our Arjuna). The hermeneutic procedure is to inventory the vocabulary of the relevant inventions—in this case, information on the manufacture of pine tar. The keyword is "distillation"—which is the chemical process involved. The word hole is *distillation* (the hole punching through every layer of event). It is a choral word, meaning that it functions "holistically," radiating through all associated forms, paronyms, semantic fields, as (mnemonic) *trace*.

The probe undertakes an inventory of terms available in the vocabulary.

Distillation. To distill: subject and process of vaporization for and condensation for purification or concentration. To extract concentrate, to drop, pass, or condense or distillate. Distillation = any concentration, essence, or abstraction. Destillare: to trickle down. Distillation: the volatilization or evaporation and subsequent condensation of a liquid, as when water is boiled in a retort and steam is condensed in a cool receiver; purify, concentrate a substance by such processes. Distiller: an apparatus for distilling, a condenser or still. Usage adds further possibilities. One of the more significant uses of "still" in theory discourse, especially relevant in our context, is the sentence of fetish logic, manifesting a condition of denial (repression), a disconnect between reason and desire (fantasy): *I know, but still* . . . Electracy inverts the fundamental logical operator of literacy—the law of non-contradiction: if contradiction emerged in an argument it signaled that the premise was false. In electracy the emergence of contradiction is a symptom of desire. Contradiction is a rhetorical boundary object. The original context in Freud is the male child's denial of sexual difference, motivated by "castration anxiety." A current example in daily life is resistance to vaccination: "I know (science) that vaccines do not cause autism, but still (emotionally) I believe they do." Hole tracks this tension or dialectical collision across the registers of human capability (the faculties of knowing, willing, feeling). As a means to trope disaster, *Still* opens a semantic field to be mapped across the event, using the definition to be found in most dictionaries.

> still 1 |stil|
>
> adjective
> not moving or making a sound : the still body of the young man.
> • (of air or water) undisturbed by wind, sound, or current; calm and tranquil : her voice carried on the still air | a still autumn day.
> • (of a drink such as wine) not effervescent; compare with sparkle .
> noun
> 1 deep silence and calm; stillness : the still of the night.
> 2 an ordinary static photograph as opposed to a motion picture,

esp. a single shot from a movie.

adverb
1 without moving : the sheriff commanded him to stand still and drop the gun.
2 up to and including the present or the time mentioned; even now (or then) as formerly : he still lives with his mother | it was still raining.
• referring to something that will or may happen in the future : we could still win.
3 nevertheless; all the same : I'm afraid he's crazy. Still, he's harmless.
4 even (used with comparatives for emphasis) : write, or better still, type, captions for the pictures | Hank, already sweltering, began to sweat still more profusely.

verb
make or become still; quieten : [trans.] she raised her hand, stilling Erica's protests | [intrans.] the din in the hall stilled.

PHRASES
still and all informal nevertheless; even so.
still small voice the voice of one's conscience (with reference to 1 Kings 19:12).
still waters run deep proverb a quiet or placid manner may conceal a more passionate nature.

DERIVATIVES
stillness noun

ORIGIN Old English stille (adjective and adverb), stillan (verb), from a base meaning 'be fixed, stand.'

still 2
noun
an apparatus for distilling alcoholic drinks such as whiskey.
ORIGIN mid 16th cent.: from the rare verb still [extract by distillation,] shortening of distill .

Phusis

Konsult addresses the disaster as Second Nature relative to First Phusis introduced by the Presocratic philosophers, identified by Heidegger as the other beginning that is a point of departure for electracy. The heuretic principle is extrapolation to our own apparatus and epoch, so the purpose is not return to some unmediated first nature, but rather, since Aristotle himself recognized artefacts as second nature, perhaps it is access to third nature (and counting), the dimension opening in electrate metaphysics: the imagination. In the contemporary machine age it seems that artefactual production has appropriated natural generation, thus flattening the distinction used to identify being as "coming out of itself." This flattening is manifested also in modernist aesthetics, with art creation rejecting mimesis of nature in favor of simulating a creator god (Genius). Conduction extends the discoveries of psychoanalysis and the arts to collective egency, to track the vectoral register, the movement of desire. Meaning at this level is inferred, emergent within figural connotation.

We receive the materiality of the historical scene as discourse, tracked through works of the imagination, to be mapped onto our specific circumstances. Pepper is the materialization of the vector in our case, invoking the history of the spice trade. Timothy Morton, *The Poetics of Spice*, explains the pattern composing our event. Pepper (spice) imagined possesses *the quality of viscosity, stickiness*. Morton illustrates the point with respect to the Romantic imagination, with reference to a poem ("The Panther") by Leigh Hunt. Morton's commentary indicates the mythological power of material qualities (element) to collect correspondences across the popcycle.

> The capitalist imaginary tends to envision spice both as flow—as in the flowing perfume of the gums in the first verse paragraph—and as density or viscosity—as in the "rich round tears" of the second verse paragraph, an allusion to *Othello* amongst other texts. This kind of viscosity is what Friedrich von Schelling called *geistige Körperlichkeit*—the kind of spectral substantiality associated with the poetics of spice. Significantly the state of frozen enjoyment, embodied in the jewel-like *jouissance* of the rich round tears, is evoked in the context of the human pursuit and capture of the gums, with "swords and spears." If this poem is an allegory about the form of enjoyment

in consumerism, then what it describes are the ways in which consumerism captures, but not entirely, the *jouissance* that sustains it—rather than the subject that might conceivably transcend it. There is an excess flow left over which the end of the poem characterizes as the scent of love, in parallel with, rather than in strict opposition to, the spicy breeze which the panther yearns for at the beginning. We have been extrapellated, rather than interpellated, in the Althusserian sense, by this traversal of capitalist ideology. The advertisement cannot entirely be bought. (Morton 213–14)

Morton is known for his account of "hyperobjects," of which global warming is the primary example—an object (event) so vast that it exceeds apprehension (it is sublime). It is relevant to note in our context that the first property of a hyperobject is "viscosity," meaning that we are stuck to it and cannot get free (it is tar baby). The *Phusis* or firstness (Peirce) of the disaster emerges through placing the material protagonist—the pine tar—in a network constellation. The marker of this vector is the viscosity, the stickiness that is a primary quality of the experience of pine tar, meaning that *Murphy* opens onto the more general catastrophe known as the Anthropocene. The second node assembled by viscosity for us is the epiphany in Jean-Paul Sartre's *Nausea*, when Roquentin (the protagonist) undergoes an experience of Phusis, which in his case triggers a crisis. The schemas and categories of conceptual thinking fall away, and Roquentin confronts bare life as force, pure energy in which all matter is equal in its striving to exist (perhaps an anticipation of what today is known as object-oriented ontology).

> That black against my foot, it didn't look like black, but rather the confused effort to imagine black by someone who had never seen black and who wouldn't know how to stop, who would have imagined an ambiguous being beyond colors. It *looked* like a color, but also . . . like a bruise or a secretion, like an oozing—and something else, an odor, for example, it melted into the odor of wet earth, warm, moist wood, into a black odor that spread like varnish over this sensitive wood, in a flavor of chewed, sweet fiber. I did not simply *see* this black: sight is an abstract invention, a simplified idea, one of man's ideas. That black, amorphous, weakly presence, far surpassed

> sight, smell and taste. But this richness was lost in confusion and finally was no more because it was too much. . . . Had I dreamed of this enormous presence? It was there, in the garden, toppled down into the trees, all soft, sticky, soiling everything, all thick, a jelly. And I was inside, I with the garden. I was frightened, furious, I thought it was so stupid, so out of place, I hated this ignoble mess. Mounting up, mounting up as high as the sky, spilling over, filling everything with its gelatinous slither, and I could see depths upon depths of it reaching far beyond the limits of the garden, the houses, and Bouville, as far as the eye could reach. I was no longer in Bouville, I was nowhere, I was floating. I was not surprised, I knew it was the World, the naked World suddenly revealing itself, and I choked with rage at this gross, absurd being. (Sartre 134)

Adding to the relevance of this scene is that Roquentin's revelation is triggered specifically by *a tree root in the park*. Tree stumps constituted one of the primary resources used in the production of pine tar. The tree is a universal symbol of life, documented in nearly every civilization. Delueze and Guattari usefully rejected "arborescent" metaphysics, which is to say "literacy," proposing to replace it with a metaphysics figured rather by nature's rhizomes, whose decentralized horizontally spreading and swarming better captures the networked systems of electracy. The figure retains the evocation of organic bare life, so that an updated *Nausea* could have Roquentin kick an anthill, for example. In terms of apparatus invention, we are exploring the capacity of material qualities such as "viscosity" to perform rhythm metaphysics.

Nocturnal

Gilbert Durand makes an important contribution to this elemental probe when he locates viscosity as a key marker of one of the three fundamental archetypal orders of world culture. The viscous dimension is affiliated with one of the two nocturnal orders (vectors), associated with mystic traditions of descent, participation and immersion in earth, distinct from and in dynamic inversion with separation and distinctness of ascent into air, associated with the individual hero. In this context we may understand Roquentin's nauseated repulsion from the revelation of bare life as the reaction of a diurnal individualized hero to nocturnal mystic immersion (loss of identity and boundary). In other words, the articulation of the new position required for an electrate narrative involves accommodation with the nocturnal order of archetypes.

> The second structure, a corollary of the first, consists in the viscosity and adhesiveness of the style of nocturnal representation. It is this characteristic which first caused psychologists to attribute to certain psychological types names derived from roots meaning viscosity or glue. Viscosity is manifested in many areas: social, affective, perceptive and representational. We have already seen the importance of thematic viscosity, which gives rise to thought consisting of a profusion of variations on that same theme, rather than of thought which makes distinctions. Ixothymia always shows "too few dissociations." Ixothymic viscosity also manifests itself on a social level. In the Rorschach test a large number of "form-color" responses is considered to be an indication of affective viscosity. In Van Gogh one finds a constant concern to make friendships, to construct an almost religious community in the "house of friends," to construct a "painters' cooperative." Viscosity appears most particularly in the structures of expression. Numerous illustrations of the mystical structures of the Nocturnal Order are to be found in both the literary and pictorial work of the painter of "Starry Nights." (Durand 262)

A guideword naming the heuretics of konsult may be derived from Durand's "ixothymic." The motivation has something to do with the signature effect of mystory, since I have used "glue" as a screen name for decades (initials G. L. U. + French "e"). What is this "ixo" fatality? The provocation of the term is its antithetical or dialectical relation with "schizoanalysis," the "schizo" naming "cut," separation. One implication is that the rhizomatics of Deleuze and Guattari might belong more appropriately not to schizoanalysis but to *ixotropics*. Schizoanalysis remains diurnal, heroic. Ixotropics is nocturnal, mystic. "Analytics" also signals a reluctance to let go of literacy. "Tropics" alludes to the figural emergent character of *signifiance* associated with vectoral rhythmics. *Ixotropics* then? Let that be a prompt for the next stage in the invention of konsult.

6 Rhythm

Chaosmosis

The possibility that *rhythm* offers a more adequate organizational model for apparatus than does structure in electracy was already suggested by one of the inventors of structuralism, Claude Lévi-Strauss, with his analogy of mythologies organized like symphonies. Henri Lefebvre reframed his earlier work on space as "Rhythmanalysis" late in his career. Konsult relates chorography to rhythm within the paradigm of Proust's *Recherche*, related to Swann's experience of Vinteuil's sonata as paragon of the sensible idea. Rhythm metaphysics is developed in one of the most ambitious philosophical developments to date of heuretics in the work of Gilles Deleuze and Félix Guattari, both in their collaborations and single-authored texts. We will use Deleuze and Guattari to review and summarize the contribution of Theory to our CATTt generator of konsult. Apparatus heuretics picks up the invention trajectory from French post-structuralism in general. It is worth noting, in the context of commentaries regarding the "closure" of metaphysics, that from the point of view of grammatology, "closure" means "completion" in the sense of telos: each apparatus has its own epochal version of metaphysics, just as it has its own version of narrative and the other practices that make civilization functional. Heidegger's argument references teleology in the decision made in the first beginning of the Western tradition: the "thing" invented by the Greeks realizes its potential in modern industrial mass production of goods.

The philosophers themselves rarely acknowledge the grammatological (including technics of language) dimension of metaphysical shift. For example, Deleuze, in his major study *Difference and Repetition*, undertakes a systematic experiment to invent an alternative to the metaphysics of Plato and Aristotle, without referencing the grounding of Greek Philosophy in the alphabetic machine. As late as *What Is Philosophy?* Deleuze and Guattari's final collaboration, they are still puzzling over exactly why philosophy began in Greece at that moment in history. This lapse is rectified on the electrate side in Deleuze's cinema books, leading beyond the consensus critique of conceptual discursive thinking, to an exposition of a possible electrate annotation. A shorthand version of their generative CATTt is: Contrast: Metaphysics of Plato and Aristotle; Analogy: Modernist arts (Proust in particular); Theory: Sciences of Complexity, Chaos, Catastrophe; Target: Practical Reason, and even "lifestyle" itself (politics, ethics, aesthetic practices seeking alternatives to Capitalist, commodity fascism); tale: philosophical treatise.

Despite a formidable innovative vocabulary that shifts with every book, Deleuze and Guattari's oeuvre is consistent, spinning out variations on a core theme. A concordance correlating the vocabularies of each book is found in Manuel Delanda's *Intensive Science and Virtual Philosophy* ("Appendix: Deleuze's Words"). The point of departure for their heuretics is Aristotle's systematizing of Plato's cosmology in *Timaeus*, which is to say that Deleuze and Guattari are addressing choragraphy. Plato introduced Chora (Space, Region) as a third kind—genos, generation, including a figure as nurse—facilitating the relationship between Being and Becoming, such that choragraphy takes up the temporality of Trace as genesis and generation. Since Chora is neither intelligible (idea) nor perceptible (matter), Plato addressed it figuratively (with "bastard" reason). His primary metaphor to evoke the function of Chora was that of threshing or winnowing, expropriating from the Eleusinian Mysteries the liknon or winnowing basket, symbol of fertility. The cosmos emerged not from nothing, but from chaos in the Greek account of creation, through a movement, violent motion, a vortex, introducing rhythm into chaos capable of sorting the undifferentiated whole into the material Elements (Earth, Air, Fire, Water). It is worth reviewing the role of Chora in Plato to clarify Deleuze and Guattari's method as heuristic, in that their invention by Contrast is not an attack or rejection of Classical metaphysics, but another variation in becoming idea (the program of the coming philosophy, in Benjamin's terms). Deleuze and Guattari update Chora while retaining Plato's figures: the ontological categorial functionality of Chora is that of *machinic rhythm*, specifically of "turbulence" in the contemporary sense elaborated in chaos theory. Deleuze and Guattari name this processual emergence *chaosmosis*, and their originality and contribution to chorography is their extensive elaboration of "turbulence" as the conductive fourth inference procedure that electracy adds to literate reasoning. (Deleuze, *Difference and Repetition*).

Aristotle collapsed Plato's dualism in his invention of substance, a composite of form (Being) and matter (Becoming). Aristotle explicated the ontological pairing in terms of actuality (energeia) and potentiality (dunamis), with reality attributed to actuality through production or realization. The question concerns the Being of life, and the relay generalized into metaphysics (covering all being) was organic growth or development over time, from seed to fruit or egg to chick. Aristotle invented the term Entelechy to name this production of things that become what they already are. Deleuze and Guattari invert Entelechy, describing Being as emergent out of Becoming, with no necessary end or telos, but only a creative processual historical evolution of potentiality. The first point of relevance is to identify these movements of life as vectors (sense as direction), to be annotated by means of rhythm as formal device. Heidegger worked with this distinction also, noting two dimensions of capability (virtue, power): first is the capability to learn (for example); second is to act upon this capacity, in order actually to learn.

Capacity and capability as framed by Amartya Sen are central notions for electrate Justice, but realization depends upon affordances and how they are exploited within specific conditions. Deleuze and Guattari do not abandon the organic relay, but rather draw on contemporary science to update it, including especially ethology. Their primary figure evoking the functioning of existential process across all matter is the rhizome, network formation, but understood in evolutionary terms of symbiotic formations such as the orchid and wasp (clover and bee), all read as troping database networks. Life as generation, the libidinal energy of reproduction, operates through devices of attraction and repulsion, and maintains itself, to survive and thrive (or not). This process has no necessary end or purpose, other than "living on" (Derrida). Part of Deleuze and Guattari's innovation is to frame the organic figure as a machine, with the machinic replacing structure in their ontology. The machine is emblematic of industrial modernism, but they define the figure transversally as a functionality of flow and interruption across all matter. The common definition of "apparatus," in any case, is "social machine," to clarify that it is an emergent blend of ideology and technology. Bratton proposes rhizome as a "design brief" for Stack *User*, following Benedict Singleton design theory, "based on *metis* and cunning, for which design is the instigations of traps. All species are at work to design their interactions with the world so as to trap what they need, and for humans the institutionalization of these traps is where design and govenmentality intersect.... Ensnared one within the other, the 'user' of each design encapsulates another while being itself encapsulated, infecting and infected at once, integrities crumbling. This is a model for communities of users one inside the other." (Bratton 288).

Desiring Machines

The insight of apparatus theory is that metaphysics is the operating system of language and technics (machinics), emerging within a matrix of technology, institution formation, and identity behaviors. Literacy realized a particular potential inherent in alphabetic writing of Indo-European natural language. Specifically, Topos as the mediating operator of literacy, became practical with Aristotle's discovery of the logical possibilities of oppositional procedures available in writing, the logical square moving through contradiction, contrariety, and complementarity—in short, dialectics, a practice continually developed from Plato's dialogues to Hegel, continuing in contemporary semiotics (Greimas's actantial deep structure). Substance is the product of dialectics sorting matter into form in the dimension created by conceptual technics. The challenge for konsult is to find an equivalent movement of sense (vector) operational in the new dimension of electracy, with Chora as scene of a new inception. The achievement of Deleuze and Guattari is not just that they recognized the historical relativity of dialectics and analyzed its inadequacy to and complicity with the problematic of modernity, but that they systematically and experimentally introduced a comprehensive alternative to dialectics (literate metaphysics). Their vocabulary correlates with and replaces Aristotle's terms, signaling at once that they are doing metaphysics but in a post-literate mode (electracy).

Deleuze and Guattari refer regularly to Proust as a touchstone for clarifying their innovations (just as Heidegger referenced Hölderlin). Proust's novel addresses life through Eros, thus continuing the tradition of invention from Courtly Love, taken as paradigmatic by Agamben, Lacan, and many others, and "The Birth of Venus" as Neoplatonic icon, all resonating with Diotima in Plato's *Symposium*. The talking cure of Anna O. belongs in this series as well. Electracy brings into metaphysics the libidinal register of this genesis—the life and death energy of embodied reproduction and generation, Geschlecht, the capacity for Jouissance, adding to orality (religion) and literacy (science) a third axis concerned with Enjoyment, and governed not by right-wrong (belief) or true-false (reason) but attraction-repulsion, pleasure-pain (thriving-destruction), joy-sadness. Courtly Love is credited as an invention not just of literature, but of behavior and attitude, even a lifestyle and worldview institutionalizing human passions—the invention of "love," as Denis de Rougement argued in his classic study, *Love in the Western World*. This historical example clarifies what is at stake in Deleuze and Guattari's experiment, and the ultimate goal of konsult as the genre of electrate education: a heuretics of lifestyle as such (Nietzsche's project, articulated in three versions: will to power, eternal return, transvaluation of all values). Guattari used the events of Tiananmen Square, when Chinese students faced off against the tanks of the Communist state, as a prototype for "lifestyle" or the manner of appropriating Being, as the issue of processual ontology.

What are the operators of thought Deleuze and Guattari make available for konsult? Chaosmosis begins not from the beginning (not from chaos itself) but continues the evolutionary game, starting in territorialized or fixed, standardized, conventional conditions of some habitus or ethos, some archive of tradition. For us that ethos is Corporate Capitalism, with the task of coming philosophy being "cartography" [choragraphy] to map the routes of potentiality for deterritorialization, lines of flight (vectors) capable of transforming a situation. There is no blank slate or starting over, but rather, invisible forces code the world and may be rendered manifest by our practice. These forces appear in territorialized terms ("territory" considered in our context as a version of "region") as Gestalts, or even as elementary catatastrophes (Thom) that is, ready-made forms that citizens recognize relative to common and good sense, manipulated (troped) as modules for comprehension, communication, and expression.

The choral function of chaosmosis, producing order or organization of the world, manifests the ontological categories of space and time as *faciality* and *refrain*. Capitalism, or any state striated regime, attempts to eliminate open potentiality and reduce all choice to a binary black and white system, a fundamental figure-ground Gestalt (melodrama) that Deleuze and Guattari describe as White Wall and Black Hole. In Capitalism the mass media circulate the Gestalt default fixed in the icons or brands of celebrities (the prototypes of Michael Jackson, Elvis Presley, Marilyn Monroe, top three "dead celebrities" in terms of annual earnings). The prosopopoeia (personification of lifestyle extending beyond iconic faces to bodies and landscapes) of lifestyle, repressive or territorializing in the West, functioned alternatively as a line of flight (vector) in China. The essential context is that identity behaviors (lifestyle) are as much a part of apparatus invention as are technologies and institutions.

These terms are not just descriptive, but rhetorical in providing means of composing as well as of reading or interpreting. Deleuze and Guattari remind us that Proust himself, and Marcel as narrator, apprentice themselves to Swann's love story, in order ultimately to learn how to create art (art-life rhizome). We follow their lead in order to learn choragraphy. The *Recherche*, as a narrative, communicates a diegesis, an imaginary world, a microcosm rendering manifest our macrocosm. A novel is a useful relay for Chora to suggest the holistic nature of electrate categories, as well as for revising the scenario genre of consulting. Novels archive imagined "dispositions," reviewing the potentiality of existence (EPS). Choragraphy inverts the analytical logics of literacy, sorted out into pure categories, differentiating into genus and species, instead to grasp and hold transversally all the strata coexisting in reality in an assemblage. Here is the crux of innovation, in the spirit of electracy, which is to open the collective dimension of sociohistorical reality to ontology. Deleuze and Guattari do not replace literate metaphysics, but supplement it, to do for collective existence and relation what literacy did for the individual self and thing. The general name for this register of thought is the Unconscious, understood not as some private inner aspect of personal mind, but as the intersubjective interdependent quantum field coexistence with others (the Other, alterity). Deleuze and Guattari enhance our Theory, doing for desidero (Unconscious) what Descartes did for cogito (consciousness).

Under the banner of schizoanalysis, Deleuze and Guattari push psychoanalysis beyond its ordination by the family romance and the Oedipal model, into an integral systems assemblage of all the institutions of society. The individual human experience of self is taken up in its participation in various group subjectivations, opening up social fractal dimensions between the individual and society. Konsult supports this group formation through social media, the encounters of alterity, towards a collective *conscientization* or collective singularity, enabling egents to experience collective agency (and not only to understand the concepts of ecology). Such is the purpose of affective capability instantiated in arts annotations: to enable egents to experience and undergo well-being against disaster. *Anti-Oedipus* is an exposition of this aspect of chaosmosis, explaining how molecular and molar (micro and macro-cosm) interrelate as desiring machines—a phrase that continues the series of guidewords in the family of Enjoyment. This insight is fundamental to fifth estate electrate politics, showing that social and cultural historical institutions are bodies without organs (BWO), functioning as collective dimensions of human organs, introducing a capacity of holistic feeling (electrate sensorium). Thus, with respect to what motivates public policy, konsult foregrounds as emblem the historical assemblage relating to the human capacity for taste (the enjoyment of pungent flavor in the literal sense, promoted as figure into metaphysical practice) by means of the institutions of trade that delivered pepper to Europe, and ultimately motivated the discovery of America. The prototype of a vector of egent desire is the trade route.

Deleuze and Guattari address the molecular level underlying these molar events and historical names, to describe and invent an electrate equivalent of literate representation, for understanding, undertaking, and undergoing (theopraxesis) ourselves the creation of subjectivation in reality. To declare this project as "metaphysics" is a reminder that what needs to be invented for digital media is the embodied felt equivalent of discursive reason for a coming global society. We know from neuroscience that feeling grounds and accompanies human thought. Literacy wrote the thought (idea); electracy traces the feeling (felt). The EmerAgency in order to perform chorography as the organizer of electrate konsulting needs to invent/learn a rhetoric of desiring machines, referring to the functioning in this circulation of corporeal organs through corporate BWOs, the mapping that organizes a global libidinal economy as simulacral erogenous zones. Here is the problematic of capacity: the human capability of sensory experience, the routes produced through the Real motivated by each sensory organ and all of them together, that configure global power dynamics instantiated in global capitalism. Corporation is prostheses of appetite, just as School is prosthesis of intellect.

The specific application in education is the second capacity: to activate and act upon the capability (the ability-to-be).

VIRTUAL OBJECTS

We are exploring how event rhythm (registering vectoral trace of life force) replaces structure for designing konsult. Electrate metaphysics operates beyond language, and (here is the "sticking" point) beyond reason, with vectoral *signifiance* created through every manner of circulation (from commodity sign to gift trace). Measure in this modality is sublime. McKenzie Wark extended "vector" to name the mode of capitalism (the vectoral class) native to electracy with its information and knowledge economy (Wark, *Telesthesia*). The vectoral circulation between corporeal bodies and BWOs is made possible by the human capacity to negotiate environment (Umwelt) by means of part objects within digital media. Theopraxesis is the rhetoric of this visceral movement (just as logic guided the inference paths through conceptual space). The functionality of rhthym systems is to enable egents to overcome alienation and reification, to experience individually the collective effects of "violent symbiosis" (Bratton) among all participants in this environment (human and non). Part objects were introduced in object-relations psychology to explain individual interaction with the world, learned through nurturing. One's manner of conduct as an adult is determined through introjection and manipulation of objects of earliest experience (beginning with the body). Especially useful for our design, Deleuze and Guattari's common example of a rhizome in this context is the primary part object relation—mother's breast to infant's mouth, forming a complex dynamic among need, desire, and demand. The infant perceives only the relevant part providing gratification. The castration complex originated in this way, the penis/phallus imagined (fantasized) as detachable, like other parts and products (milk, feces). This detachability, associated with the functioning of the body, makes organs "writable." Konsult learns from this theory the "extimate" (inside-outside moebius topology) character of the mental model as chiasmatic landscape. The inventions of modernist avant-garde poetics are required to compose this landscape, beyond mimetic or realist modes of representation, addressing the sensorium organized as lamella. Konsult designs the "glocal" place of encounter between egent bodies and vectoral global forces.

Lacan changed the definition (the object only partially represents its function), and adds to the inventory of part objects: phoneme, gaze, voice, and the nothing. The part object is folded in Lacan's notion of the object-cause-of-desire, the *objet petite a* (the little other, object @), manifesting a hybrid mode of "thing" (*das Ding*) relevant to electrate ontology. Lacan troped the Dark Lady in Courtly Love to figure the function of this Thing as inaccessible unknowable Real, relevant as a relay for inventing behavior (lifestyle, *wesen*) relative to a culture. "Thing" (das Ding) is a hinge, passage between literacy and electracy, in that the difference between the "thing" invented in the Athenian Academies through definition, and the object @ in electrate metaphysics through FX, manifests the leap, the discontinuity of this passage. The overlap of terms evokes the extent of challenge for our project, to do for object @ what School did for conceptual things.

Deleuze and Guattari gather the family of such objects into the Idea of virtual objects, including Winnicott's transitional (potential) objects: things that are extimate, relating topologically the inner and outer environments that configure Unconscious, supplying the logos of concrete and abstract assemblages. Bernard Stiegler warned that this first object (transitional, potential)—foundation of all creative imagination—has been industrialized in digital civilization, and thus requires a new educational order to help humanity adapt and thrive (Stiegler, *What Makes Life Worth Living*). It is worth remembering that this modal object functions metaphysically within the libidinal economy of electracy, expressing an ontology of Jouissance, working transversally or holistically to produce cosmos out of chaos through rhythm (mediation repetition, pattern vectors). Our design brief for konsult calls for the invention of a behavior of Justice for electracy. This ontology captures the way in which desire (libido) is an energy that saturates every plane or plateau of the world, beyond Freud's notion of sublimation. The circulation of part-objects through media and commodity channels manifested in aesthetic design is disclosive of Being, specifically of the force of desire in the electrate apparatus: voice with breast; gaze with anus, the affiliation made possible through the shared drive of appetites. Egents learn to think, act, and make within this sensorium, necessarily, although the only aspect of visceral orientation acknowledged in most contemporary pedagogy is Piaget's unthreatening sensorimotor stages of cognitive development. Here (as we keep saying) is the sticking point, the aporia in passage between literacy and electracy: konsult as pedagogy of the visceral.

Agamben's shorthand for composite (potential) objects is "fetish" (invoking usage by Marx, Freud, and avant-garde arts), to remind us that actual things encountered in experience include a dynamic virtual or potential dimension (libidinal investment), and that this investment is catalytic, triggered by aesthetically designed materiality discharging surplus value. Advertisers (sophists of visceral ontology) already compose in this way, which is useful to keep in mind when the theory becomes too opaque. We are already undergoing necessary innervation through commodity form adapting us to Liquid environment. The function of virtual objects is rhizomatic, relational, having the power of strange attractors in complexity, relying on function (rule + variable) for ratio, bringing into expression what otherwise remains Unconscious. The rhizomatic relation that replaces dialectics in chaosmosis conjoins two divergent heterogeneous asymmetrical vectoral series, producing a collapse into (dada) assemblage. The challenge addressed by konsult is that egents live inside and through the performance of these series, such that they themselves are at once author and text through the feedback loops of system networks (becoming god).

Virtual objects organize space, time, and cause, through patternings formed by pure (aesthetic) differentiation and repetition (*signifiance*). Deleuze and Guattari refer to these patterns as *existential refrains*, invoking ethology as relay: the way birds make multiple uses of a blade of grass—courting, nesting, marking territory—is a relay for understanding human use of virtual objects to de/territorialize an ecology. Deleuze and Guattari in any case are not bound by the strict definitions of their sources and affiliates, but appropriate terms for their own purposes. The coherence of a virtual object is composite.

> How do certain semiotic segments achieve their autonomy, start to work for themselves and to secrete new fields of reference? It is from such a rupture that an existential singularization correlative to the genesis of new coefficients of freedom will become possible. This detachment of an ethico-aesthetic "partial object" from the field of dominant significations corresponds both to the promotion of a mutant desire and to the achievement of a certain disinterestedness. Here I would like to establish a bridge between the concept of a partial object (object "a" as theorized by Lacan) that marks the autonomisation of the components of unconscious subjectivity, and the subjective autonomisation relative to the aesthetic object. At

> this point we rediscover a problematic highlighted by Mikhail Bakhtin in his first theoretical essay of 1924: the function of enunciative appropriation of aesthetic form by the autonomisation of cognitive or ethical content and the realization of this content in an aesthetic object—what I will call a partial enunciator. I am attempting to draw the psychoanalytic partial object that is adjacent to the body—the point of coupling of the drive—towards a partial enunciation. The expansion of the notion of partial object, to which Lacan contributed with the inclusion of the gaze and the voice in the object "a," needs to be followed up. This entails expanding the category to cover the full range of nuclei of subjective autonomisations relative to group subjects, and to instances of the production of subjectivity (machinic, ecological, architectural, religious, etc). (Guattari, *Chaosmosis* 13–14)

Guattari develops in this functionality of the virtual object nothing less than an electrate group enunciation, distinct from but a new media equivalent of the linguistic practices of alphabetic writing and literate metaphysics, to be performed by egents as Users of Stack Interface. The importance of this functionality for konsult education cannot be overstated as clarifying konsult as practice (keeping in mind that everything said here is by way of instructions). The insight is that an existential refrain is a hybrid of virtual object with modernist aesthetic object, integrated with the ethological economy of lived experience. Here is the event of epiphany that is annotated for konsult: the *Stiftung* or foundational event of the sensible idea theorized by Merleau-Ponty. The two vectoral series form a rhizome (symbiotic trapping) through a chance encounter when, in a flash, a match between an internal and external object triggers (catalyzes) a deterritorialization, a new trajectory of Becoming. Guattari theorizes the revelation precisely as catalysis (encounter as catalyst: epiphany).

> This poetic-existential catalysis that we find at work in the midst of scriptural, vocal, musical or plastic discursivities engage quasi-synchronically the enunciative crystallisation of the creator, the interpreter and the admirer of the work of art, like analyst and patient. Its efficiency lies in its capacity to promote active, processual ruptures within semiotically structured, significational and denotative networks, where it will put emergent

subjectivity to work. When it is effectively triggered in a given enunciative area—that is, situated in a historical and eco-political perspective—such an analytico-poetic function establishes itself as a mutant nucleus of auto-referentiality and auto-valorisation. This is why we must always consider it in two ways: 1. As a molecular rupture, an imperceptible bifurcation, capable of overthrowing the framework of dominant redundancies, the organization of the "already classified" or, if one prefers, the classical order. 2. In the way that it selects certain segments of these very chains of redundancy, to confer on them the a-signifying existential function I have just evoked, thereby "refraining" them and producing virulent, partial fragments of enunciation operating as "shifters" of subjectivation. The quality of the base material matters little here, as one can see in repetitive music or Butoh dance, which, as Marcel Duchamp would have wished are turned entirely towards "the spectator." What does matter is the mutant rhythmic impetus of a temporalisation able to hold together the heterogeneous components of a new existential edifice. (19–20)

The value of this proposal from the point of view of electracy, associating the virtual object as the *shifter* vehicle, is fundamental to egency. Here is the electrate equivalent of the position of "I" in literacy, designed to support the position of collective singularity, or group subject, the egent capable of receiving (with the help of the apparatus) Unconscious thought (Simulacrum, Avatar, Ereignis, Event). This innovation is the rationale for rethinking the transcendental subject as proposed by Benjamin and Agamben for coming philosophy. The question remains open: is School as it exists today capable of becoming electrate in the terms we are describing, or will it play Church to Science? The konsult CATTt says: read Theory as instructions.

Existential Refrain

Deleuze and Guattari's version of the sensible idea as basic unit of electracy (the digital equivalent of concept), whose prototype is the little phrase of the sonata articulated with Swann's love for Odette, resonates with Sen's Justice defined as a universal or inalienable right to capability—the right of conatus (striving to persevere in one's own Being, which is addressed in *Avatar Emergency*): to not give up on My desire. This striving is a force of survival, and violent in the manner of appetite, whose collective movement conducts reality and as such is annotated in konsult. It is good to recall that Heidegger's Dasein was an updating of Spinoza's conatus and Leibniz's monad, all versions of tracing the vector directing the movement or propensity of life. That conatus is a guideword for Jane Bennett's "vibrant matter" signals its status as boundary notion for the coming ontology. (Jane Bennett) A goal of konsult is to help a community receive, shape and direct this vector for thriving against disaster.

> The machine is always synonymous with a nucleus constitutive of an existential Territory against a background of a constellation of incorporeal Universes of reference (or values). The "mechanism" of this turning around of being consists in the fact that some of the machine's discursive segments do not only play a functional or signifying role, but assume the existentializing function of pure intensive repetition that I have called the refrain function. . . . The manifestations—not of Being, but of multitudes of ontological components—are of the order of the machine. And this, without semiological mediation, without transcendent coding, directly as "being's giving of itself," as giving. Acceding to such a "giving" is already to participate ontologically in it as a full right. The term right does not occur here by chance, since at this proto-ontological level it is already necessary to affirm a proto-ethical dimension. The play of intensity of the ontological constellation is, in a way, a choice of being not only for self, but for the whole alterity of the cosmos and for the infinity of times. (Guattari, *Chaosmosis* 53)

An assumption of apparatus metaphysics is that Being must be appropriated (Ereignis): Being is a potentiality that may be actualized (or not), but this realization happens through collective decision in an historical ecology. Hence the point of departure for konsult, to open a Chora revealing well-being as the virtue (power) of Justice for a community.

The program for coming philosophy established the passion of love as the most direct access in experience of Unconscious potentiality (that we are enveloped in an outside of alterity within which our egency registers as feedback). We are apprenticed to Proust's account of Swann falling in love with Odette, (we are troping Proust) to learn an imaging of sensible ideas, which we translate into instructions. Proust is described as an anthropologist or even ethologist of French society. The Verdurin salon where the founding event of catalysis occurs is a collective assemblage, with two passages or routes (vectors, directions), two inputs, meaning that it may be mapped by means of René Thom's elementary cusp catastrophe. The spatial passage is faciality: although Odette is not Swann's "type," he relates to her aesthetically by an analogy with a Botticelli fresco representing Zipporah (wife of Moses). This strategy is a defense that keeps passion at a distance (like Courtly Love). The temporal dimension of passage is refrain, materialized in this encounter in the little phrase of Vinteuil's sonata, the re-hearing of which, in the context of Odette, triggers actual passion that crystallizes a new assemblage. Deleuze and Guattari's analysis adds to the other accounts an emphasis on the machinic unconscious, that is, on the collective holistic historical quality of the encounter. Guattari, for example, reminds us that the little phrase is one *measure* (and this is the "secret word" for us, seeking a metaphysical unit of limit), carried along in a series within the history of music.

> Consider the example of the pentatonic musical refrain which, with only a few notes, catalyses the Debussy constellation of multiple Universes:—the Wagnerian Universe surrounding Parsifal, which attaches itself to the existential Territory constituted by Bayreuth;—the Universe of Gregorian chant;—that of French music, with the return to favor of Rameau and Couperin;—that of Chopin, due to a nationalist transposition;—the Javanese music Debussy discovered at the Universal Exposition of 1889;—the world of Manet and Mallarmé, which is associated with Debussy's stay at the Villa Médicis. It would be appropriate to add to these past and present influences the prospective resonances which constituted the reinvention of polyphony from the time of the Ars Nova, its repercussions on the French musical phylum of Ravel, Duparc, Messiaen, etc., and on the sonorous mutation triggered by Stravinsky, his presence in the work of Proust.
> ... (*Chaosmosis* 50)

The fictional Vinteuil is a composite figure drawn from several of Proust's favorite composers, including Debussy and César Franck among others. An equivalent in painting is the mediating role played by Japanese Ukiyo-e prints ("pictures of the floating world," that is, pleasure quarters) for Van Gogh's formal innovations. The machinic or multiple frame locates the shifter of subjectivation as a potential moving site, a threshold catastrophe (map of change), poised for triggering a convergence of diverse historical vectors of becoming, and "triggering" is how "idea" is "thought" in electracy: "involuntary"—a feature of the "little sensations." The Unconscious is the milieu constituted by the history of music and the social formation of the salon (among other things). The *measure* or little phrase is choral in catalyzing a virtual object: x object inside, x object outside, and the refrain bringing them into rhythm or pattern (felt). Guattari generalizes the event, which is fundamental for electrate learning as change.

> To illustrate this mode of production of polyphonic subjectivity, where a complex refrain plays a dominant role, consider the example of televisual consumption. When I watch television, I exist at the intersection: 1. Of a perceptual fascination provoked by the screen's luminous animation which borders on the hypnotical. 2. Of a captive relation with the narrative content of the program, associated with a lateral awareness of surrounding events (water boiling on the stove, a child's cry, the telephone . . .). 3. Of a world of fantasms occupying my daydreams. My feeling of personal identity is thus pulled in different directions. How can I maintain a relative sense of unicity, despite the diversity of components of subjectivation that pass through me? It's a question of the refrain that fixes me in front of the screen, henceforth constituted as a projective existential node. My identity has become that of the speaker, the person who speaks from the television. Like Bakhtin, I would say that the refrain is not based on elements of form, material or ordinary signification, but of the detachment of an existential "motif" (or leitmotiv) which installs itself like an "attractor" within a sensible and significational chaos. The different components conserve their heterogeneity, but are nevertheless captured by a refrain which couples them to the existential Territory of my self. (*Chaosmosis* 16–17).

The refrain is My vehicle, ordinator of Existential Positioning. In metaphysical terms, the existential refrain is interface, functioning as transversal logos, gathering and holding together a dynamic collective assemblage, managing one's positioning within the various institutions of the popcycle. Electracy accesses and annotates for further manipulation the environmental force of desire through these rhythms and patterns, just as literacy annotated and accessed physical materiality by means of propositional truth. Our assignment is to devise a practice of choragraphy to map in one's own case this Unconscious virtual region of potentiality, the flow of multiple divergent vectors through an environmental feedback system of *transference*, to create a place for epiphany (reception of Avatar). The mobility to be coordinated through ubiquitous computing uses the separability, the detachability of virtual objects correlated with refrains and faciality (electrate time and space), recording with the autonomy of filmic imaging and related post-production devices, registering a multiplicity of point(s) of view. The machinic unconscious names a circulation of flow/interruption, subject to all the dynamics of complexity (turbulence) previously described by tropology, the cardinal tropes, with "metaphor" as prototype of the ancient device updated in electracy: the word means "transport" or "vehicle," literally a "bus" in Greek. It is how computational 1/0 is lived. Mobile computing in smart environments samples the technics dimension of the digital apparatus, supporting mapping, touring, and even creating of the routes or vectors of condensation and displacement traveled by caravans of signifiers in an information economy, passage through mobile Chora. The appropriations of tropology in contemporary theory (core contribution of arts and letters to digital education) may be recovered in our context, in relation with chaosmosis and schizoanalysis (and ixotropics), to help design and test the authoring rhythms of facialities and refrains, especially when it is appreciated that the cardinal tropes correlate with all figure/ground configurations informing Gestalt (Fold) design. (McLuhan)

Meanwhile it is important in the context of konsulting to remember that when Marcel apprenticed himself to Swann's legend he was attempting to understand the experience of intense happiness that accompanied his own epiphanies. "Epiphany" (flash reason) is a keyword to name a device and an experience of correspondences between microcosm and macrocosm. Deleuze concludes his study of Proust with a footnote contextualizing Proust's image in modernist poetics.

> We should have to compare the Proustian conception of the image with other post-Symbolist conceptions: for example, Joyce's epiphany or Pound's imagism and vorticism. The following features seem to be shared: image as autonomous

link between two concrete objects insofar as they are different (image, concrete equation); style, as multiplicity of viewpoints toward the same object and exchange of viewpoints toward several objects; language, as integrating and comprehending its own variations constitutive of a universal history and making each fragment speak according to its own voice; literature as production, as operation of effect-producing machines; explication, not as didactic intention but as technique of envelopment and development, writing as ideogrammatic method (with which Proust allies himself on several occations). (*Proust and Signs* 188)

Star Maps

Proust's account of time regained, including the sensible idea, is the prototype evoking the time-space categories to be generalized for electracy as temporal rhythm. Proust's epiphanic moment is to electrate temporality what linear progress is to literacy, or the season cycle to orality, afforded by the light-speed of digital civilization. This intense holistic aesthetic shape of experience (whose rhetoric is theopraxesis) must be appropriated, augmented, designed, and extended through the institutions of the apparatus, to take up the work conducted by historiography in literacy and mythology in orality. Proust discovered his vocation as an artist by tracking his epiphanies of involuntary memory to their source in certain sensory patterns, recreating in the process the historical social order of his environment. Proust is a kind of Marco Polo of choragraphy, and the ambition of konsult is to generalize the functionality operating in Proust's happiness. Epiphany articulating *moment* (*Augenblick*) as rhythm is the syllogism of electracy.

"Chaosmosis" suggests the relevance of René Thom to this inventory of resources. Ivar Ekeland (*Mathematics and the Unexpected*) noted that René Thom's topology, a geometric formalizing of seven elementary catastrophes, albeit limited to the dissipative subset of nonlinear systems, diagrams the dynamic unfolding of such epiphanies (catastrophe = epiphany, sudden change or transformation). Phase space (chaos, complexity) is for electracy, in any case, what Euclidean space is for literacy. The information energy field of electracy is a dynamical landscape organized by movement around an attractor. Attraction and repulsion of libidinal energy (Jouissance) is a special case of energy dynamics in general (electricity), with the effect of attractors expressed formally as wells or basins. Relevant to Derrida's allegory of Trace as sun's heat (more than light), Aristotle's Entelechy (the process of a being becoming what it already is, achieving completion) is thermodynamically a kind of entropy. Ekeland's association of Proust's epiphanies with Thom's catastrophes calls attention to the family of theories guiding our topic, for Thom himself explained his project as a formalization of Greimas's actantial deep structure of narrative (mapping the event of change in narrative). Thom's topological Gestalts, schemas, or archetypes facilitate the transition from literacy to electracy, serving as a kind of Rosetta Stone translating between literary semantics (descriptions of events) and event processes as such. Literacy explained the vector of life energy as Entelechy. Electracy accounts for it as autopoiesis. These models apply to the movement of learning as well, concerned with how egents experience direction or purpose as emergent rather than as fixed goals.

One of the lessons of this work is how a virtual object functions as the shifter in a group or collective enunciation (egent they), supporting the actantial User position in Stack. The question concerns deictics of egent position constituting a collective point of view (group position, location, EPS). Wolfgang Wildgen (*Catastrophe Theoretic Semantics*) clarified that Thom's topology draws on Charles Sanders Peirce's semiotics as well as that of Greimas, to map a path through an event of sense. The catastrophe/epiphany is event of agency, "interpretant" in Peirce's terms, matching a selection operator with a stochastic process. The prototypical scene whose potentials or affordances are modeled in topology is that of two agents negotiating for one object. Wildgen suggests this could be the basic commercial relationship of commodity exchange, and we recognize it also (via Greimas) as a basic narrative conflict, including the dramas of jealousy iterated for Swann-Odette and Marcel-Albertine, not to mention the Romantic Comedies and melodramas central to Stanley Cavell's Emersonian conversations. Wildgen cites Thom's own analogy relating the elementary topology with sentence structure.

> This theory of a spatial origin of syntactic structures explains many facts: that an elementary sentence has at most four agents, and in the case of inflected languages it points to the origins of most of the cases: the nominative (ergative) case of the subject; the accusative case for the object; the dative case

for the goal of verbal expressions which corresponds to the morphology of giving, the instrumental (or ablative) case for those verbs which contain the morphology of excision (or of union). The only classical case which cannot be interpreted by this table is the genitive case (31).

The operation of these four cases is generalized in phase space, and correlates with the four-color map principle of the popcycle, and every other fouring (from Aristotle's causes to our CATTt).

Michel Serres offers important insights into the nature of the virtual collective shifter that makes egency (Avatar) functional as fifth estate. He describes it as the "third-instructed," to characterize the experience undergone in this mobile "sensible place." It is perhaps predictable that this position deliberately contrasts with the rule of the excluded middle or non-contradiction fundamental to literate reasoning. Serres accumulates figures (conceptual personae) to express the functionality of this operator—Troubadour, Harlequin (his patchwork coat), fables of the hare in the garden, and "parasite" as a choral word or "hole" (Lacan), deployed in all its senses in French, including "noise." Parasite is an exciter, trigger, coming from outside, interrupting, producing not analysis but catalysis. Its position is at the threshold of potential, capable of switching selection or attention between order and disorder, music and noise, figure and ground. Our keyword capacity (capability) is also Serres's focus.

> One day at some point, everyone passes through the middle of this white river, through the strange state of a phase change, which could be called sensitivity, a word that signifies possibility or capacity in every sense. Sensitive, for example, the scale when it seesaws up and down, vibrating, in the beautiful middle, in both directions; sensitive also the child who will walk when he throws himself into an unbalanced balance; observe him again when he immerses himself in speech, reading, or writing, cleansed, besmirched in sense and nonsense. How hypersensitive we were, stuck-up, sowing our wild oats, when crossing all the thresholds of youth. That state vibrates like an instability, a metastability, like a nonexcluded third between equilibrium and disequilibrium, between being and nothingness. Sensitivity haunts a central and peripheral place—in the form of a star (*The Troubadour of Knowledge* 9).

The concern with "balance" evokes one of the attributes of Lady Justice (her scales). Lévi-Strauss's mythologies showed how to track transformations across thresholds (myth defined precisely as pattern persisting through continuous transformations across systems and strata of discourses and cultures). In terms of phase space, the desired topology for Serres is the one known as the "butterfly" catastrophe. Wildgen's context establishes that the "star" pattern references the butterfly topology. This higher formation maps "the archetype of passage or mediated effect" (Wildgen 65). This passage includes events of transfer, of giving (which is no doubt why Serres adopted it as the dynamic of learning). Butterfly phase space is four-dimensional, so it may only be graphed with sections, but Wildgen's description of the route through this phase space gives the flavor of the dimension relevant to konsult as vector and rhythm of change. "The path which leads to Thom's archetype of giving (our archetype of transfer) must seek its way under the 'roof,'" Wildgen states, referring to his diagram, "and through the pocket inside the intersection of right and left parts of the 'roof'" (72). A number of bifurcation points may be crossed along the way, with the potential to trigger abrupt change (catastrophes). Thom's phrase describing giving (gift) was *morphologie du don*, alerting us to the association with the donor or helper actant in Greimas's narrative structure, as well as with Derrida's Trace or Heidegger's *Seyn*, mapping how Being sends or gives through time space (*il y a, es gibt*), with konsult designed to receive this gift. The central archetypes derived from the butterfly are: compromise, transfer indirect action/ instrumental interaction. The simple "localistic" description is of "one domain where two areas overlap (a zone of common influence). Lacan documented this locale with the klein bottle (two spheres, each inside the other). In this domain, separated by a conflict-line (a fold), a third domain emerges, which can achieve a kind of metastable dominance creating thus a 'compromise pocket' between the two conflicting attractors. This complicated situation can be associated with political domains and neutral zones between two opposed blocks" (76). The "star" configuration appears through recursion of the butterfly passage (its opening and closing may be observed through animation), adding the archetype of gradual birth/death (84). It is important to note that these figures describe everyday life processes (just as complexity geometries may be used to generate natural geological or botanical shapes). Thom's prototype for all transitive action is *predation*, manifesting not love but hunger as the basic drive, his example being cat-mouse predation. He has in mind the same interdependence described in Deleuze and Guattari's rhizome, referenced in Bratton's Stack Interface as Users's setting traps for one another. (Thom, *Semio Physics: A Sketch*). Heidegger, too, identified an irreducible violence in being, the *Riss* of pursuer and pursued. Thom borrows Gestalt vocabulary to describe the salience of a mouse entering a zone created by the *prägnanz* of the cat's hunger, and his caveat reveals a secret of all behavior (perhaps). The caveat is that the cat must *recognize* the prey as such to trip the *autotropic* trigger, producing *camouflage* as a way of life. Indeed, an alternative allegory for konsult could be the chase genre in general, and the cat and mouse animated cartoon specifically (something by Chuck Jones preferably). Konsult addresses "separation from the star" (dis-aster) by applying phase space in choragraphy, to disclose the attractor basins (wells) capturing the forces configuring the scene. The moral of the cartoon fable is: keep the game going (dis/satisfaction), a symmetry of caricature and camouflage. Here is how Justice among predators may be managed in electracy.

Quasi-Modal Circulation

This book has developed at length the *Theory* resource of the CATTt guiding the invention of konsult as genre for electrate learning, assuming for realization the digital affordances of Stack. One lesson of this accumulation of resources is the agreement in general that digital metaphysics concerns Enjoyment operating through aesthetics. Konsult as genre of education organizing a transition from literacy to electracy, is a retrieval and updating of virtue (power) for electracy (Justice). The effect of designing konsult is a collective experience of the force of virtue, of in/capacity, im/potence. Every apparatus addresses power, but the metaphysics is different in each case, organizing differing realities (technologies, institutions, identities). Michel Serres is representative of contemporary philosophy in his explicit contrast with literate (Aristotelian) metaphysics of substance, committing instead to turbulence (element). In our terms this is the configurational shift from structure to rhythm. As was the case with Heidegger's "destruction" (deconstruction) of the first beginning, Serres also returns to the Classical epoch to find a new point of departure: Lucretius (Atomism). The difference is worth noting, since it has direct bearing on our theme of potentiality (*dunamis*). Aristotle's solution to the paradox of Being was Entelechy (beings fulfill their potential in becoming necessarily what they already are, finding their place, their proper end).

> With the idea of original multiplicity (everything that is may be unitary, but there is a countless number of such units), atomism introduced at once a new theory of movement and an alternative doctrine of contingency. Where Aristotle could only regard chance as an interruption in a pre-determined causal sequence, atomism allowed for contingency as the outcome of an indeterminate beginning. In Lucretius, this fundamental indeterminacy is articulated via the clinamen, which cannot therefore be interpreted as a cause of any kind. To be a cause—even as accidental or chance—is to be isolable. The clinamen, however, is by definition concealed beneath the lowest possible threshold of measurement. Its angle of deviation is indiscernible (David Webb, qtd. in Serres, *The Birth of Physics* xi).

Teleological growth is replaced as the model of "life" in digital rhythmics with "fluctuations of turbulence." Hence the emphasis on potentiality in electrate metaphysics: actualization becomes invention. "Without the vantage point required to survey the whole, thinking and writing chart their own paths as they find their way along, producing local cartographies that reflect the specificity of environments, both physical and epistemological" (Webb). Choragraphy is ontology.

Aristotle's categories, and the concepts generated by procedures of definition applying the categories, were positioned as overviews, surveying, looking down on the whole (God's universal vantage point). The positioning of the group shifter supporting egents, the virtual object that Serres calls the quasi-object (associated with all the versions of electrate "thing"), is in contrast fundamentally local, in the midst of a milieu. One of Serres's instructive models for the quasi-object (*furet*) is (again) a game (soccer), providing an analogy for shifter in egent utterance. His description of the ball game as model of turbulent discourse addresses our central question about how the shifter works to support a group subject (egent). "The furet is the animal, the ferret, as well as the marker in a game somewhat like hunt-the-slipper or button, button, who's got the button?"

> This quasi-object is not an object, but it is one nevertheless, since it is not a subject, since it is in the world; it is also a quasi-subject, since it marks or designates a subject who, without it, would not be a subject. He who is not discovered with the furet in his hand is anonymous, part of a monotonous chain where he remains undistinguished. He is not an individual; he is not recognized, discovered, cut; he is of the chain and in the chain. He runs, like the furet, in the collective. The thread in his hands is our simple relation, the absence of the furet; its path makes our indivision. Who are we? Those who pass the furet; those who don't have it. This quasi-object, when being passed, makes the collective, if it stops, it makes the individual. If he is discovered, he is "it" (mort). Who is the subject, who is an "I," or who am I? The moving furet weaves the "we," the collective; if it stops, it marks the "I." (Serres, *The Parasite* 225)

Serres then proposed the "ball" as furet. "Playing is nothing else but making oneself the attribute of the ball as a substance. The laws are written for it, defined relative to it, and we bend to these laws. Skill with the ball supposes a Ptolemaic revolution of which few theoreticians are capable, since they are accustomed to being subjects in a Copernican world where objects are slaves. The ball circulates just like the furet" (226). These passages resonate with Lacan's object @ and Trace of the part-object extended through exchange economies, whether of commodity or gift.

> This quasi-object that is a marker of the subject is an astonishing constructer of intersubjectivity. We know, through it, how and when we are subjects and when and how we are no longer subjects. "We": what does that mean? We are precisely the fluctuating moving back and forth of "I." The "I" in the game is a token exchanged. And this passing, this network of passes, these vicariances of subjects weave the collection. I am I now, a subject, that is to say, exposed to being thrown down, exposed to falling, to being placed beneath the compact mass of the others; then you take the relay, you are substituted for "I" and become it; later on, it is he who gives it to you, his work done, his danger finished, his part of the collective constructed. The "we" is made by the bursts and occultations of the "I." The "we" is

made by passing the "I." By exchanging the "I." And by substitution and vicariance of the "I." (*The Parasite* 227)

Serres shows why Bratton noted the User of Stack Interface will not have been Subject but actant (a position for rent, so to speak). The importance of televised sports as apparatus ritual is similarly noted (ESPN as electrate *Popol Vuh*). Each theory we have reviewed refines the invention further, thus adding further guidance for our own experiments, keeping in mind that everything reviewed here constitute instructions, not information. The terminology is critical—exchange, substitution, circulation. The ball game, in any sport, models metaphysics. The task of choragraphy as pedagogy is to assist annotation and navigation of this circulation, this vectoral rhythm, with the egents playing "they." The metaphysical context of the game allegory was noted previously in *Avatar Emergency*.

> The historical prototype is polo, invented in Ancient Persia. The sacred dimension of this game as ritual provided an allegory of life: you are the ball, the club is chance, the goal is destiny, god is the player (not you, you are not the player but the object in play). In dream logic (hole), we understand that we are the addressee of every aspect of the scene. The word "polo" means "ball," derived from Tibetan "pulu." This allegory was made most explicit in *The Ball and the Polo Stick*, by Arifi of Herat, a fifteenth-century Sufi's account of ecstatic self-sacrificing love (Huson 21). Huson notes that the allegory is invoked also in the *Rubaiyat* of Omar Khayyam (eleventh-century Sufi poet and astronomer) to figure human helplessness before god. The added value in our context is that the emblems representing the four elements making possible polo play (ball, stick, hole or goal, and stroke) are the historical basis for the four suits of playing cards, most importantly the four suits of the minor arcana of the Tarot (pentacles, wands, cups, swords). Tarot (and also the *I Ching*) is image metaphysics, primary sources available for retrieval as relays for an Internet education system. Divination is how the relationship between player and avatar was managed in the pre-modern habitus. A task for concept avatar is the secularization and updating of these traditional image metaphysics, to do for

electrate civilization what the oracles did for pre-modern cultures. (Ulmer 166)

Serres's heuristic, as we saw before with the goose's game relay, is that the ball game too is a phenomenal schema, a pattern. The four elements of the game (dramatizing case grammar articulating relations between perception and language) refer precisely to Element as the replacement for substance in electrate metaphysics. The four operators are "machinic" Deleuze and Guattari would say, and Serres has discussed *motor* as a model for the dynamic circulation we are mapping. Gregory Bateson's description of *system as motor* shows the correlation of the basic engine with circulating furet, in the paradigm of thermodynamic heat.

> Imagine a machine in which we distinguish, say, four parts, which I have loosely called "flywheel," "governor," "fuel," and "cylinder." In addition, the machine is connected to the outside world in two ways, "energy input" and "load," which is to be imagined as variable and perhaps weighing upon the flywheel. The machine is circular in the sense that flywheel drives governor which alters fuel supply which feeds cylinder which, in turn, drives flywheel. Because the system is circular, effects of events at any point in the circuit can be carried all around to produce changes at that point of origin (*Mind and Nature* 104).

The match with the elements or suits of polo are evident: cylinder = hole; flywheel = bat; governor = ball; fuel = stroke, with "god" as "energy input." In any case, the machinic is universal, present in the cultures of all the major civilizations. China codified the elements in a system of five phenomena, used as categories or mnemonic classifications: wood, fire, earth, metal, water. The thermodynamic scene is recognizable in some of the presentations, showing the positive and negative directions of possible relations among the elements (building a fire to boil water in a pot). The four figures interacting in Herriman's *Krazy Kat* provide an emblem for motor: *Kat, Mouse, Pup, Brick*. Perhaps Herriman is the prototypical metaphysian of electracy.

It is relevant in the context of Chora to include Buckminster Fuller's *Synergetics*, since his point of departure for modeling the fundamental principles of all systems is the Platonic solids, the polyhedrons. Fuller demonstrated that the minimum system (at every scale) may be modeled as a tetrahedron, with four vectors of constraint.

Assuming we can imagine an element that doesn't itself have any substance (the Greeks' dimensionless "point"), let's begin with two of them. There now exists a region between the two points—albeit quite an unmanageable region as it lacks any other boundaries. The same is true for three points, creating a triangular "betweenness," no matter how the three are arranged (so long as they are not in a straight line). In mathematics, any three noncollinear points define a plane; they also define a unique circle. Suddenly with the introduction of a fourth point, we have an entirely new situation. We can put that fourth point anywhere we choose, except in the same plane as the first three, and we invariably divide space into two sections: that which is inside the four-point system and that which is outside. Unwittingly, we have created the minimum system. Any material can demonstrate the procedure. The mathematical statement is unaltered by our choice: a minimum of four corners is required for existence. This minimum system was given the name tetrahedron (four sides) by the Greeks, after the four triangular faces created by the set of four vertices and their six edges (Edmondson 26–27)

Tetrahedron is the first of the five "solids" Plato introduced as building blocks of his cosmology in *Timaeus*. Fuller accepted the Greek nomenclature, although *Synergetics* assumed that "there are no solids, no continuous surfaces, only energy event complexes and relationships." Fuller's use of point, line, and plane as vectors to model the energy system productive of shape in space resonate with Paul Klee's poetics of graphic arts, in which the formal affordances of design model the energies of life. Most importantly, "synergy" is another example of emergence, naming the fact that the whole is greater than the sum of its parts. The strength of a geodesic dome, for example, exceeds considerably what would be predicted from the materials alone. This transmedial transversal minimum system grounds electrate metaphysics, giving an account of reality—an understanding to be applied in konsult to education for electrate Justice: fix the motor driving disaster.

GAMESCAPE

Choragraphy composes/designs within a group point of view (egency), and the function of konsult is to orient egents to their movement in an energy landscape. Theoria also was a group of tourist sages, whose enterprise we update from fourth to fifth estate. The mental model or interface of education is a phase space, a figure of which is found in Tarkovsky's *Stalker* (the Zone). Serres's proposal to open a Northwest Passage connecting the different divisions of knowledge makes his work helpful for understanding manifestations of phase space in phenomena, reminding us that complexity, topology, thermodynamics and the like, however abstract in their scientific principles, describe everyday reality. His texts are hybrids of literature, science, philosophy, autobiography, in which he proposes numerous quotidian models and relays with which to study the principles. One such model is the *jeu de l'oie* (goose's game):

> This game uses a board containing sixty-three squares arranged in a spiral configuration beginning from the outside and moving toward the center (hence the reference in Serres's text to a closed path circling back upon itself). A player throws two dice to advance a token along the squares. When a player lands on certain key squares, he is required to make special moves, for example, on the well square, the bridge square, the hotel square, the prison square, or the goose's square—Ed. (Serres, *Hermes* 40)

Serres proposed this children's board game as an emblem of the pattern he found in Zola's "Rougon-Macquart" cycle of novels (novels as archive of disposition). The pattern is generalizable as a vector map not just of narrative diegeses but as archetypes similar to the elementary catastrophes that inventory transformational potential in the lifeworld. The game model is a happy choice in our context because of its resonances with other sources guiding chorography: the archetypal locations (well, bridge, labyrinth . . .) evoke the naming formula of the elementary catastrophes of course, but also the system of chronotopes that Bakhtin found structuring various genres, one genre per locale. The sixty-three squares correlate with the sixty-four hexagrams of the *I Ching*, an image metaphysics relay relevant to electracy, and the spiral path references the vortex of Chora and thermodynamics. What interests Serres is the invariant path that insists in the pattern across a diverse archive of texts (vortex/t).

> Let us go back to the game's vignettes or emblems: bridge, well, labyrinth, hotel, prison, and death. . . . The bridge is a path that connects two banks, or that makes a discontinuity continuous, or that crosses a fracture, or that patches a crack. The space of

an itinerary is interrupted by a river; it is not a space of transport. Consequently, there is no longer one space; there are two without common boundaries. They are so different that they require a difficult, or dangerous, operator to connect their boundaries—difficult since at the very least a pontiff is necessary, dangerous since most of the time a devil of some sort stands watch or the enemies of Horatius Cocles stand ready to attack. Communication was interrupted; the bridge re-establishes it vertiginously. The well is a hole in space, a local tear in a spatial variety. It can disconnect a trajectory that passes through, and the traveler falls in, the fall of the vector, but it can also connect spatial varieties that might be piled upon one another: leaves, layers, geological formations. The bridge is paradoxical: it connects the disconnected. The well is more paradoxical still: it disconnects the connected, but it also connects the disconnected. The astronomer falls in (Thales); the truth comes out. The killer dragon lives there, but one draws the water of immortality from there. Mad aunt Dido throws the key into it, the key to the text, mind you, but the well (*puits*) contains all the seeds. And suddenly I am speaking with several voices; I can no longer draw the line between narrative, myth, and science. Is this bridge the Königsberg Bridge where Euler invented topology, a bridge over the Viorne or the Seine in the Rougon-Macquart cycle, or the whole group of bridges revealed in mythical discourse? No, I no longer have the choice, and it is the same bridge. Is this well a hole in Riemannian spatial varieties, a well of potentiality in which, at its lowest ebb, appears the germinating point, as in Thom, or the Plassans well, or Jacob's? No, I no longer have this choice, and it is the same well. In every case, and so much the worse for classification, connection and non-connection are at stake, space is at stake, an itinerary is at stake. And thus the essential thing is no longer this particular figure, this particular symbol, or this particular artefact; the formal invariant is something like a transport, a wandering, a journey across separated spatial varieties. Circumnavigation of Ulysses or of Gilgamesh and topology. (*Hermes* 42–43)

Such is transmedial rhetoric, useful for designing Interface as imaginal world. Serres makes explicit our intution of a mandala principle at work across all dimensions (plateaus) of Stack: these patterns do indeed register an isotopy, homology of layers we call popcycle. Humans are capable of fouring, although there are many more plateaus, but four suffice for User Interface. This topological archetypal "well" resonates with the "well" in "well-being" and the wellfield in "Murphy's Well-Being." The strata of konsult's mental model interpenetrate through keywords that function as wormholes transversing institutions and systems. The well of well-being is this choral well described by Serres. These dynamics are harnessed in the configuration of the mental model as elementary landscape. Serres's discussion of phase space in terms of game design is relevant to understanding composition of konsult as the construction of a "mental map" or "memory palace," a landscape of flesh, as interface for all the interactive systems of global education. Learning is an instance of a complex adaptive system, and our purpose is to explore the extent to which there is a certain isomorphism transversing all such systems (nature, culture, biography, history). Electrate learning is describable within a systems perspective, beginning with the popcyle of institutions within which identity is constructed.

Mystory (electrate equivalent of historiography) maps the position of a subject within the popcycle of institutions, to support learning ecology. In this respect, Bratton's insight into Stack Interface is fundamentally important, concerning the emergence of an image of wide scope from mystory, as the focus of education for heuretics (Ulmer, *Internet Invention*).

> This conceptual gathering refers to how a massively discontinouous assemblage line, bound toghether by exceedingly complex interfacial relays linking continents, must be understood and represented as if it were a single pattern or machine. For the Stack, such apparently comprehensive interfacial images of assemblage lines that themslevs comprise interfacial relays, are, for the *User*, a necessary tool to manage otherwise illegibly complex chains of interaction. It draws the discontiguous assemblage line into that resolved diagram, but to do so, it must, like all diagrams necessarily reduce and conceal the complexity of the processes it represents. . . . Ultimately the provision of an affectively compelling and instrumentally effective image of a composite interface chain becomes a strategic expertise, as information designers carve out a niche to provide convincing images of organization, tempo, and narrative. For *Users*, they compose cognitive maps of multiple layers of exchange drawn

at once, gathered into provisional total images (for which pattern recognition and intentional, motivated interpretation can start to merge). Moreover, such image interfaces are not only maps of flows as they exist according to whatever logic of reduction they invoke; they are also tools that reproject and extend their conceptual gathering of relations back out onto the world. (Bratton 234)

We understand now the value of Brodsky's composite city as EPS allegory of konsult. The ratio of Justice is micro-macrocosm correspondence, a fit between egent singular wide image and Absolute (Stack). Electrate education is heuretic, taking the long view, that living on in the coming community depends upon human capability, being-able, especially being capable of original invention, even at the level of fundamental values: capable of creating new values institutionalizing well-being against disaster.

Figure 8. Seminar Konsult, Jack Stenner, with Steve Rowell and students, 2015.

Interlude

Murphy's Well-Being (6)

MWB is a konsult experiment undertaken by the Florida Research Ensemble. It is not a template or model, but an example of one approach to designing an interface passage: hybrid of disciplinary knowledge and sensible idea. Part of the purpose of including these interludes in the book is to ground everything proposed in the CATTt Theory, including everything regarding quasi-objects as shifters, in Pepper as Trace. Pepper, afterall, may be ground. What is the demand of metaphysical Usufruct? Once Pepper was identifed behind Pine Tar as the motor of appetite in the genesis of commodities, a further insight followed, that became the theme of MWB pedagogy. Becoming electrate means *mise-en-machine* of autotropic FX, modeled in everything from Proust's involuntary memory to laughing at a joke. We can't help it! That is the pivot of vanguard modernism, revolution in the arts creating devices to author and design with the "little sensations" of digital metaphysics. Mark Seltzer cites Daniel Smail on "the emergence and spreading of autotropic commodities from the long eighteenth century on: self-stimulants such as alcohol, caffeine, chili pepper, opiates, tobacco, chocolate, sugar, gossip, sports, music, new media, religiosity, recreational drugs, sex for fun, and pornography. Last and not least is novel-reading and related forms of literary leisure." (Seltzer 41–42). Such is the flow (Tao) that belongs to us, pleasure-pain, not idea but buzz. MWB proposed in the medium and genre of interactive fable to introduce our community to its embodiment. Here is an outline of the venture.

Design Concept (Outline)

I. Konsult

A. EmerAgency Frame

1. Collective pedagogy = consulting. Goal: to provide the community, both citizens and decision-makers, insight into a policy problem based on discipline knowledge.

2. Konsult is a genre, with its own constraints and affordances. It is not entertainment, propaganda, activism, advocacy, documentary, or even story, finally.

3. Konsult appropriates "art" as method, in that it shares many features with various schools of modernist and postmodernist practices, but its function is consulting, as a form of institutional collective pedagogy.

B. Knowledge Insight

1. Chora: "Chora" means "region," functioning in metaphysics as interface between necessity (reality, what is, Being) and change (Becoming). It is a holistic or composite space-time, supporting the intersection or intertextuality of the primary discourses recording and shaping events in any particular location. "Reality" may be comprehended allegorically through the pattern emergent in the juxtaposition of these discourses (the popcycle): experience, mythology, history, philosophy. Gainesville, Florida, is Chora, for example. To understand "what happened" requires access to the full popcycle account.

2. Well-Being: Human civilization is organized to seek improvement of the human condition, our embodied sensory nature. This striving for improvement in quality of life produced ultimately the present order of industrial technology, the corporation and capitalist economy, the commodity form of exchange. Pine tar production at the Superfund site is an industrial commodity.

3. Insight: any commodity is a gift/poison (Pharmakon), meaning that it has costs as well as benefits, by-products and side effects. Pine tar is a "gift" in this sense.

C. Cabot-Koppers Superfund Site

1. There are ten Regions in the Superfund project. Florida is in Region Four, and is one of 1280 active sites of environmental disaster remediation in the United States.

2. Cabot corporation (for example) is a global enterprise, producing "performance materials to improve products," and as such is typical of the institutional form.

3. Pine tar historically is a detail in one of the central threads of world history, stretching from the spice trade in ancient times, through colonialism, to the present. The original purpose of pine tar (final cause) was to preserve the hulls of wooden ships used by the East India Company (the first modern corporation) and its equivalents to carry out European trade with Asian. The discovery of America is one of the "accidents" of this history.

D. Deliverable

1. Our Superfund disaster is "normal," a cost of doing business in industrial capitalism. Accidents are calculated in cost/benefit terms. This social model is founded on a fundamental value within a worldview and as such is not reparable, (or requires changing the value). The consequences of this civilizational decision may be ameliorated to some greater or lesser degree.

2. All citizens participate in this world order, and hence are complicit with it, and responsible for the risks. Some few citizens are sacrificed as "hostages" of fortune, exposing a position of "anyone."

3. The intended or desired insight is an experience of identification with the testimonials collected in the archive, at least to the degree of recognizing responsibility as community for "anyone."

II. Figure

A. Wellfield = Well-Being

1. The ordinating form is a figure, an analogy, informing the primary interface metaphor of the design: the condition of Murphree (Murphy) Wellfield may be understood figuratively as a measure of well-being of the community. The literal threat to our physical health is also a threat to our ethical stature. As Ben Franklin once said, we either hang together, or hang separately.

2. A Well of Stories: The installation platform, including all the equipment of the installation, the touchscreen map accessing the database of video clips, introduces vusers to the figure.

3. A trailer is the default video, constituting instructions by simulating not only the well in action but contextualizing it with some commentary, rationale.

B. "Murphy"

1. A principle of conductive logic native to electracy is that "nothing is hidden," or that at least the starting point of a konsultation should be the lexicon associated with a disaster. One of the oldest con games is the "Murphy Game," as it was called in the nineteenth century. The scammer uses a lure appealing to the mark's naiveté and/or greed, to switch the bait for something worthless.

2. The commodity structure, transposing use value into exchange value, is inherently a process of substitution, replicating in the economy the fundamental nature of language and rhetoric. One proof that a system is a true language is that it supports lies.

3. The name of Murphy Wellfield suggests that we are in a Murphy Game, and so is anyone who relies on commodities (or language). Any con game may evoke this condition. The analogy is loose, in that the switch leaves its marks not with something useless, but dangerous.

C. Insight

1. The installation tale as interactive narrative is an allegory (extended metaphor, figure).

2. A primary intended signification: a) We've been duped; b) It is our own fault.

III. Narrative

A. Fable

1. The figure is expressed through allegory. The allegory effect is created through a rhythm of repetitions across the tracks of the popcycle, each track including clips from narratives and documentaries. The basic effect is that of micro-cosm rendering legible the order of the macro-cosm.

2. Fable is structured as a particular anecdote suggesting a lesson or moral derived by generalizing the anecdote situation to other kinds of situations (it is a didactic form).

3. Testimonials (Stephen Foster neighbors): the denizen interviews, whatever they might "mean" on their own, are remotivated in context to express the insight of the konsult.

B. Cinematography

1. The General Cultural Interface (GCI) today is cinema, such that devices of montage, mise-en-scene and the like are familiar and legible.

2. The two-screen display supports a montage juxtaposition, correlated with the fable anecdote + moral. It proposes an implicit equation, leaving the final lesson open to interpretation.

3. Popcycle: the second screen or track is supplied by the popcycle discourses, supplying with mythology, history, or philosophy a context whose juxtaposition with the denizen anecdote produces a comment effect.

IV. Interactivity

A. Participation

1. Interactivity is a distinct feature of composition, on a par with narrative, with its own constraints and affordances. The assumption of interactivity is that some degree of control over the construction of the narrative and figure is entrusted to the user.

2. The Well interface prompts users to make selections, and the subsequent events of display solicit further investment of the user in the experience. The tradeoff in author control is potential greater vuser ownership of the meaning.

B. Competence

1. Interface metaphors guiding participation draw on cultural constructs already familiar to vusers.

2. Our design assumes general familiarity with cinematography, con games, fables, and consumer culture.

C. Crowdsourcing

1. Further engagement with both the spirit of fables and of konsulting is encouraged by inviting users to rate the value or insight of the presentation they selected (1 to 5 stars)
2. The assumption is that in any case each set of choices is recorded by the database, to allow some analysis later of signification generated through the process.
3. Users may annotate the rating, entering some text (tweet length) making explicit the moral of their fable.

V. Implementation

A. Selection and Sequence

1. In principle, given the reliance on repetition for the creation of meaning effects through patterning and montage, the popcycle archive maximizes testimonial clips, to be paired with a selective collection of clips representing the rest of the popcycle. The design idea is that testimonial clips are unlikely to repeat, while lesson clips are more likely to repeat across different testimonials, thus establishing through repetition the sense of the konsult.
2. Choice: vusers first select a testimonial. The clip is short, but they may choose to continue the interview, up to a certain limit of clips from that denizen. Then they choose a category to pair with the anecdotes for the second screen. The choice is restricted to one clip from each category (mythology, history, philosophy).
3. The reason for restricting popcycle matches to a maximum of one from each track is not to mix the metaphor, and thus dilute or confuse the fable. It is the same principle that discourages querents of an oracle to keep trying the system until they get the answer they prefer.
4. Vusers may run the choice sequence as often as desired.

B. Control

1. There are several options for the design of clips and their combination.
2. Simulation: complete control of clip content and which clips may combine with which is retained by the authors. This control is partially masked, and vusers' selection is limited to the

number of edits they initiate. This option requires more work from the authors, and returns less feedback about community experience.

3. Randomizing: at the other extreme from simulation is randomized access to a lightly edited archive of clips. This option turns over to crowdsourcing the task of generating possible significance, within the fable framing. The risk is that many of the combinations are "surreal" or nonsense, discouraging participation.

4. A third option is somewhere between simulation and randomizing.

5. Users know when the work is finished when the repetitions accumulate and they recognize the pattern: they get "it" (the figure).

C. Effect

1. The final determination of design depends upon desired effect. A related criterion might be effects we want to avoid.

2. Given the brief time many vusers are likely to spend with the installation, it is desirable to select the more pithy minutes of the interviews and other videos. As for control of matches, there is a tradeoff between eliminating unwanted ironies or matches that contradict our intention (on the one hand), and losing the potential for unanticipated insights (on the other).

3. Selection of clips for the lesson screen should have in mind the production of potentially interesting, moving, and or provoking combinations with the anecdotes.

4. Shot lists.

Murphy's Well-Being: A Trailer

https://youtu.be/A2Hs1K495Pc

The following text is a transcript of a trailer posted on YouTube referencing the EmerAgency konsult, entitled "Murphy's Well-Being."

1. [MONTAGE of Denizen portraits]

VO: Murphy's Wellbeing is a konsult, a genre for community deliberation on a Superfund emergency. There is a disturbance in the Wellness Field of North Central Florida. There is an appeal, a call from our neighborhoods, and from one neighborhood in particular, named for the songwriter Stephen Foster. It is a test of response-ability. What is that feeling: is it obligation? The stickiness of pine tar is an allegory of what bonds us with our neighbors.

2. [MUSIC FADES in: "Old Folks At Home." Clip: Gone With the Wind. Music continues under throughout trailer]

VO: How can the Stephen Foster neighborhood serve as a fable about the wellness of America? First, because Stephen Foster is acclaimed as the Father of American music. Composing "Old Folks At Home" for a blackface troupe in 1851, Foster needed a name for the river referred to in the lyrics. Foster never visited the South, but he found the name "Swanee" in a dictionary. A version of the song, bowdlerized to remove reminders of the slavery institutionalized in the antebellum South, is now the State Song of Florida. Stephen Foster imagined our plantation as an image of happiness. If only it was as easy to purify our water as it is to clean up history!

3. [Clip: Citizen Kane, Orson Welles, conclusion, the mansion "Xanadu."]

VO: Who else imagined our happiness? Samuel Taylor Coleridge, in "Kubla Khan," one of the greatest poems of the Romantic imagination, invented a composite city called "Xanadu." "In Xanadu did Kubla Khan a stately pleasure dome decree." Coleridge based his description of the pleasure dome mostly on Bartram's Travels, published in the late eighteenth century, in which Bartram described the karst topography of North Central Florida. Four sites are composited in Xanadu: Shangdu (Kubla Khan's capital city), the mountains of Kashmir, the caves of Abyssinia, and the sinkholes and underground river of Alachua County. In other words, what happens to us, is happening in Xanadu! Xanadu is polluted, and the old folks at home testify to the disaster.

4. [Clip: Demo of the Well with vuser using the touch screen, making choices, scenes appearing on the two screens, making more choices . . .]

VO: The Florida Research Ensemble produced Murphy's Wellbeing, to help us understand our fix. Other consultants inform the community about engineering options, or corporate calculations of cost-benefit outcomes. EmerAgency consultants add the insights of Arts and Letters expertise, concerned with the measure of wellbeing, which we know is "priceless." The testimony of our neighbors is a call not just to duty, but to Xanaduty.

5. [Demo continues, now a simulation . . . A Denizen Interview]

VO: The Well of Stories is a database Xanadu, a potential fable to remind us that the local is global. As Xanaduans, we live in four places simultaneously: Alachua County, India, Hollywood, and Utopia. Four forces shape our destiny, recorded in four subplots, the first of which consists of the testimonies of neighbors, reporting from the disaster zone. The second track is the history of pine tar. It is the story of corporations, going back to the discovery of America by Europeans trying to get to India to trade in pepper and other spices. They treated the hulls of their ships with pine tar. The third subplot is our mythology, dramatized in Hollywood tales of superheroes that express our belief in the capacity of individuals to change the world. The fourth subplot is philosophy, the voice of wisdom, explaining our ideals about wellbeing, about how the world should be.

6. [Still: Chinese Ideogram "Happiness," FADE to chorus singing, FADE to Demo of the Well in use]

VO: If the story of Murphy's Wellbeing is a fable of Xanaduty, its moral remains to be constructed by interacting with the Well. What is our answer to the ancient question, "how should we live?" The Well is an archive of narrative tracks, to be explored in basic montage units, a collective fable composed one ideogram at a time. The fable emerges by juxtaposing neighbor testimonies with passages from the other Xanadu places. You consult with the Well by selecting neighbors, and relating them to one or more of the subplots shaping their world—History, Mythology, Philosophy (repeat as often as you like). The inventors of cinema learned from Asian ideograms how to express thought by means of images. An ideogram combines two sensory properties to evoke an immaterial thought. The Chinese character for "Happiness" combines the figure of "Music" (a hand striking a drum) with "Singing" (an open mouth). "Happiness" is a feeling like that expressed in a song, a song such as "Old Folks at Home," way down upon the Murphy Wellness Field. How do these ideograms make you feel?

7. [Demo continue]

VO: A clue to the moral of the fable is in the very name of "Murphy's Wellfield," since "the Murphy Game" is a classic confidence trick, a bait and switch scam native to American folk culture. We wanted pepper, and got poison. If you used pepper today, you helped pollute Xanadu. The pine tar commodity produced at the Cabot-Koppers site is a kind of tar baby, like the one created by Br'er Fox and Br'er Bear to catch Br'er Rabbit, in the fables adapted to cinema in Walt Disney's *Song of the South*. But is that really our song, our South? There is a note of optimism in these stories, since the trickster rabbit always extricated himself from the fix. Let us hope that is also our story.

Works Cited

Agamben, Giorgio. *Stanzas: Word and Phantasm in Western Culture*. Translated by Ronald L. Martinez, U of Minnesota P, 1992.

—. *Potentialities: Collected Essays in Philosophy*. Translated by Daniel Heller-Roazen, Stanford UP, 2000.

—. *Language and Death: The Place of Negativity*. Translated by Karen Pinkus, U of Minnesota P, 2006.

—. "What Is an Apparatus?" *and Other Essays*. Stanford UP, 2009.

Augst, Bertrand. "The *Défilement* Into the Look." *Cinematographic Apparatus: Selected Writings*, edited by Theresa Hak Kyung Cha, Tanam P, 1980, pp. 249-59.

Azari, Ehan. *Lacan and the Destiny of Literature*. Continuum, 2009.

Bacon, Francis. *The Advancement of Learning*. CreateSpace Independent Publishing, 2016.

Bataille, Georges, et al., *Encyclopaedia Acephalica*. Translated by Iain White, et al., Atlas P, 1995.

Barber, Benjamin R. *Jihad Vs. McWorld: How Globalism and Tribalism are Reshaping the World*. Ballantine, 1996.

Barthes, Roland. *Critical Essays*. Translated by Richard Howard, Northwestern UP, 1972.

—. "Theory of the Text," *Untying the Text: A Post-Structuralist Reader*, edited by Robert Young, Routledge and Kegan Paul, 1981, pp. 31-47.

Bateson, Gregory. *Mind and Nature: A Necessary Unity*. Bantam, 1979.

Baudelaire, Charles. *Baudelaire: Selected Writings on Art and Literature*. Penguin Classics, 1993.

Bennett, Jane. *Vibrant Matter: a Political Ecology of Things*. Duke University Press, 2010.

Bloom, Harold. *Omens of the Millennium: The Gnosis of Angels, Dreams, and Resurrection*. Riverhead Books, 1997.

Blumenberg, Hans. *The Legitimacy of the Modern Age*. Translated by Robert M. Wallace, MIT P, 1985.
Bois, Yves-Alain, and Rosalind Kraus. *Formless: A User's Guide*. Zone Books, 1997.
Boym, Svetlana. *The Future of Nostalgia*. Basic Books, 2001.
Bratton, Benjamin H. *The Stack: On Software and Sovereignty*. MIT P, 2015.
Briggs, John. *Fire in the Crucible: The Alchemy of Creative Genius*. St Martin's P, 1988.
Brodsky, Joseph. *Watermark*. Farrar, Straus, and Giroux, 1993.
—. "The Condition We Call Exile." *Altogether Elsewhere: Writers on Exile*, edited by Marc Robinson, Harvest, 1994, pp. 3-11.
—. "A Place as Good as Any." *On Grief and Reason: Essays*. Farrar, Straus and Girous, 1997, pp. 35-43.
—. *Collected Poems in English*. Farrar, Straus and Giroux: 2000.
Brogan, Walter A. *Heidegger and Aristotle: The Twofoldness of Being*. SUNY P, 2006.
Calvino, Italo. *Invisible Cities*. Translated by William Weaver. Harcourt Brace Jovanovich Press, 1978.
Carbonne, Mauro. *La visibilité de l'invisible*. Georg Olms Verlag, 2001.
Cavell, Stanley. *Cities of Words: Pedagogical Letters on a Register of the Moral Life*. Harvard UP, 2005.
Chaitin, Gilbert D. *Rhetoric and Culture in Lacan*. Cambridge UP, 1996.
Cheetham, Tom. *The World Turned Inside Out: Henry Corbin and Islamic Mysticism*. Spring Journal Books, 2003.
Chernyakov, Alexei. *The Ontology of Time: Being and Time in the Philosophy of Aristotle, Husserl and Heidegger*. Springer Publishers, 2002.
Chocano, Carina, "Revolution Blues." *The New York Times Magazine*, August 16, 2015. https://www.nytimes.com/2015/08/16/magazine/how-rock-star-became-a-business-buzzword.html
Clark, T. J. *The Painting of Modern Life: Paris in the Art of Manet and His Followers*. Revised ed., Princeton UP, 1999.
Coates, Ta-Nehisi Paul. "Why "Tar Baby" Is Such a Sticky Phrase. *Time*, 1 Aug, 2006. http://content.time.com/time/nation/article/0,8599,1221764,00.html#ixzz1csSoAMEv.
Cristin, Renato. *Heidegger and Leibniz: Reason and the Path*. Translated by Gerald Parks, Springer, 1998.
Damisch, Hubert. *Jana Sterbak: Waiting for High Water*. Canadian Cultural Centre, 2006.
Darley, Andrew. *Visual Digital Culture: Surface Play and Spectacle in New Media Genres*. Routledge, 2000.
Deleuze, Gilles. *Difference and Repetition*. 1968. Translated by Paul Patton, Columbia UP, 1994
—. *Proust and Signs*. 1964. Translated by Richard Howard, Athlone P, 2000.

Derrida, Jacques. *Margins of Philosophy*. Translated by Alan Bass. Chicago: U of Chicago P, 1982.
—. "Geschlecht: sexual difference, ontological difference," *Research in Phenomenology*, volume XIII, 1983, pp. 65-83.
—. *Edmund Husserl's "Origin of Geometry," An Introduction*. Translated by John P. Leavey, Jr., U of Nebraska P, 1989.
—. "Artefactualités." *Echographies, de la* television, edited by Jacques Derrida and Bernard Stiegler, Galilée-INA, 1996.
—, et al., *Chora L Works: Jacques Derrida and Peter Eisenman*. The Monacelli P, 1997.
—. "To Unsense the Subjectile." *The Secret Art of Antonin Artaud*. Translated by Mary Ann Caws, MIT P, 1998, pp. 61-167.
—. *Parages*. Translated by John Leavey, et al., Stanford UP, 2010.
"The Duchess." Shmoop.com, 2019. https://www.shmoop.com/alice-in-wonderland-looking-glass/duchess.html.
Durand, Gilbert. *The Anthropological Structures of the Imaginary*. Translated by Margaret Sankey and Judith Hatten, Boombana Publications, 1999.
Edmondson, Amy C. *A Fuller Explanation: The Synergetic Geometry of R. Buckminster Fuller*. EmergentWorld, 2009.
Ekeland, Ivar. *Mathematics and the Unexpected*. U of Chicago P, 1988.
Emonet, Pierre-Marie. *The Dearest Freshness Deep Down Things: An Introduction to the Philosophy of Being*. Crossroad Publishing Company, 1999.
Fernald, James. *English Synonyms and Antonyms*. Ulan P, 2012. http://www.gutenberg.org/ebooks/28900.
Fletcher, Angus. *A New Theory for American Poetry: Democracy, the Environment, and the Future of Imagination*. Harvard UP, 2004.
French, Philip. "Le Quatro Volte—Review." *The Guardian*, May, 2011. http://www.theguardian.com/film/2011/may/29/le-quattro-volte-michelangelo-frammartino.
Freud, Sigmund. *Abstracts of the Standard Edition of the Complete Psychological Works of Sigmund Freud*. International Universities P, 1973.
Gregory, Paola. *New Scapes: Territories of Complexity*. Birkhäuser, 2003.
Greimas, Algirdas Julien, and Jacques Fontanille. *The Semiotics of Passions: From States of Affairs to States of Feelings*. Translated by Paul Perron and Frank Collins, U of Minnesota, 1993.
Guattari, Félix. *Chaosmosis: An Ethico-Aesthetic Paradigm*. 1992. Translated by Paul Bains and Julian Pefanis, Power Publications, 1995
—. *The Machinic Unconscious: Essays in Schizoanalysis*. 1979. Translated by Taylor Adkins, Semiotext(e), 2011.
Hansen, Mark B. N. *Embodying Technesis: Technology Beyond Writing*. U of Michigan P, 2000.
Hardt, Michael, and Antonio Negri. *Empire*. Harvard UP, 2001.

Havelock, Eric. *The Greek Concept of Justice: From Its Shadow in Homer to its Substance in Plato*. Harvard UP, 1978.
Haven, Cynthia L. ed. *Joseph Brodsky: Conversations*. UP of Mississippi, 2002.
Heidegger, Martin. "The Thing." *Poetry, Language, Thought*, translated by Albert Hofstadter, Harper and Row, 1971, pp. 163-80.
—. *Early Greek Thinking*. Translated by David Farrell Krell and Frank A. Capuzzi, Harper and Row, 1975.
—. *On Time and Being*. Translated by Joan Stambaugh, U of Chicago, 2002.
Holton, Gerald. "Presuppositions in the Construction of Theories." *Science and Literature: New Lenses for Criticism*, edited by M. Jennings, Anchor Books, 1970, pp. 23762.
Huson, Paul. *Mythical Origins of the Tarot*. Destiny Books, 2004.
Inferno Summary. Sparknotes, 2019. http://www.sparknotes.com/poetry/inferno
"Institute-Wide Task Force on the Future of MIT Education: Final Report." MIT, July 28, 2014.
Irigaray, Luce. *Speculum of the Other Woman*. Translated by Gillian C. Gill, Cornell UP, 1985.
Isozaki, Arata. *Japan-ness in Architecture*. Translated by Sabu Kohso, MIT, 2006.
Janicaud, Dominique. *Heidegger from Metaphysics to Thought*. Translated by Michael Gendre, SUNY P, 1994.
Jencks, Charles. "Madelon Seeing Through Objects." http://madelonvriesendorp.com/wp-content/uploads/2015/03/Jenx-piece.pdf
Kentridge, William. *Six Drawing Lessons*. Harvard UP, 2014.
Klossowski, Pierre. *Diana at her Bath. The Women of Rome*. Translated by Stephen Sartarelli and Sophie Hawkes, Eridanos P, 1990.
Koder, Selim. "Interview with Peter Eisenman." *Intelligent Environment. Ars Electronica Archive*, http://90.146.8.18/en/archives/festival_archive/festival_catalogs/festival_artikel.asp?iProjectID=8672). August 19, 2015.
Koestler, Arthur. *The Act of Creation*. Dell, 1964.
Kristeva, Julia. *Revolution in Poetic Language*. Translated by Margaret Waller, Columbia UP, 1984.
—. "The Subject in Process." *The Tel Quel Reader*, edited by Patrick French and Roland-François Lack, Routledge, 1998, pp. 133-78.
—. *Hannah Arendt: Life Is a Narrative*. Translated by Ross Guberman, Columbia UP, 2001.
Lacan, Jacques. *The Ethics of Psychoanalysis, Book VII (The Seminar of Jacques Lacan)*. Translated by Dennis Porter, Norton, 1997.
—. *The Four Fundamental Concepts of Psychoanalysis, Book XI (The Seminar of Jacques Lacan)*. Translated by Alan Sheridan, Norton, 1998.
—. *Seminar XII, Crucial Problems for Psychoanalysis, 1964–1965*. Translated by Cormac Gallagher, Karnac Books.,nd. http://www.lacaninireland.com/web/published-works/seminars/

—. *Seminar XIV, The Logic of Phantasy, 1966–1967.* Translated by Cormac Gallagher, Karnac Books, nd. http://www.lacaninireland.com/web/published-works/seminars/

—. *Seminar XVIII, On a Discourse that might not be a Semblance, 1970–1971.* Translated by Cormac Gallagher, Karnac Books, nd. http://www.lacaninireland.com/web/published-works/seminars/

—. *Seminar XX, On Feminine Sexuality, The Limits of Love and Knowledge (Encore).* Translated by Bruce Fink, W. W. Norton & Company, 1999.

___. Seminar XXII, R. S. I.: 1974-1975. Translated by Jacqueline Rose http://www.lacaninireland.com/web/translations/seminars/

___. Seminar XXIII, The Sinthome. Translated by A. R. Price, Edited by Jacques-Alain Miller, Polity Press, 2016.

—. "Lituraterre," Translated by Jack W. Stone, http://web.missouri.edu/~stonej/Lituraterre.pdf) (2/14/2015).

Lawlor, Robert. *Sacred Geometry.* Thames and Hudson, 1982.

Lefebvre, Henri. *Rhythmanalysis: Space, Time, and Everyday Life.* Translated by Gerald More and Stuart Elden, Bloomsbury Academic, 2013.

Lenfield, Spencer. "William Kentridge: 'In Praise of Shadows.'" *Harvard Magazine,* July 30, 2015, http://harvardmagazine.com/2012/03/william-kentridge-in-praise-of-shadows.

Lévi-Strauss, Claude. *The Raw and the Cooked: Introduction to a Science of Mythology: I.* Translated by John and Doreen Weightman, Harper and Row, 1969.

Lingis, Alphonso. "Translator's Preface." *Maurice Merleau-Ponty. The Visible and the Invisible,* Northwestern UP, 1969.

Long, Christopher P. *The Ethics of Ontology: Rethinking an Aristotelian Legacy.* SUNY P, 2004.

McEwen, Indra Kagis. *Socrates' Ancestor: An Essay on Architectural Beginnings.* MIT P, 1993.

MacFadyen, David. *Joseph Brodsky and the Baroque.* McGill-Queen's UP, 1998.

McLuhan, Marshall, and Eric McLuhan. *Laws of Media.* Toronto, Canada: U of Toronto P, 1992.

Maranhao, Tulio, Ed. *The Interpretation of Dialogue.* Chicago: U of Chicago, 1990.

Mathieu, Georges. *De la révolte à la renaissance: Au-delà du Tachisme.* Paris: Gallimard, 1972.

Merleau-Ponty, Maurice. *The Visible and the Invisible,* Ed. Claude Lefort, Translated by Alphonso Lingis, Northwestern UP, 1968.

Miller, Jacques-Alain. "A Note Threaded Stitch by Stitch," in Jacques Lacan, Seminar XXIII, 2016.

Morton, Timothy. *The Poetics of Spice: Romantic Consumerism and the Exotic.* Cambridge UP. 2006.

—. *Hyperobjects: Philosophy and Ecology After the End of the World*. U of Minnesota P, 2013.

Mundy, Jennifer, ed. *Surrealism: Desire Unbound*. Princeton UP, 2001.

Myall, Steve. "Malala Yousafzai tells of the moment she was shot in the head by the Taliban." Mirror, 13 October, 2013. https://www.mirror.co.uk/news/uk-news/malala-yousafzai-tells-moment-shot-2365460.

Naifeh, Steven, and Gregory White Smith. *Van Gogh: The Life*. Random House, 2011.

Oates, Joyce Carol. "Inspiration and Obsession in Life and Literature." *The New York Review of Books*, August 13, 2015. https://www.nybooks.com/articles/2015/08/13/inspiration-and-obsession-life-and-literature/

Polt, Richard. *The Emergency of Being: On Heidegger's "Contributions to Philosophy."* Cornell UP, 2006.

Protevi, John. *Time and Exteriority: Aristotle, Heidegger, Derrida*. Bucknell UP, 1994.

Proust, Marcel. *The Past Recaptured*. Translated by Andreas Mayor, Vintage Books, 1970.

Rapaport, Herman. *Heidegger and Derrida: Reflections on Time and Language*. U of Nebraska P, 1991.

Rilke, Rainer Maria. "The Duino Elegies." July 30, 2015, http://www.poetryintranslation.com/PITBR/German/Rilke.htm#anchor_Toc509812215.

Rothstein, Edward. *Emblems of Mind*. Avon Books, 1995.

Ruskin, John. *The Stones of Venice*. Da Capo Press; 2nd Edition, 2003.

Ruthven, K. K. *The Conceit*. Methuen, 1969.

Sartre, Jean-Paul. *Nausea*. Translated by Lloyd Alexander, New Directions, 1964.

Schmidt, Dennis J. *Between Word and Image: Heidegger, Klee, and Gadamer on Gesture and Genesis*. Indiana UP, 2013.

Seltzer, Mark. *The Official World*. Duke UP, 2016.

Sen, Amartya. *Development as Freedom*. Anchor Books, 2000.

—. *The Idea of Justice*. Harvard UP, 2009.

Serres, Michel. *The Parasite*, Translated by Lawrence R. Schehr. Baltimore: Johns Hopkins UP, 1982.

—*Hermes: Literature, Science, Philosophy*. Edited by Josué Harari and David F. Bell, Johns Hopkins UP, 1982a.

—. *The Troubadour of Knowledge*. Translated by Sheila Faria Glaser with William Paulson, U of Michigan P, 1997. (Published in France, 1991, as *Le Tiers-Instruit*).

—. *The Birth of Physics*. Translated by Jack Hawkes, Clinamen P, 2001.

Sloterdijk, Peter. *Rage and Time: A Pschopolitical Investigation*. Translated by Mario Wenning, Columbia UP, 2010.

Smith, Cyril Stanley. "Structural Hierarchy in Science, Art, and History." *On Aesthetics in Science*, edited by Judith Wechsler, MIT P, 1978, pp. 9-53.

Spieker, Sven. *The Big Archive: Art from Bureaucracy*. MIT P, 2008.
Stiegler, Bernard. *What Makes Life Worth Living: On Pharmacology*. Translated by Daniel Ross, Polity P, 2013.
Stoichita, Victor I. *The Pygmalion Effect: From Ovid to Hitchcock*. Translated by Alison Anderson, U of Chicago P, 2008.
Thom, René. *Semio Physics: A Sketch*. Translated by Vendla Meyer, Addison-Wesley Publishing, 1990.
Thomas, Lewis. *The Lives of a Cell: Notes of a Biology Watcher*. Penguin Books, 1978.
Ulmer, Gregory L. *Teletheory: Grammatology in the Age of Video*. Routledge, 1989.
—. *Heuretics: The Logic of Invention*. Johns Hopkins UP, 1994.
—. *Electronic Monuments*. U of Minnesota P, 2005.
—. *Avatar Emergency*. Parlor P, 2012.
—. *Miami Virtue: Choragraphy of the Virtual City*. Small Cities Imprint, vol. 3, no. 2, 2012a. http://smallcities.tru.ca/index.php/cura/issue/view/5.
Villa, Dana R. *Arendt and Heidegger: The Fate of the Political*, Princeton UP, 1996.
Wark, McKenzie. *Telesthesia: Communication, Culture, and Class*. Polity P, 2012.
Webb, David. "Introduction." *The Birth of Physics* by Michel Serres, 2001.
Weber, Samuel. *Benjamin's -abilities*. Harvard UP, 2008.
Wenders, Wim. *Once*, D.A.P., 2010.
Winterson, Jeanette. "Venice, City of Mazes." June 11, 2007. http://www.jeanettewinterson.com/journalism/venice-city-of-mazes/
Wildgen, Wolfgang. *Catastrophe Theoretic Semantics*. John Benjamins Publishing, 1982.
Williams, William Carlos. *Asphodel: That Greeny Flower and Other Love Poems*. New Directions, 1994.
Yousafzai, Malala. "Speech to the United Nations." http://www.bbc.com/news/world-asia-23291897.
Žižek, Slavoj. *Looking Awry: An Introduction to Jacques Lacan through Popular Culture*. MIT P, 1991.

Index

Absolute, 5, 11, 16, 19, 20, 25, 30, 40, 79, 93, 97, 140, 192, 245
accident, 40, 59, 63, 66, 137, 159, 167
actant, 5, 7, 20, 95, 112, 114, 121, 139, 155, 168, 194, 209, 235, 239
advertising, 131, 164
Aesop, xvi, 119, 123
aesthetics, xxiv, 21, 99, 124, 137, 143, 146, 171, 193, 198, 212, 236
Agamben, Giorgio, 4, 60, 176–179, 185–186, 189–194, 198, 220, 225, 227
aletheia, 62, 70, 177, 184, 198
algorithm, 124, 133
alienation, 85, 93, 95–96, 101, 112–113, 122, 186, 203, 223
allegory, ix, 14–17, 20, 26, 28, 30, 32–33, 38, 40, 46, 49, 53, 55–56, 69, 70, 72, 78, 96, 128, 158, 168, 170, 173, 192, 200, 212, 233, 236, 239, 245, 250–251, 254
alphabetic writing, 13, 41, 50, 62–63, 65, 67, 135, 138, 198, 219, 226

analogy, x, xv–xix, 5, 8–10, 14, 32, 41, 53, 70, 73, 88, 99, 104, 109, 127–128, 140, 142, 157, 165, 173, 198, 200, 216, 229, 233, 237, 250
Anaximander, 64–67, 68, 72, 89, 129, 134, 144–145, 152, 200
Anna O., 33, 34, 104, 220
annotation, xix, xxii, 137, 139, 146, 152, 156, 170, 175, 182, 200, 217, 239
Anthropocene, 64, 69, 213
anthropomorphism, xvii
Antigone, 65, 97, 107, 135
anxiety, 32, 49, 118, 210
aporia, xv, xxii, 17, 27, 65–66, 69, 94, 97, 100, 106, 108–110, 171–172, 185, 193, 224
apparatus, x–xi, 3–5, 7–10, 16–17, 19–21, 24–26, 29–30, 50–51, 60–61, 66–67, 71, 86–91, 98–103, 110–111, 133–135, 143–145, 147, 176–178, 188–189, 194–195, 198–201, 210–212, 227–228, 231–232
apparatus theory, xi, 17, 64, 219
appetite, xxiv, 30, 50, 62, 86, 89, 104, 121, 151, 163, 170–171, 222, 228, 247

265

appropriation, 31, 66, 70, 92, 137, 147, 149, 152, 164, 181, 189, 195, 226
arbitrage, 51
archive, x, xx, xxv, 11, 13, 44, 47, 56, 62, 105, 110, 117–118, 123, 166, 187, 192, 200–201, 207, 220–221, 242, 249, 252–253, 255
Arendt, Hannah, xxiv, 74–75, 94, 160
Aristophanes, 10, 142–143
Aristotle, xxiv, 10, 19, 29, 41, 56–57, 59, 60, 63–64, 73, 74, 91, 105–106, 135, 166–167, 170–174, 176–178, 180, 182–185, 188–190, 193, 196, 198, 200–201, 204, 212, 217–219, 233–234, 236, 237
Artaud, Antonin, 148–149, 151, 152, 153
artefact, 64, 243
Até, 135, 165
attitude, 4, 6, 8, 33, 41, 97, 119, 120, 160, 179, 196, 207, 220
attraction-repulsion, xxiii, 9, 16, 19, 29, 34, 39, 77, 89, 94, 102, 113, 131–132, 148, 150, 181, 184, 190, 195, 204, 218, 220
attunement, xv, 32, 43, 77, 143
Augenblick, 76, 232
aura, 47, 51
autodidactic, 3, 11
autotropic, 236, 247
avatar, xv, 4–5, 16, 19–21, 83, 239; concept, 239

Bachelard, Gaston, 139
bachelor machine, xxiv, 10, 60, 112, 131, 133, 157, 174, 194
Bacon, Francis, 57
Badiou, Alain, 27
Bakhtin, Mikhail, 226, 230, 242

Barber, Benjamin R., 9, 10
Barthes, Roland, 90, 100, 133, 148, 161
Bataille, George, xxiii, 94, 131, 132, 133, 140, 147, 148
Bateson, Gregory, 240
Battlestar Galactica, 124
Baudelaire, Charles, 110, 112, 137, 161, 180, 182, 203
Baudrillard, Jean, 10
beauty, 11, 16, 21, 41, 54, 68, 88, 94, 120, 128, 177, 180
being, ix– xiii, 10–11, 17–19, 29–32, 55–61, 63–68, 89–92, 100–102, 106–109, 120–121, 135–136, 172–174, 187–192, 195–197, 200–204, 212, 213, 218–220, 233–238, 244–245
Benjamin, Walter, xix, 9, 40, 75, 79, 110, 160, 178, 179, 180, 181, 182, 185, 193, 198, 199, 217, 227
Bennett, Jane, 228
bethinking, xx, 21
Bhagavad Gita, xv, 5, 19; Arjuna, xv, 5, 20, 209; Krishna, xv, 5, 20, 209
Blanchot, Maurice, xxi, 21, 85, 147, 156, 157
Bloom, Harold, 7, 15, 114, 118
Bluebeard, 94
Blumenberg, Hans, 5, 20, 175
body, 9, 16, 25, 31–34, 42, 44, 89– 94, 100–103, 111–112, 125–126, 148–153, 200–202, 210, 223, 226
bootstrapping, xii, 61
Botticelli, Sandro, 16, 32, 229
boundary object, xv, xvi, xxii, 17, 210
brand, 4, 5, 20

Bratton, Benjamin, xix, 79, 85, 95, 168, 194, 219, 223, 236, 239, 244, 245
bridge, 71, 145, 225, 242
Brillat-Savarin, Jean Anthelme, 189
Brodsky, Joseph, 50, 51, 52, 53, 55, 61, 64, 72, 73, 76, 77, 78, 87, 95, 133, 136, 141, 170, 186, 195, 245; *Watermark*, 50, 51, 52, 53, 54, 55, 59, 72, 78, 133, 139
Burke, James, 39; Connections, 39
Burke, Kenneth, 60

cabaret, 10, 130
Cabot-Koppers, xxv, 37, 39, 40, 164, 167, 249, 256
calculus, 128
calligraphy, 141, 142, 143
Calvino, Italo, 47
Cameron, James: Avatar, 38
camouflage, 236
capabilities, xxiii, 25, 57, 71, 74, 75, 176, 193, 198
capacity, 9, 13, 17–18, 26–30, 74, 155, 171, 181–189, 191–196, 201–203, 214, 218, 220–223, 226, 234, 236,
caricature, 119, 173, 202, 236
Carroll, Lewis, 119
catabasis, 83
catalysis, 44, 104, 117, 120, 192, 200, 226, 229, 234
catastrophe theory, 159
category, xii, 24, 38, 54, 59, 61, 63, 65, 66, 83, 99, 226, 252
CATTt, xii, xiv, xxi, xxii, xxiii, xxiv, 55, 60, 70, 87, 88, 122, 125, 133, 144, 170, 190, 216, 217, 227, 234, 236, 247
Cavell, Stanley, 26, 27, 28, 30, 32, 33, 52, 90, 92, 106, 108, 157, 233
celebrity, 63

Cézanne, Paul, 139, 201, 202, 204
chaosmosis, 218, 220, 222, 225, 231
character, xiv, 24, 32, 49, 90, 123, 142, 168, 208, 215, 223, 255
chora, 39, 70, 95, 149, 176, 193, 200
choragraphy, xviii, xix, xxii, 39, 78, 92, 114, 126, 127, 176, 177, 185, 186, 188, 190, 195, 202, 216, 217, 220, 221, 222, 231, 232, 236, 239, 242
circulation, 86, 110, 120, 222, 223, 224, 231, 239, 240
climate change, 17, 158
cogito, 90, 91, 95, 96, 101, 132, 204, 221
collaboration, x, xiv, xvi, xxii, xxv, xxvi, 39, 45, 56, 81, 217
commodity, 73, 86, 101, 102, 104, 120, 163, 164, 196, 217, 223, 224, 225, 233, 238, 248, 249, 250, 256
conatus, xx, xxiii, 25, 30, 89, 227
conceit, 72, 73, 74, 77, 84, 87, 98
conceptual persona, xxi, 49, 50, 87, 144, 170, 186, 195, 234
conduction, 86, 133, 139, 159, 174
constraint, 240
contamination, 37, 82, 195, 209
contradiction, 90, 93, 108, 131, 185, 201, 204, 210, 219, 234
Corbin, Henry, 7, 21, 71, 107
corporation, xi, 9, 17, 85, 121, 151, 163, 164, 209, 248, 249
cosmology, ix, 8, 21, 67, 76, 95, 98, 103, 108, 126, 136, 139, 151, 157, 159, 200, 203, 217, 241
counsel, 169, 207
courtly love, 193
crossing, 96, 112, 199, 234

crossroads, 76, 91
Cubism, 201
cyberspace, 4

Dadaism, 10, 146
Daedalus, 68, 72, 78, 129, 157
daidala, 68, 69, 70
Damisch, Hubert, 47
Dante Alighieri, 38, 82, 83, 117, 191
Dasein, xx, 11, 25, 26, 43, 66, 92, 96, 136, 188, 203, 228
database, xxv, 41, 44, 56, 118, 123, 134, 207, 218, 250, 252, 255
decision, 21, 27, 42, 62, 63, 67, 73, 95, 122, 135, 147, 170, 180, 183, 184, 186, 192, 216, 228, 248, 249
deconstruction, 62, 63, 172, 198, 236
definition, xi, xvi, xviii, xxiv, 5, 13, 27, 30, 41, 54, 58, 65, 104, 112, 124, 136, 148, 164, 167, 204, 209, 210, 219, 224, 237
Delanda, Manuel, 217
Deleuze and Guattari: *What Is Philosophy?*, 217
Deleuze, Gilles, xxiii, 19, 44, 110, 165, 181, 186, 199, 201, 215, 216, 217, 218, 219, 220, 221, 222, 223, 224, 225, 227, 229, 231, 236, 240
demansion, 140, 143, 147, 150, 153, 175, 190
Derrida, Jacques, xvii, xix, xxiii, 39, 62, 70, 81, 85, 118, 127, 138, 144, 145, 146, 147, 151, 152, 153, 154, 155, 156, 157, 158, 164, 172, 173, 174, 175, 176, 177, 178, 179, 181, 183, 185, 186, 188, 194, 218, 233, 235
Descartes, René, 91, 221

descent, 4, 16, 19, 27, 83, 85, 132, 133, 214
desidero, 92, 95, 96, 101, 105, 108, 132, 139, 221
desire, xxiii, xxiv, 10, 16, 19, 26, 27, 30-34, 92–96, 103–104, 110–111, 126–132, 147–151, 175, 189–193, 202–204, 210-212, 222-225, 228, 231
desiring machine, xxiii, 97, 106, 172, 222
destiny, 20, 24, 25, 65, 107, 184, 239, 255
detritus, 100, 102, 103, 113, 126, 127, 132, 140, 149
dialectic, xii, xxi, 34, 50, 60, 61, 88, 94, 100, 105, 110, 127, 133, 137, 182, 186
dialogue, xii, xv, xxi, 14, 26, 28, 30, 33, 46, 50, 53, 55, 59, 60, 70, 88, 100, 104, 126, 170, 176, 189, 192
differend, 11, 57, 165
digital media, 135, 138, 141, 143, 154, 170, 174, 195, 222, 223
digital technology, x, 29, 70, 85, 104, 188
disaster, xxi–xxv, 17–21, 39–41, 81, 84–88, 97, 100, 119–123, 163–167, 171–175, 208–213, 249, 250
disposition, xx, 11, 29, 43, 45, 77, 78, 171, 188, 242
distillation, 167, 210, 211
diurnal, 22, 27, 28, 52, 158, 214, 215
drive, xxiii, 49, 103, 110, 111, 130, 131, 132, 149, 153, 224, 226, 236
Duchamp, Marcel, 131, 227
dunamis, 64, 105, 120, 164, 171, 172, 178, 182, 183, 185, 218, 236

Durand, Gilbert, 214, 215
dwelling, 77, 202

East India Company, 164, 249
écriture, 90, 101
egent, xv, xxi, xxii, xxiv, 6, 12, 25,
  34, 42, 81, 88, 91, 93, 99, 100,
  123, 126, 127, 140, 143, 149,
  152, 155, 156, 157, 171, 188,
  189, 197, 204, 222, 223, 227,
  233, 237, 245
Einstein, Albert, xix, xx, 43, 44
Einstellung, 158, 160, 161
Eisenman, Peter, xvii, xviii, 39, 81
electracy, ix–xii, xv, xvii–xviii,
  xx–xxiv, 3–14, 17–30, 39–42,
  60–62, 64–67, 71–77, 84–87,
  91–95, 98–108, 112, 114,
  120–126, 129–134, 140–150,
  170–179, 190–200, 210–214,
  216–221, 227
element, 54, 139, 173, 179, 184,
  202, 212, 236, 241
emblem, 15, 28, 78, 94, 120, 127,
  155, 167, 186, 200, 207, 222,
  240, 242
embodiment, 83, 103, 120, 138,
  164, 187, 202, 204, 248
EmerAgency, xiv, xix, xxi, xxv, 4,
  11, 12, 18, 39, 55, 83, 98, 102,
  134, 176, 186, 222, 248, 253,
  255
emergence, 9, 10, 25, 60, 64, 68,
  70, 73, 75, 76, 78, 84, 85, 93,
  95, 100, 102, 107, 113, 117,
  118, 136, 145, 146, 152, 159,
  165, 172, 174, 180, 189, 203,
  210, 218, 241, 244, 247
Emerson, Ralph Waldo, 14, 24,
  26, 28, 30, 56, 99, 144
émouvoir, 204
encounter, 21, 23, 27, 50, 51, 64,
  65, 67, 79, 87, 90, 113, 117,
  121, 140, 141, 144, 171, 196,
  199, 223, 226, 229
enjoyment, 66, 67, 68, 88, 89, 90,
  91, 94, 102, 107, 126, 127, 134,
  135, 141, 145, 146, 152, 212,
  222
entelechy, 183, 185, 189, 198
entertainment, xi, xxiii, 8, 9, 45,
  50, 58, 60, 91, 101, 108, 121,
  122, 137, 248
Entstellung, 160
Ephron, Nora, 27
epiphany, 112, 115, 139, 161, 182,
  187, 192, 196, 213, 226, 231,
  232, 233
epoch, x, xv, xxiii, 3, 5, 9, 12, 19,
  66, 135, 150, 158, 177, 180,
  212, 236
EPS: existential positioning system,
  xv, xxiv, 16, 21, 38, 52, 67, 74,
  76, 92, 95, 99, 114, 140, 143,
  152, 155, 157, 160, 173, 183,
  188, 189, 192, 221, 233, 245
Erfahrung, 75, 110, 118, 119, 121,
  149, 192, 194, 196
Eros, 16, 33, 219
ethics, xxiv, 18, 19, 39, 75, 89, 92,
  144, 147, 158, 170, 171, 185,
  188, 217
ethos, xv, 5, 7, 20, 39, 56, 68, 100,
  120, 122, 158, 171, 195, 196,
  209, 220
event, 11, 27, 40–44, 57–62, 66,
  68–74, 85–86, 96–98, 107–109,
  119–120, 136–137, 156–158,
  177–183, 187–192, 195–200,
  203, 207–213, 223, 226,
  229–233, 241
everyday life, xx, 22, 26, 28, 35,
  56, 115, 117, 122, 135, 157,
  184, 235
exile, 50, 51, 68, 77, 141
existential refrain, 225, 226, 230

270 *Index*

experience, xii, xix, xxiv, 4, 5, 11–12, 20–28, 41–45, 51–56, 62–64, 76–78, 88–91, 98–102, 105–108, 110–112, 117–124, 134–137, 143–150, 175–180, 185–192, 198–203, 221–223, 228–233
experiment, xix, xxiv, 25, 45, 61, 77, 85, 87, 91, 119, 121, 182, 207, 217, 220, 247
expression, 8, 90, 111, 168, 176, 189, 190, 199, 201, 209, 215, 220, 225

fable, 39, 85, 86, 122, 123, 165, 168, 169, 208, 236, 248, 251, 252, 253, 254, 255, 256
faciality, 220, 229, 231
fantasy, 51, 71, 95, 111, 119, 133, 158, 159, 210
fashion, 54, 78, 180, 202
fatal, 63, 167, 177, 184
fate, 25, 56, 75, 167, 196
feedback, xxi, 85, 95, 100, 106, 110, 117, 118, 136, 137, 140, 178, 188, 192, 194, 195, 196, 203, 209, 225, 228, 231, 253
feeling, xxiv, 29, 43, 44, 52, 67, 72, 96, 104, 109, 114, 115, 124, 127, 150, 153, 157, 168, 171, 181, 185, 196, 199, 200, 202, 210, 222, 230, 254, 255
felt, 15, 49, 52, 62, 65, 67, 75, 91, 108, 127, 144, 148, 149, 175, 199, 200, 222, 230
fetish, 102, 108, 124, 190, 193, 200, 210, 225
fifth estate, xvii, xxii, 4, 12, 22, 28, 29, 51, 55, 56, 58, 61, 78, 88, 100, 107, 134, 136, 137, 138, 153, 158, 176, 195, 222, 234, 242

figure, xvi–xviii, 14, 31–34, 49, 50, 62, 65–68, 78, 109, 142, 156, 170, 172, 180, 182, 200, 208, 217–218, 221–224, 231, 234, 242–243, 250, 251, 253
firstness, 127, 137, 199, 213
flash reason, 86, 182, 192, 231
Flaubert, Gustave, 137, 203
Fletcher, Angus, 22, 29, 61, 62
Florence, 83
Florida Research Ensemble, viii, xiv, xxv, xxvi, 2, 247, 255
formless, 135, 187
Foucault, Michel, 127, 179
fourfold, 73, 74, 76
Frammartino, Michelangelo, 165, 166
Freud, Sigmund, xix, 31, 32, 33, 34, 69, 71, 84, 89, 91, 102, 104, 105, 108, 110, 113, 114, 126, 130, 138, 150, 189, 193, 209, 210, 224, 225
Frye, Northrop, 38
Fuller, Buckminster, 240, 241
fumisme, 33
function, 128–134

game, xiii, xix, 84, 86, 87, 127, 134, 149, 164, 178, 220, 236, 237, 238, 239, 240, 242, 244, 250
gaze, 95, 103, 104, 106, 110, 127, 128, 132, 139, 160, 200, 203, 224, 226
Gehry, Frank, 43, 44
Gelernter, David, 44
genesis, 16, 60, 68, 93, 146, 147, 152, 172, 173, 174, 175, 177, 189, 195, 209, 217, 220, 225, 247
Geschlecht, 174, 175, 189, 220
gestalt, 63, 128, 148, 199, 208, 221, 231, 236

gesture, 29, 44, 148, 149, 172, 193, 198
Gibson, William, 5
gift, xviii, xx, 43, 51, 74, 77, 85, 132, 137, 152, 156, 158, 163, 164, 167, 177, 184, 209, 223, 235, 238, 249
Goethe, Johann Wolfgang von, 144
Gradiva, 30, 31, 32, 33, 34, 69, 157
grammatology, 138, 185, 198, 216
Greeks, 17, 26, 41, 44, 59, 63, 69, 135, 177, 183, 184, 203, 216, 241
Greimas, Algirdas Julien, 85, 95, 118, 124, 167, 168, 194, 195, 197, 198, 219, 233, 235
Guattari, Félix, xxiii, 44, 110, 165, 198, 214, 215, 216, 217, 218, 219, 220, 221, 222, 223, 224, 225, 226, 227, 228, 229, 230, 236, 240

habitus, 37, 39, 42, 56, 122, 196, 220, 239
Hades, 26, 72, 83
Hansen, Mark, 70
happiness, 18, 27, 28, 49, 52, 104, 158, 167, 174, 175, 193, 208, 231, 232, 254
Hardt, Michael, 12
haunting, 151, 154
Havelock, Eric, 12
hegemony, 86, 91, 193
Heidegger: *Ereignis*, 26, 39, 66, 67, 88, 92, 99, 119, 120, 156, 157, 158, 181, 183, 189, 195, 198, 202, 203, 227, 228
Heidegger, Martin, xx–xxiii, 26, 34, 42–43, 62–68, 70–75, 77, 78, 84, 87–92, 94–98, 134–137, 144–146, 151–158, 174–178, 180–188, 198–203, 212, 216–219, 235–236
Heraclitus, 163
Herriman, George, 240
heuretics, ix, xi, xviii, xx, xxi, xxvi, 21, 22, 24, 43, 49, 62, 87, 115, 126, 177, 179, 184, 185, 188, 195, 215, 216, 217, 220, 244
Hindu (religion), xv, 5, 7, 19, 20, 23, 83
hinge, 70, 91, 98, 105, 120, 131, 151, 155, 171, 199, 201, 204, 224
Hobbes, Thomas, 18
Hölderlin, Friedrich, 74, 184, 219
hole, 91, 98, 106, 107, 120, 134, 141, 144, 209, 234, 239, 240, 243
Hollander, John, 61, 62, 118, 143
Holton, Gerald, xx, 42, 43
Homer, 12, 13, 69, 118
hospitality, 158
hyperobject, 17, 213
hypotyposis, 53

iconography, 84, 153
idea, 29, 46, 54, 64, 112, 127, 128, 129, 145, 148, 174, 177, 180, 181, 186, 199, 200, 201, 202, 204, 213, 217, 222, 230, 237, 247, 252
identity, xvii, xviii, xix, xxiii, 4, 5, 7, 9, 11, 20, 24, 25, 26, 27, 30, 83, 85, 91, 92, 94, 95, 107, 123, 124, 129, 134, 138, 139, 148, 165, 177, 181, 214, 219, 221, 230, 244
ideogram, 143, 207, 208, 255
image metaphysics, 239, 242
image of wide scope, xx, 42, 43, 244
image-sign, 136
imaginal realm, 14

272 *Index*

imagination, xx, xxiv, 8, 19, 30, 48, 70, 71, 78, 79, 95, 107, 111, 119, 121, 127, 139, 171, 180, 192, 199, 212, 224, 254
inception, 37, 62, 64, 68, 69, 74, 100, 134, 138, 147, 219
industrial revolution, 4, 84, 100, 101, 146
innervation, 86, 194, 225
inspiration, xii, xix, xxvi
Instagram, 137
intensity, 153, 154, 155, 168, 190, 198, 228
interactive design, 117, 165
interface, x, xii, xv, xvi, xix, xxi, xxii, 5, 13, 16, 25, 39, 41, 43, 45, 50, 56, 60, 76, 77, 78, 100, 108, 118, 123, 140, 143, 155, 171, 186, 189, 192, 194, 195, 196, 197, 207, 230, 242, 244, 247, 248, 250, 251
Internet, xiii, xvi, xvii, xix, xx, 12, 55, 84, 88, 134, 158, 176, 239, 244
intuition, 29, 41, 42, 44, 97, 200
invention, ix–xxiii, 4, 5, 10–14, 20–25, 38, 41, 55, 59, 62–69, 87–91, 98–106, 120–121, 135–138, 140–148, 170–179, 181–185, 188–194, 198, 201, 203, 213–221, 236–239
Irigaray, Luce, 55, 115
Isozaki, Arata, 99
ixotropics, 215, 231

Jakobson, Roman, 114
Jencks, Charles, xviii
Jensen, Wilhelm, 31, 32, 33, 34
jointure, 65, 69, 70, 73, 76, 91, 92, 94, 96, 97, 98, 107, 114, 126, 129, 131, 132, 133, 134, 141, 143, 145, 147, 150, 151
joke, 93, 98, 114, 247

jouissance, 10, 34, 89, 90, 92, 93, 100, 103, 107, 108, 113, 138, 140, 142, 146, 150, 212
journalism, xvii, 12, 22, 29, 55, 60, 177
Joyce, James, 118, 138, 139, 140, 145, 231; Finnegans Wake, 138, 145, 157
judgment, xxiv, 8, 30, 35, 83, 170, 171, 180, 186
justice, 11, 12, 17, 18, 22, 31, 44, 57, 58, 65, 89, 120

Kafka, Franz, 44
Kant, Immanuel, xxiii, xxiv, 28, 30, 35, 41, 56, 70, 71, 75, 91, 92, 94, 108, 122, 136, 139, 149, 159, 180, 181, 185
kenosis, 131
Kentridge, William, 15, 26
Klossowski, Pierre, xxiii, 106, 111, 200
Koestler, Arthur, 114, 135
Kristeva, Julia, 75, 138, 147, 148, 149, 150, 151, 200
Kuntzel, Thierry, 204

labyrinth, 72, 99, 193, 242
Lacan, Jacques, 89–109, 125–159, 192–194, 199–203, 209, 224, 225, 234, 235, 238
lamella, 86, 103, 125, 223
Las Vegas, 10, 130
Lautréamont, Comte de, 131
Lefebvre, Henri, 216
Leibniz, Gottfried Wilhelm, xx, 60, 128, 201, 228
letter, 7, 101, 104, 106, 127, 136, 139, 140, 141, 142, 203
libidinal economy, 102, 154, 222, 224

Index 273

limit, 6, 19, 64, 69, 92, 94, 97, 128, 138, 144, 147, 154, 157, 158, 181, 229, 252
literacy, x–xiii, xvi, xvii, xxi–xxiv, 3–7, 9–14, 18, 20, 21, 22, 24, 26, 29, 32, 34, 40, 41, 49, 59–71, 86–95, 101–106, 114, 117, 119, 132–133, 141–150, 174–182, 185, 188, 190, 193, 195, 198–200, 219–22
littoral, 54, 139, 140, 141, 142, 143, 153, 155, 156, 157, 158, 159, 190
lituraterre, 137, 138, 139, 141, 143
Lotman, Jurij, 117, 143
love, 8, 16, 27, 28, 31, 32, 33, 34, 52, 54, 105, 114, 124, 154, 189, 191, 192, 193, 196, 198, 213, 220, 221, 227, 228, 236, 239
Lyotard, Jean-François, 11, 165

MacFadyen, David, 72, 73
manner, 10, 13, 15, 29, 30, 39, 40, 54, 56, 63, 64, 66, 67, 68, 72, 73, 75, 93, 102, 117, 120, 123, 125, 131, 134, 136, 153, 172, 180, 182, 195, 202, 204, 207, 211, 220, 223, 228
map, xviii, xxii, xxiv, 28, 40, 61, 68, 78, 95, 117, 126, 140, 143, 145, 166, 220, 230, 231, 233, 234, 242, 244, 250
Marc, Franz, 136
Marx, Karl, 18, 86, 100, 102, 108, 152, 208, 225
Masson, André, 32
matheme, 103
Mathieu, Georges, 128, 129, 148
McLuhan, Marshall, xii, 5, 91, 103, 127, 175, 231
McWorld, 9, 10, 12, 58
measure, xvii, xviii, 6, 13, 18, 19, 38, 41, 57, 58, 61, 68, 69, 84, 93, 100, 129, 131, 134, 138, 144, 158, 183, 189, 201, 229, 230, 250, 255
melodrama, 27, 33, 52, 221
memory, xv, xxiv, 31, 38, 42, 43, 44, 45, 47, 49, 51, 52, 76, 77, 85, 105, 110, 122, 123, 133, 143, 150, 152, 154, 155, 191, 198, 201, 232, 244, 247
Merleau-Ponty: Flesh, 17, 32, 46, 139, 173, 198, 199, 200, 202, 203, 204, 244
Merleau-Ponty, Maurice, 139, 181, 198, 199, 200, 201, 202, 203, 204, 226
metalepsis, 109, 118, 194
metaphysics, x–xiii, xvii–xviii, xxii–xxiv, 8–21, 26–34, 40–46, 57–65, 68–74, 82–83, 85–91, 94–96, 101–108, 118–121, 131–135, 138–146, 150–159, 170–172, 175–193, 200–201, 216–228, 236–241
metis, 219
Michael (film), 12, 27, 221
microcosm-macrocosm, 5, 21, 39, 47, 73, 98, 99, 136, 157, 201, 221, 231
middle voice, 3, 140, 203
miniaturization, ix, 40, 47
mise-en-abyme, xix, 15, 47, 50, 127, 140
modality, 4, 12, 97, 120, 171, 176, 180, 181, 185, 190, 192, 223
modernism, xi, 39, 100, 110, 128, 129, 135, 161, 203, 218, 247
moment, 5, 10, 20, 22, 32, 48, 52, 75, 76, 83, 107, 109, 111, 127, 131, 137, 146, 149, 152, 160, 177, 181, 182, 185, 197, 198, 217, 232
momentous site, 21, 23, 25, 34, 108, 155, 182, 197

274 Index

monad, 25, 201, 228
montage, 47, 127, 130, 143, 181, 182, 207, 208, 251, 252, 255
moral perfectionism, 28, 30, 31, 108
Morton, Timothy, 17, 212, 213
motto, xxv, 24, 39, 83, 151, 194
multitude, 37
Murphy game, 84, 164
My, 6, 24, 56, 91, 93, 94, 95, 100, 104, 127, 136, 140, 144, 155, 158, 160, 187, 197, 227, 230
mystic, 7, 107, 113, 114, 129, 186, 203, 214, 215
mystory, xix, 19, 23, 25, 29, 51, 53, 76, 77, 79, 94, 166, 215, 244
mythology, 11, 34, 38, 52, 70, 74, 105, 114, 138, 151, 157, 165, 171, 232, 248, 251, 252, 255

natality, 63, 68, 152, 183, 191
necessity, 30, 64, 65, 84, 88, 104, 145, 146, 176, 200, 248
neighborhood, xxv, 38, 40, 74, 76, 77, 78, 119, 155, 159, 161, 208, 254
Neoplatonic, 16, 32, 38, 78, 220
neuroaesthetics, 127
Nietzsche: eternal return, 220
Nietzsche, Friedrich, 24, 71, 92, 99, 193, 220
Nussbaum, Martha, 19

object @, 129, 149, 167, 175, 224, 238
obscenario, xxiv, 25
Okakura, Tenshin, 99
ontology, xvii, xxiv, 17, 41–45, 65–69, 100–102, 118, 124–125, 134, 139, 151–153, 168–173, 182, 185, 188, 198–199, 201–205, 220–228
Overwhelming, 97, 140

parasite, xvii, 234
parergon, 153
Paris, xxiii, 10, 33, 39, 110, 130, 137, 146, 154, 161, 182, 203; Montmartre, xxiii, 10, 33, 130, 137, 146
Parmenides, 132, 183
parody, 118, 119
part object, 98, 103, 104, 111, 121, 123, 126, 150, 154, 223, 224
Pasolini, Pier Paolo, 47, 135
passage, xvi, xxiii, 5, 14, 26, 69, 70, 72, 82, 118, 121, 124, 132, 141, 151, 152, 155, 166, 172, 175, 178, 183, 187, 194, 196, 200, 224, 229, 231, 235, 247
passion, 124, 175, 187, 189, 192, 193, 197, 228
pastiche, 118
pathos, 34, 100, 114, 120, 151, 195
pedagogy, ix, xi, xiv, xv, xviii, xix, xx, xxi, xxiii, 3, 16, 24, 45, 69, 87, 88, 94, 95, 99, 108, 110, 119, 121, 134, 144, 170, 176, 190, 193, 224, 239, 247, 248
Peirce, Charles Sanders, 137, 213, 233
pepper, 119, 121, 125, 222, 247, 255, 256
personification, 221
phase space, 234, 235, 242, 244
Photosynth, 169
phronesis, 12, 27, 170
Phusis, 41, 63, 64, 66, 67, 69, 73, 75, 85, 88, 92, 100, 102, 113, 126, 127, 134, 136, 145, 152, 175, 182, 201, 203, 209, 212, 213
pine tar, 39, 164, 166, 167, 209, 213, 214, 249, 254, 255, 256

pivot, 81, 145, 199, 201, 204, 247
Plato, xi– xv, xix, 10–17, 26, 28, 30, 32, 34, 38, 39, 41, 44, 46, 47, 49, 50, 53, 54, 55, 58–60, 62–64, 70–74, 87–92, 125–126, 130–136, 170–172, 187–194, 217–220, 241; Timaeus, xix, 39, 59, 70, 71, 187, 194, 217, 241
pleasure, 3, 9, 39, 93, 94, 106, 110, 148, 150, 175, 181, 200, 209, 220, 230, 247, 254
poetics, xii, xiv, xx, xxii, xxiii, xxiv, 23, 61, 69, 73, 74, 104, 110, 114, 115, 118, 121, 139, 143, 147, 152, 159, 160, 180, 182, 191, 193, 195, 212, 223, 231, 241
policy-formation, 18
pollution, xiv, xxv, 37, 81, 83, 96, 100, 209
polo, 239, 240
popcycle, xviii, xix, xxii, xxv, 3, 7, 19, 20, 27, 32, 38, 40, 44, 53, 76, 77, 95, 118, 144, 155, 166, 184, 207, 212, 231, 234, 244, 248, 251, 252
popular culture, 3, 4, 9, 10, 26, 76, 115, 123
poststructuralism, xxiii, 138, 179
potentiality, 19, 28, 30, 64, 68, 105, 175, 176, 178, 179, 181, 182, 183, 184, 185, 186, 187, 188, 189, 191, 192, 195, 196, 198, 200, 201, 202, 203, 218, 220, 221, 228, 231, 236, 237, 243
Pound, Ezra, xix, 40, 143, 208, 231
practical reason, 18, 19, 35, 39, 180
Presocratics, 64, 68, 70, 134, 203
procession, 15
prosopopoeia, 221

Protevi, John, 26, 170, 171, 172, 183, 195, 201
Proust, Marcel: The Past Recaptured, 32, 48, 52, 139, 195, 196, 197, 198, 204, 216, 217, 219, 221, 228, 229, 231, 232, 233, 247
prudence, 168
public sphere, 12, 18, 22, 29, 51, 75, 79, 88, 120, 137, 160, 176
pun, 93, 101, 128, 140, 152
Pythagoras, xii, 70, 166

quasi-object, 103, 127, 237, 238, 247

ratio, xvii, 14, 53, 54, 68, 70, 76, 77, 91, 92, 99, 100, 107, 120, 126, 127, 129, 133, 134, 141, 144, 145, 147, 157, 159, 179, 225, 245
rebus, xix, 102, 103, 209
recognition, 4, 31, 43, 46, 94, 107, 139, 146, 245
reflective judgment, xxiv, 75, 136, 139, 149, 199, 203
rehearsal, 188
remarriage comedy, 27, 31, 33, 34
remediation, 81, 82, 84, 249
reoccupation, 7, 14, 15, 20, 33, 50, 53, 57, 59, 61, 87, 91, 95, 98, 129, 159, 179, 181
retrieval, 13, 21, 45, 87, 107, 110, 176, 181, 236, 239
rhetoric, xxiv, 26, 39, 47, 61, 110, 111, 114, 120, 144, 151, 156, 177, 184, 191, 207, 222, 223, 232, 243, 250
rhizome, 117, 121, 218, 221, 223, 226, 236
rhythm, 28, 44, 82, 118, 120, 126, 128, 150, 153, 158, 166, 172, 178, 182, 207, 214, 216, 217,

218, 223, 224, 230, 232, 235, 236, 239, 251
Rilke, Rainer Maria, 21, 22, 74, 98, 195
Ruskin, John, 47
Russell, Bertrand, 46, 129

sacrifice, 38, 74
Sade, Marquis de, 94
Sanskrit, 4, 16, 62, 83
Sartre: *Nausea*, 108, 109, 113, 147, 213, 214
Sartre, Jean-Paul, 108, 109, 113, 114, 147, 175, 213, 214
satisfaction, 19, 34, 103, 104, 107, 110, 209, 236
savoir-y-faire, 139, 149
scarab, xvi, 101, 136, 142, 149, 160
scenario, xiv, 16, 22, 25, 28, 40, 51, 60, 74, 75, 78, 88, 124, 128, 134, 135, 144, 155, 164, 165, 176, 192, 194, 221
Schelling, Friedrich Wilhelm Joseph, 212
schizoanalysis, 110, 165, 215, 221, 231
Second Life, 4
self, xvii, xviii, 4, 5, 11, 20, 26, 34, 51, 72, 95, 96, 97, 105, 106, 114, 119, 124, 133, 136, 148, 152, 159, 168, 173, 187, 188, 193, 201, 221, 228, 230, 239, 247
Seltzer, Mark, 247
Sen, Amartya, 18, 19, 22, 23, 24, 28, 29, 90, 92, 157, 170, 171, 175, 218, 227
sensible idea, 139, 181, 182, 198, 199, 201, 203, 204, 216, 226, 227, 228, 232, 247
sensorium, 86, 101, 103, 125, 132, 171, 181, 188, 222, 223, 224

sentient doll, 123, 125, 196, 209
Serres, Michel, xvi, 234, 235, 236, 237, 238, 239, 240, 242, 243
shifter, 227, 230, 233, 234, 237
shock, 110, 112, 152
signifiance, xxiv, 67, 90, 91, 100, 102, 107, 139, 142, 144, 145, 148, 152, 155, 157, 170, 178, 181, 190, 195, 199, 201, 215, 223, 225
signifier, 90, 100, 101, 102, 104, 106, 128, 133, 141, 142, 148, 150
simulacrum, xxii, 29, 111, 125, 165, 192, 193, 194, 195, 196, 197, 199, 200, 204, 208
simulation, 44, 253, 255
singularity, 26, 172, 201, 222, 227
sinthome, 100, 139
slime mold, xvii, xviii
Sloterdijk, Peter, 115
social media, xvi, xvii, 4, 22, 29, 56, 88, 134, 137, 157, 222
Socrates, xii, xxi, 8, 13, 16, 21, 34, 49, 50, 55, 58, 59, 62, 68, 69, 88, 100, 104, 143, 144, 186, 198
solidification, 81, 82, 84
somatic markers, 42, 44, 45, 122
souffrance, 105, 106, 107, 110, 135
spectacle, 59, 111, 154, 195, 196
spice trade, 39, 164, 209, 212, 249
Spinoza, Baruch, xxiii, 228
stance, 186, 203
Sterbak, Jana, 46, 50, 51, 55, 56, 61, 72, 133, 136, 137, 195
steresis, 19, 105, 171, 189
Stiegler, Bernard, 224
stigmergy, xvi, xvii
striving, xx, 16, 25, 30, 213, 227, 248
style, 18, 73, 77, 90, 99, 120, 133, 138, 141, 151, 153, 202, 204, 215, 232

subjectile, 151, 153, 154, 155
sublime, 17, 41, 42, 94, 213, 223
Sufi, 7, 14, 21, 71, 132, 239
Superfund, xxi, xxv, 37, 39, 40, 84, 123, 164, 171, 209, 248, 249, 254
surveillance, 56, 104, 110, 134, 200
symptom, xix, 11, 91, 100, 113, 122, 128, 139, 210
syncretism, xvi, xx, 7, 16, 17, 25, 30, 71, 136, 143

take, xvii, 6, 11, 21, 25, 28, 29, 30, 53, 56, 88, 91, 119, 134, 142, 160, 166, 171, 178, 193, 198, 201, 232, 238
talking cure, 33, 104, 220
Tao, 67, 98, 99, 247
tar baby, 123, 169, 213, 256
Tarkovsky, Andrei, 96, 242
Tarot, xii, 239
taste, 121, 180, 181, 214, 222
tawhid, 57
technics, 40, 124, 182, 203, 209, 217, 219, 231
Tel Quel, 75, 90, 104, 138, 143, 146, 147, 204
template, xii, 13, 49, 50, 55, 87, 100, 174, 175, 178, 184, 195, 247
terror, 9, 21, 22
testimony, 12, 25, 51, 127, 136, 255
theme park, 10, 121
theopraxesis, xvii, 14, 25, 30, 38, 44, 50, 51–61, 69–75, 79, 85–89, 94, 96, 107–109, 139, 141, 144, 147, 150–154, 168–171, 180–197, 222, 232
Thespis, 85, 165
thing, 29, 51, 52, 62, 63, 65, 66, 73, 91, 102, 104, 124, 129, 130, 153, 166, 172, 177, 187, 190, 200, 202, 216, 221, 224, 237, 243
Thom, René, xvi, xxv, 143, 220, 229, 232, 233, 235, 243
Thoreau, Henry David, 30, 56
threshold, xi, 70, 132, 159, 171, 181, 189, 230, 234, 237
thymos, 139, 151, 155, 168
time, xv–xvi, 3, 6, 7, 14–17, 20–25, 32, 44–48, 51–54, 61–64, 75–78, 93–102, 109–113, 125–131, 141–142, 151–159, 173–178, 181–183, 186, 197, 199, 204, 211, 218, 220, 225, 229, 231–235
topics, 18, 39, 60, 191, 193, 196
topoi, 191
topology, 100, 109, 126, 130, 151, 190, 193, 223, 232, 233, 235, 242, 243
topos, 156, 190, 191, 193
trace, xvi, xvii, xxiii, 28, 43, 82, 85, 95, 118, 141, 144, 145, 146, 152, 154, 155, 160, 172, 183, 187, 188, 210, 223
tradition, xi, xii, xvi, xvii, 7, 9, 13, 14, 18, 19, 24, 26, 27, 28, 30, 31, 40, 57, 62, 63, 70, 83, 107, 114, 118, 125, 129, 134, 139, 144, 160, 170, 171, 172, 175, 177, 180, 182, 185, 186, 216, 220
tragedy, 13, 26, 65, 70, 97, 135, 165
trait, 106, 139, 141, 142, 156, 161, 178
transference, 34, 107, 109, 146, 149, 152, 231
transitional object, 125, 127, 149, 200
transversal, 44, 82, 209, 230, 241
Travolta, John, 27

trickster, 256
trobar, 191, 193, 198
trope, 62, 72, 103, 155, 194, 210
tropology, 35, 103, 114, 117, 131, 159, 231
troubadours, 191
truth, xx, 27, 29, 32, 34, 53, 57, 58, 59, 60, 62, 66, 68, 88, 92, 134, 142, 177, 178, 184, 188, 231, 243
turbulence, 134, 135, 218, 231, 236, 237
turn, ix, xx, xxiii, 3, 14, 16, 26, 48, 64, 65, 69, 78, 91, 118, 126, 128, 135, 142, 143, 144, 145, 147, 151, 169, 173, 177, 179, 203, 207, 240

ubiquitous computing, ix, xv, xvii, 134, 148, 156, 183, 202, 231
Ulmer, Gregory: *Electronic Monuments*, 57; *Internet Invention*, xix, xx, 244; *Miami Virtue*, xiv, 61, 171
uncanny, 27, 65, 78, 97, 105, 160
unconscious, 140, 225, 229, 231
University of Florida, xxv, xxvi
usage, 4, 5, 20, 58, 64, 65, 66, 68, 69, 73, 74, 88, 89, 90, 91, 94, 101, 121, 134, 135, 145, 146, 150, 151, 179, 192, 199, 225
User, xix, 76, 79, 95, 106, 112, 123, 134, 144, 155, 168, 194, 219, 233, 239, 244
usufruct, 68, 88, 89, 94, 104, 200

value, xvi, xxvi, 7, 8, 30, 48, 57, 72, 73, 98, 101, 102, 108, 110, 120, 121, 130, 147, 152, 156, 160, 164, 182, 190, 194, 195, 196, 197, 225, 227, 239, 245, 249, 250, 252

Van Gogh, Vincent, 8, 151, 153, 154, 215, 230
Velázquez, Diego, 127
Venice, 46, 47, 48, 49, 50, 51, 52, 53, 56, 61, 64, 72, 76, 77, 78, 87, 95, 136, 137, 140, 141, 143, 155, 156, 170, 186, 195
Villa, Dana, 75, 229
Virilio, Paul, 137, 172
virtue, xxiv, 12, 17, 18, 19, 24, 27, 30, 61, 69, 84, 93, 105, 170, 171, 184, 202, 218, 228, 236
viscosity, 113, 212, 213, 214, 215
vital anecdote, 186

Wark, McKenzie, 223
Weber, Samuel, 178, 179, 181
well-being, xxiii, 10, 13, 18–19, 21–29, 34–39, 61–66, 75, 102, 104, 120–122, 130, 163–167, 170–178, 195, 208, 209, 222, 228
Wenders, Wim, 159
Wesen, 133, 136, 137, 146, 153, 202, 204
Whitman, Walt, 61, 69, 118
Wildgen, Wolfgang, 233, 235
will, vii, x, xi, xiii, xv, xvii, xviii, xxiv, 19, 57, 75, 84, 96, 122, 152, 180, 181, 189, 192, 220
Williams, William Carlos, 53, 56
Winnicott, Donald, 125, 149, 200, 224
Winterson, Jeanette, 48
wisdom, 13, 68, 97, 99, 108, 121, 122, 164, 169, 255
writing, 21, 24, 61, 101, 153

Xanadu, 254, 255, 256

Yousafzai, Malala, 6, 7, 11, 60

About the Author

Gregory L. Ulmer is Professor Emeritus, English and Media Studies, University of Florida. He is Coordinator of the Florida Research Ensemble, and Joseph Beuys Chair of the European Graduate School. His recent books include *Electracy* (2015), *Avatar Emergency* (2012), and *Miami Virtue* (2012). His current project is Konsult Experiment (www.konsultexperiment.com) a blog affiliated with the Electracy and Transmedia Studies series, edited by Jan Holmevik and Cynthia Haynes for Parlor Press.

Figure 9. "Florida Research Ensemble, Feb 21, 2017."

www.ingramcontent.com/pod-product-compliance
Lightning Source LLC
Chambersburg PA
CBHW021652230426
43668CB00008B/602